Varieties of ol

ORIGINALLY PUBLISHED BY HARVARD UNIVERSITY PRESS

Varieties of Police Behavior

THE MANAGEMENT OF LAW AND ORDER IN EIGHT COMMUNITIES

by James Q. Wilson

ATHENEUM NEW YORK
1976

TO MATTHEW AND ANNIE

Published by Atheneum
Reprinted by arrangement with Harvard University Press

Library of Congress catalog card number 68-54027
ISBN *0-689-70224-8*
Manufactured in the United States of America by
The Murray Printing Company,
Forge Village, Massachusetts
Published in Canada by McClelland & Stewart Ltd.
First Atheneum Printing January 1970
Second Printing August 1971
Third Printing February 1972
Fourth Printing September 1972
Fifth Printing January 1973
Sixth Printing September 1973
Seventh Printing September 1974
Eighth Printing April 1975
Ninth Printing December 1976

Acknowledgments

My principal debt is to the students who, over the last few years, have helped me gather materials on and speculate about the American police. Mark Adams, Paul Halpern, Martin Levin, Martin Shefter, John Stuart Smith, and Paul Weaver proved themselves to be indefatigable researchers and stimulating critics. My only regret is that considerations of space, decorum, or libel prevent me from using some of the better anecdotes they collected. I, of course, bear full and final responsibility for such materials of theirs as I have used.

Early drafts of this manuscript benefited substantially from the comments and suggestions of Edward C. Banfield, Peter B. Clark, Charles Fried, John Gardiner, Harvey Mansfield, Jr., Walter B. Miller, Martha Derthick, Judith Shklar, and Arthur L. Stinchcombe.

In every community I visited I had the cooperation and assistance of the principal officials of the police department and the local government. Not all of them will approve of everything I have written in this book, but I hope it is some consolation to them to know that I learned a great deal about law, order, and the police from them and I feel myself very much in their debt. This is not the book they would have written, but at least it is a book informed by a realization of the immense complexity and difficulty of the problems they face. To protect those who were helpful to me, I have wherever possible avoided attributing any remark to them by name.

Several organizations provided financial support for this study. The faculty committee of the Joint Center for Urban Studies of M.I.T. and Harvard allowed me, while I was its director, to use some of its funds to begin these explorations and my successor, Daniel Patrick Moynihan, has subsequently given me every possible support and encouragement. At a crucial stage in the research Don K.

Price, Dean of the Kennedy School of Government at Harvard University, made funds available to me that kept the project alive. Completing the research and writing the manuscript were made possible by a generous grant from the Committee on Governmental and Legal Processes of the Social Science Research Council.

Important information was made available to me by the Division of Research of the New York State Department of Corrections, the Uniform Crime Reporting Section of the Federal Bureau of Investigation, and the International City Managers' Association. I thank all these groups, the fact givers equally with the fund givers, for their help.

Mrs. Susan Michaelson was my research assistant during the latter stages of this project and accordingly had to read this manuscript in its many versions more times than anyone should, as did Mrs. Judith Augusta, my typist. I offer both of them my sympathy as well as my thanks. George Greenberg helped develop some of the statistical materials and Marlin Gordon edited the final draft. My wife prepared the index, the fourth she has done for me and each better than the last.

J.Q.W.

Contents

Tables

Varieties of Police Behavior

One Introduction

Increasingly, our lives are touched by the activities of large government organizations that educate our children, regulate our businesses, draft our sons, inspect our food, support our indigents, and warn us of the hazards of cigarette smoking. Increasingly, we complain that these organizations are inefficient, unresponsive, unfair, ponderous, or confusing; the common epithet is "bureaucratic." Such complaints, once made only by the political right, which felt the government was doing "too much," today are expressed by liberals, radicals, moderates, and almost everybody in between. Conservatives once feared that a powerful bureaucracy would work a social revolution. Radicals now fear this same bureaucracy is working a conservative reaction. And moderates fear the bureaucracy is not working at all.[1] Accordingly, the schools, the police, and the welfare agencies, among many others, are today under attack either for trying to do the wrong thing or for doing the right thing the wrong way. Efforts are being made to change these organizations by curtailing their activities, decentralizing their structures, reviewing their decisions, and insisting that their clients (or members) have a voice in the setting of objectives and the conduct of affairs.

These are matters, one might suppose, to which scholars would have devoted their attention. With a few exceptions, this has not been the case. Studies of the behavior of government agencies are rare in any event, but those that try to discover how effectively, or efficiently, they attain their objectives or to estimate the quality of the service provided the client are especially infrequent except

1. The material in these paragraphs is adapted from James Q. Wilson, "The Bureaucracy Problem," *The Public Interest*, No. 6 (Winter, 1967), pp. 3–9.

in a few areas (hospitals, for example).[2] Most studies analyze only one organization (a "case study"), or an isolated part of several organizations (studies of small work groups or of "decision makers"), or but one aspect of the organizations' behavior — for example, the rate of innovation or the distribution of authority — not immediately relevant to the interests of the client. Students of organizations have been interested less in how the members of an organization deal with the client and more in how they deal with each other.[3]

Any study of organizations that is addressed to what is popularly called the "bureaucracy problem" must have as its central focus

2. Some of the few studies evaluating how government organizations deal with their clients are reviewed in Peter M. Blau and W. Richard Scott, *Formal Organizations* (San Francisco: Chandler Publishing Co., 1962), Chap. III. Hospitals have been analyzed from this perspective more than any other kind of organization; these studies are summarized and criticized in Charles Perrow, "Hospitals: Technology, Structure, and Goals," in James G. March, ed., *Handbook of Organizations* (Chicago: Rand McNally & Co., 1965), pp. 910–971. A major effort to discover how various attributes of the public school system affected one output of that organization — pupil performance on an achievement test — is, of course, the so-called "Coleman Report": James S. Coleman et al., *Equality of Educational Opportunity* (Washington: Government Printing Office, 1966), esp. Chap. III. Other studies relating school inputs to education outputs are reviewed in Charles E. Bidwell, "The School as a Formal Organization" in March, *Handbook of Organizations*, esp. pp. 988–989. There is an abundant literature on prisons. Though very little of it offers any systematic analysis of the extent to which such organizations achieve their purposes, the accounts of the different "styles" of prison management, and of the special problem of managing the discretion of guards and prisoners, are quite relevant to the problems of the police: see the review article by Donald R. Cressey, "Prison Organizations," in March, *Handbook of Organizations*, pp. 1023–1070, and especially the excellent monograph by Gresham M. Sykes, *The Society of Captives* (Princeton: Princeton University Press, 1958). The way welfare agencies and workers exercise their discretion with respect to their clients is treated in Alan Keith-Lucas, *Decisions About People in Need* (Chapel Hill: University of North Carolina Press, 1957) and Martha Derthick, "Intra-State Differences in Welfare Administration" in James Q. Wilson, ed., *City Politics and Public Policy* (New York: John Wiley & Sons, 1968).

3. Especially in the vast literature on "human relations" in industry, a great deal is said about how to raise the morale, increase "interpersonal sensitivity," or improve job satisfaction of workers but relatively little about how these change their productivity or the way they handle clients. See Warren G. Bennis, "Bureaucracy and Social Change: An Anatomy of Failure," Sloane School of Industrial Management, MIT, 1962 (mimeographed); George Strauss, "Some Notes on Power Equalization," in Harold J. Leavitt, ed., *The Social Science of Organization* (Englewood Cliffs: Prentice-Hall, Inc., 1963), pp. 39–84; Harold J. Leavitt, "Applied Organizational Change in Industry," in March, *Handbook of Organizations*, esp. pp. 1166–1167.

the problem of getting the front-line worker — the teacher, nurse, diplomat, police officer, or welfare investigator — to do "the right thing." What *is* the right thing, of course, may be very much a matter of dispute. We want him to deal "effectively" with the problem at hand, but we also want him to do other things as well — follow the boss's orders, be fair to the clients, help clients cut through "red tape," avoid wasting money, refrain from stealing, and so on. To the extent these objectives conflict, we expect the worker to "use his judgment," but we rarely tell him what "judgment" is or how to use it and we stand ready to criticize him after the fact if he uses it in ways we dislike.

The police, for reasons I trust are obvious, are an especially interesting case of the "bureaucracy problem." First of all, to the extent they suffer from the problem at all, it cannot be solved by deciding that their functions should no longer be performed or should be returned to private enterprise. The need for law enforcement, and law enforcement under public rather than private auspices, is not now, though it once was, in doubt. Second, there is hardly any public agency — the schools are an obvious exception — that affects the lives of more people. In 1965, over five million arrests were made and uncounted millions of traffic tickets were issued; in addition, the police provided all kinds of services having little to do with law enforcement. Third, there are thousands of police agencies in this country — about forty thousand, in fact — each of which is organized in roughly the same way under comparable, if not identical, legal codes, each of which performs similar functions, and each of which is responsible to a separate governmental jurisdiction having its own political processes and institutional arrangements. Because of this, we can compare the way in which the police are managed under different circumstances and thus learn something about the extent to which police behavior can be changed. But finally and most important, the ability of the police to do their job well may determine our ability to manage social conflict, especially that which involves Negroes and other minority groups, and our prospects for maintaining a proper balance between liberty and order.

4

The purpose of this book is to describe how the police patrolman behaves with respect to the more frequently applied laws; to analyze the problems facing the police administrator both in deciding what the patrolman ought to do and in getting him to do it; to discover how, if at all, patrolmen in various cities differ in performing their functions; and finally to inquire whether — or under what circumstances — such differences as exist are based on explicit community decisions.

A citizen interested in how the police are governed might well ask these questions in reverse order. He would want to know first how or by whom decisions affecting police policy are made, then what problems police administrators have in getting patrolmen to carry out that policy, and finally what consequences — in terms of law, order, and justice — these police policies have for various segments of the community. In this book we begin with what the patrolman does and end with what the community can do because the possibility (and the consequences of) various community decisions are best understood in terms of the legal and organizational constraints on the individual officer. A major theme of the book is that these constraints arise out of the nature of his function and thus place real limits on the degree to which his behavior can be modified by organizational directives.

The police function that is the subject of this book is that of the patrolman insofar as he enforces laws and maintains order. This is not, of course, all that he does. In addition to catching criminals and preventing crime, he recovers stolen property, directs traffic, provides emergency medical aid, gets cats out of trees, checks on the homes of families on vacation, and helps little old ladies who have locked themselves out of their apartments.[4] The "service" functions of the police — first aid, rescuing cats, helping ladies, and the like — are omitted from this study because, unlike the law enforcement functions, they are intended to please the client and no one else.

4. A recent study estimated that only one third of all police radio calls involve criminal matters that *may* result in an arrest and in only about 5 per cent of all calls does an arrest actually ensue. President's Commission on Law Enforcement and Administration of Justice, *Task Force Report: Science and Technology* (Washington: Government Printing Office, 1967), p. 93.

There is no reason in principle why these services could not be priced and sold on the market. It is only a matter of historical accident and community convenience that they are provided by the police; one can just as easily imagine them sold by a private, profit-making firm ("Emergency Services, Inc."). The transaction between buyer and seller exhausts the value of the service — there are few, if any, external benefits or costs that are imposed on third parties or on society generally.[5]

To the police administrator, these services have the advantage of not raising questions of legal standards, community objectives, or the interests and opinions of third parties. The task of service administration is accordingly easier than that of law administration, when the "client" cannot be the sole judge of the quality of police performance. (Service administration still has its problems, of course, especially since the police, being tax-supported, provide the service "free" to any given client. Inasmuch as he need not pay for it, he is encouraged to ask for as much as he cares to; inasmuch as the police — typically — do not charge for it, they have no way of rationing the service other than by more or less arbitrarily deciding how many requests of what kind they will respond to and in what ways.) When a law is being enforced — a burglar sought, a car thief arrested, a traffic ticket issued, a public disturbance suppressed — the "client," if he is the suspect, is not allowed to decide whether or not he wishes police service. If the "client" is the victim, his preferences are given more weight, but still not to the exclusion of other considerations — he cannot, for example, expect the police summarily to execute the suspect (even suspects have rights); he cannot demand that the police drop everything else to find the man who victimized him (other victims must be served, after all); and he cannot take matters into his own hands and deal with the suspect by some form of private vengeance.

This study, then, is concerned with those police activities the quality of which the client cannot be allowed to judge for himself:

5. For a discussion of the difference between divisible or individual goods and collective or public goods, see Richard Musgrave, *The Theory of Public Finance* (New York: McGraw-Hill, 1959).

in short, with police efforts to enforce laws and maintain order. These activities create special problems of administration, for they require the organization to deal with conflict over the meaning and importance of the law, the definition of "public order," and the trade-off between protecting individual rights and protecting the community. But even with regard to law enforcement, some police activities raise these issues more than others. Hardly anyone, for example, will argue that homicide, except in self-defense, is ever right or that the police should overlook it. The police are not thought of as having — and do not think of themselves as having — discretion with respect to serious crimes that produce victims.

But only a tiny fraction (two tenths of 1 per cent) of all persons arrested are charged with homicide and only a small fraction (less than 10 per cent) are charged with *any* of the seven serious offenses that make up the FBI "Crime Index."[6] The vast majority of arrests, and of citizen-police contacts that involve an offense but do not lead to an arrest, are for such matters as drunkenness, disorderly conduct, assault, driving while intoxicated, gambling, vandalism, and the like. People do differ as to whether such matters are important, or such conduct "really wrong," or even what constitutes the proscribed conduct in question. "Disorderly conduct," for example, is not easily defined or to everyone the same thing. A riot is clearly an instance, but a drunken argument may not be. To some delicate souls, a rough shove may be an assault; to others, nothing short of an armed attack may be worthy of the legal name and thus of legal intervention. A traffic violation — speeding, for example — may be legally unambiguous, but both the motorist and the officer know that many similar violators are not caught and one or both may feel that it is not a "serious" offense, especially if the driver was only going "a few miles" over the limit.

It is with the enforcement of the laws dealing with these common offenses that this study is primarily concerned, partly because, being common, they affect so many persons,[7] but primarily because they

6. Federal Bureau of Investigation, *Uniform Crime Reports, 1965* (Washington: Government Printing Office, 1965), p. 112.

7. Of the ten most common nontraffic offenses, eight are misdemeanors or infractions, which together account for two thirds of all arrests made in the United

raise in particularly clear form the question of administrative discretion. A murder, in the eyes of the police, is unambiguously wrong and beyond question serious; murderers are accordingly arrested. But with respect to a street-corner scuffle or a speeding motorist, the police exercise discretion *whether* to intervene (should the scuffle be stopped? should the motorist be pulled over?) and, if they do, just *how* to intervene (by an arrest? a warning? an interrogation?).

Formally, the police are supposed to have almost no discretion: by law in many places and in theory everywhere, they are supposed to arrest everyone whom they see committing an offense or, with regard to the more serious offenses, everyone whom they have reasonable cause to believe has committed an offense.[8] In fact, as all police officers and many citizens recognize, discretion is inevitable — partly because it is impossible to observe every public infraction, partly because many laws require interpretation before they can be applied at all, partly because the police can sometimes get information about serious crimes by overlooking minor crimes, and partly because the police believe that public opinion would not tolerate a policy of full enforcement of all laws all the time.

In almost every public organization, discretion is exercised — indeed, from the client's viewpoint, the problem arises out of how and whether it is exercised — but the police department has the special property (shared with a few other organizations) that within it discretion increases as one moves *down* the hierarchy. In many, if not most, large organizations, the lowest-ranking members perform the most routinized tasks and discretion over how those tasks are to be performed increases with rank: the foreman has more discretion than the worker, the supervisor more than the foreman, the man-

---

States — drunkenness, disorderly conduct, larceny, driving under the influence of alcohol, simple assault, vagrancy, gambling, and violations of the liquor laws. See President's Commission on Law Enforcement and Administration of Justice, *The Challenge of Crime in a Free Society* (Washington: Government Printing Office, 1967), p. 20.

8. See Wayne R. LaFave, *Arrest* (Boston: Little, Brown & Co., 1965), pp. 75–82, and Joseph Goldstein, "Police Discretion Not to Invoke the Criminal Process: Low-Visibility Decisions in the Administration of Justice," *Yale Law Journal*, 69 (March 1960), esp. pp. 556–562.

ager more than the supervisor, and so on. In some cases this condition exists because of the worker's task: he does one or a few things over and over again, as in a manufacturing plant. In other cases it is because the worker's task, though not so routinized, is continuously under the observation of a supervisor, as in a clerical office or a retail store. In still other cases, though the worker performs a complex task free from continuous observation, there is some more or less objective and obvious means of measuring his performance: an insurance agent, for example, works alone and without close supervision, but he can be judged roughly on the basis of how much insurance he sells. A "successful" agent is one who has pleased the client and the client's pleasure is unambiguously recorded — a premium is paid.

The police have a complex, not a simple, task; they work alone or in pairs, and not under continuous supervision; and they cannot let the client be the sole judge of their nonservice function. These attributes are not unique. Schoolteachers, welfare workers, doctors in a hospital, and parish priests in the Catholic church share them, and as a result school superintendents, welfare supervisors, hospital administrators, and bishops share the police chiefs' special concern for the problem of discovering, evaluating, and modifying the ways their organization's operatives deal with clients. Unlike his colleagues, however, the police chief must perform his administrative task under some special and, I believe, unique constraints; these will be discussed in the next two chapters.

For now, it is enough to note that the lowest-ranking police officer — the patrolman — has the greatest discretion and thus his behavior is of greatest concern to the police administrator. The patrolman is almost solely in charge of enforcing those laws that are the least precise, most ambiguous (those dealing with disorderly conduct, for example), or whose application is most sensitive to the availability of scarce resources and the policies of the administrator (those governing traffic offenses, for example). Detectives, by contrast, are concerned with the more precisely defined and more serious offenses (primarily felonies — crimes that may be punished by death or by imprisonment in a state prison, usually for one year or longer) and only after the crime has been committed. The patrolman handles matters about which there are apt to be great differences of public opinion; the detectives, except those dealing with vice and narcotics, deal with crimes whose definition and seriousness are not, typically, in dispute. Further, the patrolman is supposed not only to enforce laws but to maintain order and keep the peace; detectives are concerned almost entirely with law enforcement and hardly at all with peace keeping. Finally, patrolmen when not responding to a particular call are supposed to "prevent" crime, look for "suspicious" activities, and make "on view" arrests of persons breaking a law even though no one has summoned the police. The detective, on the other hand, does not begin his work until a crime has been reported (again, except for vice), he does not usually try to "prevent" a crime (other than by arresting a person who has already committed one crime and might, if left alone, commit another), and he rarely makes "on view" arrests by, for example, picking up drunks or handing out traffic tickets. The detective, in short, does his work (other than on the vice squad) because people have, in effect, asked for his help and under conditions such that he has a reasonably clear and noncontroversial objective; the patrolman often intervenes when people have not asked for him (and would prefer he stayed away) and under circumstances where what constitutes a successful intervention is unclear or in dispute.

For all these reasons, one would expect that the behavior of detectives, except for vice work, would display more uniformity, within departments and among different departments in different cities, than that found in the behavior of patrolmen.[9] The functions of the patrolman make the problem of administration (that is, controlling discretion) more difficult and thus make differences in administration more apparent. Of course, not all men with the *rank* of patrolman, the lowest but most populous rank, do patrol *work*. Some are assigned to a specialized part of the uniformed force — traffic enforcement, for example. Others, though retaining the rank

9. For an account of police work that gives special attention to the work of detectives, as well as to vice squad officers, see Jerome H. Skolnick, *Justice without Trial* (New York: John Wiley & Sons, 1966).

of patrolman, are taken out of uniform and given quasi-investigative duties — as juvenile officers, for example. And in a few departments, patrolmen out of uniform are given assignments on the vice squad. Even in these capacities, however, the patrolman confronts the problem with which this book is concerned: enforcing laws that involve conflicts among citizens, that are necessarily ambiguous in their definition, or that require the police to intervene on their own initiative without a citizen to serve as either a victim or a complainant.

A comprehensive study of the patrol function would, ideally, examine police-citizen contacts from the perspective of all participants and from start to finish — from initial police intervention to final disposition, if any, by the courts and the correctional institutions. This study is partial in that it examines only the police, not the citizen, limits its attention to police treatment of citizens, and considers only indirectly the treatment accorded citizens by other criminal justice agencies. Only a shortage of resources precluded the larger study. There is a risk that in examining only the police one will be led wrongly or unknowingly to accept their premises and conclusions. No effort at "scientific detachment" can be strong enough to avoid this altogether, though I have tried to be on my guard. The problem is stated here so the reader can be on his guard, too.

Thus, this is not a study of "the administration of justice" in the American city — it is far from clear that what the police administer *is* justice (though the constraint of justice is at least as relevant to their work as to the work of schoolteachers or tax collectors). In any case there are other institutions, not here described, that share in the (just or unjust) disposition of lawbreakers and disturbers of the peace. I try to describe the behavior of patrolmen discharging their routine law-enforcing and order-maintaining functions, to explain how that behavior is determined by the organizational and legal constraints under which patrolmen work, to discover the extent to which it varies among police departments, and to determine insofar as the evidence permits what accounts for these differences and especially how local politics contributes to them.

Though this study has intellectual rather than practical objectives, it is not without policy implications. Any attempt to change the way in which patrolmen use their discretion should take into account the extent to which police officers can or cannot be induced to act in accordance with the intentions of police administrators, city officials, or others. One argument will be that the principal limit on managing the discretionary powers of patrolmen arises, not from the particular personal qualities or technical skill of these officers, but from the organizational and legal definition of the patrolman's task.

The eight communities included in this study were selected by first casting the net very widely and more or less at random — at the outset, I did not know how or why local police departments differed in their handling of minor crimes and offenses, and so the first task was to get some sense of the range of variation. In the summer of 1964, students under my direction who lived in certain major metropolitan areas across the country studied and compiled lengthy written reports on at least two local police departments, one in a high-income suburb and one in a working-class city. This first round of reports produced exploratory accounts of the police departments and local courts in twelve cities. During the following academic year, these reports were discussed informally and in a graduate seminar. In the summer of 1965, additional field studies were carried out but this time with an effort to select cities randomly, in order not to choose places because they were thought to fit some preconceived model or theory.

For this second foray, only places within New York State were picked so that differences that might be attributed to legal codes or statewide requirements and constraints could be ignored. All New York cities over 100,000 population, excepting New York City (which was too big for anyone to handle), were listed; there were seven, three with a council-manager form of government and four with the mayor-council form. Four were picked for initial inquiries.[10] In addition, because I suspected that city size might make an im-

10. Albany and Syracuse (both mayor-council cities) and Rochester and Yonkers (both council-manager cities).

portant difference in police behavior, all places, both cities and townships, in New York were listed if they had a 1960 population between 15,000 and 30,000 and had, as of 1962, five or more full-time police employees. Because the social class of such communities was likely to affect both crime rates and police behavior, the list was divided into two extreme groups — those places with a 1960 median family income of less than $6,000 (there were seventeen) and over $8,000 (there were seven). From the seventeen low-income places, seven were picked, partly at random, partly to minimize travel costs, for study.[11] From the seven high-income places, five were picked.[12] Finally, one county that had the equivalent of an urban police department was added. Seventeen communities were thus visited for one or two weeks each by a research assistant to acquire some first impressions, collect available statistics and reports, and interview police chiefs, patrolmen, judges, prosecutors, city officials, and the like.

These reports were examined and, at a conference of all researchers, seven communities were chosen for intensive and prolonged study.[13] Three to six weeks were spent in each place and long reports were written during the late summer and fall of 1965. These reports were discussed in a graduate seminar in the spring of 1966.

As the organization and planning of this book took shape during the 1966–67 academic year, of the twenty-five places reported on, I chose eight for detailed analysis and visited each for varying lengths of time. Six were in New York — Albany, Amsterdam, Brighton, Nassau, Newburgh, and Syracuse — and two elsewhere — Highland Park, Illinois, and Oakland, California. Thus, it is not easy to answer the obvious question "Why did you pick these eight communities?" In the last analysis, they were picked because they were "interesting" — that is, they seemed to exhibit important differences in police behavior and political culture. But they were not

11. Amsterdam, Cohoes, Dunkirk, Glens Falls, Newburgh, Saratoga Springs, and Yorktown Township.

12. Brighton, Garden City, Lynbrook, Rockville Centre, and Scarsdale.

13. Albany, Amsterdam, Brighton, Nassau County, Newburgh, Syracuse, and Yonkers.

picked to fit some theory: such categorization as is offered in this book was arrived at more or less inductively, not deductively, and reflects the empirically observed patterning among places initially picked pretty much at random.

Are these eight communities "typical" of all American cities? Obviously not. They were chosen because of their differences, not their similarities. Within their various categories of size and socio-economic status, they are "extreme" in some sense; that is what makes them interesting. But neither are they wholly atypical. What is said here about Amsterdam, for example, could have been said without too much change about Saratoga Springs or Glens Falls or Dunkirk. What is said about Brighton might have been said, with only a few modifications, about Scarsdale or Rockville Centre. The absence of any southern city is deliberate: the problem of the Negro, and the deep involvement of politics and the police in civil rights issues makes southern cities, if not unique, then very special. In a sense, the South presents the easy case to someone wishing to explore the relationships among police behavior, administrative exigencies, and political environment — there, as Gunnar Myrdal has observed, one of the most important consequences of excluding Negroes from the political process has been the biases this exclusion has introduced into law enforcement.[14] The more recent findings of the United States Commission on Civil Rights seem to bear this out.[15] The North, one supposes, offers the more "normal" case — how do the police behave in communities where all groups can vote and hold office?

In an exploratory study such as this, it is rarely possible to collect precise, numerical data sufficient to permit rigorous analysis. To answer the question of *what* is to be measured, or whether anything *can* be measured, is one reason for doing an exploratory study in the first place. The problem of evidence is not, however, solved by offering such excuses. Much of what is said in this book is asserted, or illustrated, or suggested, but not *proved*. Why should the reader

14. Gunnar Myrdal, *An American Dilemma* (New York: Harper, 1944), pp. 497–498, 538–545.

15. United States Commission on Civil Rights, *1961 Report*, Book I, Part III, esp. p. 187.

believe it? Why especially should he believe it, since what is being asserted so often is a pattern or an attitude that cannot, unlike assertions about scandals or dramatic issues, be checked against newspaper files and the records and memories of other participants? If the subject were not so controversial, perhaps this checking would be a minor scholarly travail, but I am under no illusion that, regarding the police, people in or out of uniform are disposed to have their intensely held convictions about "what everybody *knows*" and "the way it happened to me" set aside in favor of what some professor has written.

The only rejoinder possible is that my assistants and I have visited and written reports about twenty-five police departments. Each of the cities included in this book was visited at least twice and usually three or four times for periods of no less than three weeks and in some cases for nearly two months by at least two researchers, who then compared notes. Each account of the workings of a local police agency or political system was submitted to key local informants to have the facts checked and the interpretations commented upon. Finally, I have studied first hand and written about for other purposes the police departments of Chicago, Detroit, and Boston in addition to the eight places in this book. Despite this, some facts are still in dispute and others, no doubt, will eventually be proved wrong. But we have given what appears to us (or to me, since, despite the help of others, the responsibility for error and interpretation is mine alone) a true account.

Because I believe the question of evidence is an important one, because I feel that the reader should bring to bear on my account of these cities such contextual or background knowledge he may have of them, and because I want other researchers to feel free to check my findings by visiting the cities themselves, I have departed from the usual scholarly convention of giving pseudonyms to the places one describes. The cities in this book retain their real names. To save helpful local officials and informants from needless embarrassment and to honor the promise of confidentiality I made to them, no remarks — except those already a matter of public record — are attributed to a named source.

One final note. The penal law of the state of New York was revised recently and the new code went into effect in September 1967. All references to the law and to police practices under it in New York are based on the unrevised penal law in effect in 1965. And some of the communities may have changed as well. This is an account of what they looked like in 1965–67 and does not pretend to be an account of what they may be like today.

Two The Patrolman

The patrolman's role is defined more by his responsibility for *maintaining order* than by his responsibility for enforcing the law.[1] By "order" is meant the absence of disorder, and by disorder is meant behavior that either disturbs or threatens to disturb the public peace or that involves face-to-face conflict among two or more persons. Disorder, in short, involves a dispute over what is "right" or "seemly" conduct or over who is to blame for conduct that is agreed to be wrong or unseemly. A noisy drunk, a rowdy teenager shouting or racing his car in the middle of the night, a loud radio in the apartment next door, a panhandler soliciting money from passersby, persons wearing eccentric clothes and unusual hair styles loitering in public places — all these are examples of behavior which "the public" (an onlooker, a neighbor, the community at large) may disapprove of and ask the patrolman to "put a stop to." Needless to say, the drunk, the teenager, the persons next door, the panhandler, and the hippies are likely to take a different view of the matter, to suggest that people "mind their own business," and to be irritated with

1. The distinction between order maintenance and law enforcement is similar to distinctions made by other authors. Michael Banton notes the difference between "law officers" and "peace officers" in his *The Policeman and the Community* (London: Tavistock, 1964), pp. 6–7. Egon Bittner distinguishes between "law enforcement" and "keeping the peace" in his analysis of patrolmen handling derelicts: "The Police on Skid Row: A Study of Peace-Keeping," *American Sociological Review*, 32 (October 1967), pp. 699–715. At a higher level of generality, Eugene P. Wenninger and John P. Clark note that the police have both a value maintenance and a goal attainment function: "A Theoretical Orientation for Police Studies," in Malcolm W. Klein, *Juvenile Gangs in Context* (Englewood Cliffs: Prentice-Hall, 1967), pp. 161–172. Though I employ concepts similar to those used by others, the implications of the distinction developed in this chapter are my own responsibility. The distinction may have implications larger than those relevant to the police, for it suggests that the police help perform two of the functional imperatives of any society — what Talcott Parsons calls "goal attainment" (part of which is law enforcement as here defined) and "pattern maintenance" (here, order maintenance). The relevance is suggested by Wenninger and Clark and developed somewhat in James Q. Wilson, "Dilemmas of Police Administration," *Public Administration Review* (forthcoming).

the "cop" who intervenes. On the other hand, a fight, a tavern brawl, and an assault on an unfaithful lover are kinds of behavior that even the participants are not likely to condone. Thus, they may agree that the police have a right to intervene, but they are likely to disagree over who is to blame and thus against whom the police ought to act.

Some or all of these examples of disorderly behavior involve infractions of the law; any intervention by the police is at least under color of the law and in fact might be viewed as an "enforcement" of the law. A judge, examining the matter after the fact, is likely to see the issue wholly in these terms. But the patrolman does not. Though he may use the law to make an arrest, just as often he will do something else, such as tell people to "knock it off," "break it up," or "go home and sober up." In his eyes even an arrest does not always end his involvement in the matter. In some sense he was involved in settling a dispute; if and how he settled it is important both to the parties involved and to the officer himself. To the patrolman, "enforcing the law" is what he does when there is no dispute — when making an arrest or issuing a summons exhausts his responsibilities. Giving a traffic ticket is the clearest case: an infraction of the law is observed and familiar, routinized steps are taken to make the offender liable to the penalties of the law. Similarly, if the patrolman comes upon a burglary in progress, catches a fleeing robber, or is involved in apprehending a person suspected of having committed a crime, he is enforcing the law. Other agencies will decide whether the suspect is in fact guilty; but *if* he is guilty, then he is to blame. Guilt is at issue in both order-maintaining and law-enforcing situations, but blame is at issue only in the former. The noisy neighbor or the knife-wielding lover may say, "Don't blame me"; the fleeing robber, on the other hand, will say, "I'm not guilty."

The Maintenance of Order

The problem of order, more than the problem of law enforcement, is central to the patrolman's role for several reasons. First, in at least the larger or more socially heterogeneous cities, the patrolman encounters far more problems of order maintenance than opportunities for law enforcement, except with respect to traffic laws. Table 1 shows all the radio calls to police cars made by the

Table 1. Citizen complaints radioed to patrol vehicles, Syracuse Police Department, June 3–9, 1966 (based on a one-fifth sample of a week's calls).[a]

Calls		Number in sample	Full count (sample multiplied by 5)	Per cent
Information gathering		69	345	22.1
Book and check	2			
Get a report	67			
Service		117	585	37.5
Accidents, illnesses, ambulance calls	42			
Animals	8			
Assist a person	1			
Drunk person	8			
Escort vehicle	3			
Fire, power line or tree down	26			
Lost or found person or property	23			
Property damage	6			
Order maintenance		94	470	30.1
Gang disturbance	50			
Family trouble	23			
Assault, fight	9			
Investigation	8			
Neighbor trouble	4			
Law enforcement		32	160	10.3
Burglary in progress	9			
Check a car	5			
Open door, window	8			
Prowler	6			
Make an arrest	4			
Totals		312	1,560	100.0

[a] Not included are internal calls — that is, those originating with another police officer (as, for example, when an officer requests a check on the status of a person or vehicle or requests the wagon, and so forth) — or purely administrative calls.

Syracuse Police Department during a one-week period in June 1966. About one fifth required the officer to gather information ("get a report") about an alleged crime for which no suspect was thought still to be on the scene. The patrolman's function in this case is mainly clerical — he asks routine questions, inspects the premises, and fills out a form. About a third of the calls were for services that could as easily be provided — and in many cities are — by a different government agency or by a private firm. Only about one tenth of the calls afforded, even potentially, an opportunity to perform a narrow law enforcement function by stopping a burglary in progress, catching a prowler, making an arrest of a suspect being held by another party, or investigating a suspicious car or an open window. In fact, very few of *these* will result in arrests — there will be no prowler, except in a woman's imagination, the open window will signify an owner's oversight rather than a thief's entry, the "suspicious" car will be occupied by a respectable citizen, and the burglar, if any, will be gone. Almost a third of all calls — and the vast majority of all nonservice calls — concern allegations of disorder arising out of disputes, public and private, serious and trivial.[2]

Second, the maintenance of order exposes the patrolman to physical danger, and his reaction in turn may expose the disputants to danger. Statistically, the risk of injury or death to the patrolman may not be great in order maintenance situations but it exists and, worse, it is unpredictable, occurring, as almost every officer interviewed testified, "when you least expect it." In 1965 there were reported over twenty thousand assaults on police officers, nearly seven thousand of which resulted in injury to the officer; eighty-

2. The workload of the police in dealing with noncriminal matters, especially interpersonal problems, is analyzed in Elaine Cumming, Ian Cumming, and Laura Edell, "Policeman as Philosopher, Guide and Friend," *Social Problems*, 12 (Winter, 1965), pp. 276–286. The importance of order-maintenance calls in Chicago, especially those involving minor family conflicts, is discussed in Raymond I. Parnas, "The Police Response to the Domestic Disturbance," *Wisconsin Law Review* (1967), pp. 914–960. During the week studied, the Syracuse police dispatched about 7.9 operational, that is, nonadministrative, radio messages per thousand population. The message rate for the same week was somewhat higher in Oakland (11.1 per thousand population) and lower in Albany (6.4 per thousand); the distribution of messages within the various categories was about the same in all three cities.

three officers were killed and only thirty of these by auto accidents.[3] There is no way to tell what proportion of these deaths and injuries occurred in the restoring of order as opposed to the pursuit and subduing of a criminal, but patrolmen almost universally contrast the random, unexpected nature of danger involved in handling, say, a domestic quarrel with the "routine" and taken-for-granted nature of danger when chasing a bank robber. Jerome Skolnick considers the preoccupation with danger an important element of the police officer's "working personality."[4] I would add that the risk of danger in order maintenance patrol work, though statistically less than the danger involved in enforcing traffic laws or apprehending felons, has a disproportionate effect on the officer partly because its unexpected nature makes him more apprehensive and partly because he tends to communicate his apprehension to the citizen.

Chasing a speeding motorist, the officer is running risks of his own choosing. Chasing a fleeing robber, he anticipates violence — weapons are drawn, gunfire is expected, and the issues are clear. But when he walks into a room where a fight is under way or stops to question a "suspicious" person, the *possibility* of danger makes the patrolman suspicious and apprehensive. To those fighting or to the person stopped, the patrolman seems "hostile" or "edgy," and if, as is often the case, the citizen has no intention of attacking the officer, he sees the patrolman as "unjustifiably" suspicious, hostile, or edgy. If the citizen then shows his resentment, the officer is likely to interpret it as animosity and thus to be even more on his guard. Both sides may be caught in an ascending spiral of antagonisms.

3. Federal Bureau of Investigation, *Uniform Crime Reports, 1965* (Washington: Government Printing Office, 1965), pp. 152–153. An even larger number of people are killed by the police. Between 1950 and 1960, an average of 240 persons per year were fatally injured by the police. The total on-duty death rate of police officers (33 per 100,000, as of 1955) was less than the comparable death rate in mining, agriculture, construction, and transportation. See Gerald D. Robin, "Justifiable Homicide by Police Officers," *Journal of Criminal Law, Criminology, and Police Science*, 54 (1963), pp. 225–231, and President's Commission on Law Enforcement and Administration of Justice, *Task Force Report: The Police* (Washington: Government Printing Office, 1967), p. 189.

4. Jerome H. Skolnick, *Justice without Trial* (New York: John Wiley & Sons, 1966), pp. 42–48.

But most important, the order maintenance function necessarily involves the exercising of substantial discretion over matters of the greatest importance (public and private morality, honor and dishonor, life and death) in a situation that is, by definition, one of conflict and in an environment that is apprehensive and perhaps hostile.

Discretion exists both because many of the relevant laws are necessarily ambiguous and because, under the laws of many states governing arrests for certain forms of disorder, the "victim" must cooperate with the patrolman if the law is to be invoked at all. Statutes defining "disorderly conduct" or "disturbing the peace" are examples of laws that are not only ambiguous, but necessarily so. In New York State, disorderly conduct is a breach of the peace occasioned by, among other things, offensive behavior or language, disturbing other people, begging, having an "evil reputation" and "consorting with persons of like evil reputations," and "causing a crowd to collect." In California disturbing the peace includes "maliciously and wilfully" breaching the peace of a neighborhood or person by, among other things, "loud or unusual noise," "tumultuous or offensive conduct," or using "vulgar, profane, or indecent language within the presence or hearing of women or children." [5] One might object, as some have, that such statutes are vague and one might expect the courts to rule (again, as some have) all or parts of them unconstitutional for failing to specify a clear standard, but one would be hard pressed to invent a statute that would cover all possible cases of objectionable disorder in language that would leave little discretion to the officer. Most criminal laws define *acts* (murder, rape, speeding, possessing narcotics), which are held to be illegal; people may disagree as to whether the act should be illegal, as they do with respect to narcotics, for example, but there is little disagreement as to what the behavior in question consists of. Laws regarding disorderly conduct and the like assert, usually by implication, that there is a *condition* ("public order") that can be diminished by various actions. The difficulty, of course, is that public order is nowhere

5. New York, *Penal Law*, sec. 722; California, *Penal Code*, sec. 415.

defined and can never be defined unambiguously because what constitutes order is a matter of opinion and convention, not a state of nature. (An unmurdered person, an unraped woman, and an unpossessed narcotic can be defined so as to be recognizable to any reasonable person.) An additional difficulty, a corollary of the first, is the impossibility of specifying, except in the extreme case, what degree of disorder is intolerable and who is to be held culpable for that degree. A suburban street is quiet and pleasant; a big city street is noisy and (to some) offensive; what degree of noise and offense, and produced by whom, constitutes "disorderly conduct"?

One could, of course, throw up his hands and say that there is no such thing as public order and thus disorderly conduct cannot be a crime. This is precisely what we have tended to do with an analogous legal situation, that pertaining to obscenity. Being unable to agree on what constitutes a decent book or picture, we — that is, the courts — have decided that, except in the undefined "extreme" case of "hard-core pornography," obscenity does not exist as a legal matter.[6] However, this reaction is unlikely in the case of disorderly conduct because such conduct can impose real costs on other persons whereas obscenity, except when it is displayed in ways such that the innocent person cannot avoid it, imposes costs, if at all, only on the person who knowingly and voluntarily consumes it.

Certain forms of disorderly or disputatious behavior can be given a relatively unambiguous legal definition — assault or battery, for example. Striking or wounding another person is legally definable because we can agree on what an unstruck or unwounded person looks like. But here another difficulty arises — the need for victim cooperation. Most crimes the patrolman is concerned with are misdemeanors, that is, any crime not a felony, which in turn is — generally speaking — a crime punishable by death or by imprisonment in a state prison, usually for one year or longer. But under the law of many states, an officer can make an arrest for a misdemeanor only when the act has been committed in his presence or upon the properly sworn complaint of a citizen in whose presence it was com-

6. See *Roth v. United States*, 354 U.S. 476 (1957) and *Manual Enterprises, Inc., v. Day*, 370 U.S. 478 (1962).

mitted.[7] If the law, like the disorderly conduct statute or, in some states, the public intoxication statute, is ambiguous enough, the officer can always find some grounds for asserting that the offensive act was committed in his presence — he can "see" people being "disturbed" or a man being "intoxicated in a public place." But to make an arrest for an assault or a battery (misdemeanors in most states) when he has not seen the fight (as is usually the case, since most people stop fighting as soon as the police arrive), he must often obtain a sworn complaint from the victim so that the victim, in effect, makes the arrest and the officer simply takes the suspect into custody.

But it is the exception, not the rule, for the "victim" to cooperate in this way. In over half (54 per cent) of the 125 cases of simple assault turned up by the household survey sponsored by the President's Crime Commission, the police were not notified at all. And in over half (57 per cent) of these unreported cases, the reasons given were that the victim "did not want to harm the offender," regarded the affair as a private matter, or was afraid of reprisal.[8] In short, the victim didn't want to "get involved." A study of the files of the Oakland Police Department shows that between May 5 and May 31, 1967, there were 163 batteries reported to the police.

7. See New York, *Code of Criminal Procedure*, sec. 177 and California, *Penal Code*, sec. 836. In Illinois, however, the police can arrest on probable cause for any offense, including a misdemeanor. See *Illinois Revised Statutes*, Chap. 38, sec. 107–2(c).

For an empirical study of the application of the misdemeanor arrest law as it exists in most states, see John D. O'Connell and C. Dean Larsen, "Detention, Arrest and Salt Lake City Police Practices," *Utah Law Review*, 9 (Summer, 1965), pp. 593–625. A nineteenth-century Boston police chief, who was also an author and poet of modest distinction, was able in one paragraph to describe the law of arrest as it then governed the maintenance of order of the streets: "The offenses for which persons may be legally arrested without a warrant, are, felony (crime punishable in State's Prison), assault and battery *in your presence*, persisting in disturbing the peace, and drunkenness. Simple larceny is not included in the statute, but common practice will, I think, justify an officer in taking a person charged with that crime to the Station House, for the direction of his captain. Other cases may occur, which will require much good judgment and discretion to determine what is proper." Edward H. Savage, "Advice to a Young Policeman," *Recollections of a Boston Police Officer, or, Boston by Daylight and Gaslight*, 2d ed., rev. (Boston, 1865), p. 344.

8. Philip H. Ennis, *Criminal Victimization in the United States*, A Report of a Research Study Submitted by the National Opinion Research Center to the President's Commission on Law Enforcement and Administration of Justice (Washington: Government Printing Office, 1967), pp. 42, 44.

In 85 per cent of the cases, the attacker was known to his victim but in only 30.1 per cent of such cases was an arrest made — in the others, the victim did not want to press charges.[9]

Even though he or she may not want to swear out a complaint, especially if this requires going downtown the next morning, the victim usually wants the police to "do something." A typical case, one which I witnessed many times, involves a wife with a black eye telling the patrolman she wants her husband, who she alleges hit her, "thrown out of the house." The officer knows he has no authority to throw husbands out of their homes and he tells her so. She is dissatisfied. He suggests she file a complaint, but she does not want her husband arrested. She may promise to make a complaint the next morning, but the patrolman knows from experience that she will probably change her mind later. If the officer does nothing about the quarrel, he is "uncooperative"; if he steps in, he is in danger of exceeding his authority. Some patrolmen develop ways of mollifying everyone, others get out as quickly as they can, but all dislike such situations and find them awkward and risky.

The difficulty of maintaining order is further exacerbated by the fact that the patrolman's discretion is exercised in an emotional, apprehensive, and perhaps hostile environment. Even though the vast majority of Americans report, in opinion polls, that they think the police are doing a good job, are properly respectful, and are honest, and even in those neighborhoods — middle-class ones, and especially white middle-class ones — where sentiments favorable to the police are most widespread,[10] police-citizen contacts in any but routine matters are likely to leave both parties dissatisfied.

The police are like various professionals, without themselves being a profession, in that they handle on a routine basis what to others are emergencies.[11] When the police arrive to look for a

9. The Oakland data are cited because, of the cities studied, its police keep the most careful and complete records of offenses and arrests. A crime report is prepared on every reported battery, even if the victim does not wish to prosecute. In some other cities, minor assaults are not even recorded as having occurred unless there is an arrest or a good chance of one.

10. Ennis, *Criminal Victimization*, p. 53.

11. Everett Hughes argues that one defining characteristic of a profession is the tendency of its members to treat as routine what to others is a crisis and to talk in

prowler, examine a loss, or stop a fight, the victim and suspect are agitated, fearful, even impassioned. But the police have seen it all before and they have come to distrust victim accounts (to say nothing of suspect explanations) of what happened. Instead of offering sympathy and immediately taking the victim's side, the police may seem cool, suspicious, or disinterested because they have learned that "victims" often turn out not to have been victimized at all—the "stolen" TV never existed or was lost, loaned to a boyfriend, or hidden because the payments were overdue; the "assault" was in fact a fight which the "victim" started but was unable to finish. A genuine victim, of course, is dismayed by the routine manner in which his crisis is being attended to and irritated because the police do not instantly and fully accept his version of what happened. To him, a serious matter is being mishandled or even lightly dismissed. If the police knew he was a genuine victim, they might be more sympathetic—and in fact the better officers try to develop an appropriate "bedside manner"—but they often suspect that he is not genuine or that, though genuine, he is exaggerating the incident or giving an inaccurate or incoherent account of it.

A citizen who calls an officer usually meets him for the first time and, having recounted his grievance—a missing television set or a broken jaw—rarely meets him again. If there is a suspect still on the scene, the patrolman must decide whether to make an arrest; if he does not, he usually fills out a report. In either case, he soon leaves. Unless an arrest is made—which occurs in only about 7 per cent of all calls to patrolmen[12]—the client is likely to feel "nothing" has been done.

In truth, there is often little the police *can* do. Most crimes are crimes against property, and these are rarely solved because there are neither clues nor witnesses. Even when a suspect is identified, the police are often unable to make an arrest because, if the offense was a misdemeanor, they can only arrest when it is committed in

---

"shocking terms" about intimate matters. *Men and Their Work* (New York: Free Press, 1953), pp. 80–85.

12. Calculated from data in President's Commission on Law Enforcement and Administration of Justice, *Task Force Report: Science and Technology* (Washington: Government Printing Office, 1967), pp. 7–8.

their presence or if they have a signed complaint. Other times the police appear to do too much: they make an arrest when no grounds are evident because they sense danger, recognize a known criminal, or feel a challenge to their authority. Or if a proper arrest is made, the man may be back on the street again within a day, in which case the public may blame the police when in fact the courts have released him on bail or, if he is a juvenile, the probation department or the family court intake office has "settled" the matter with a warning.

Because the patrolman, unlike the schoolteacher or the doctor, cannot himself give a complete and visible response to the needs of his "client" and because those needs are often, to the client, of the highest importance, a citizen's evaluation of an officer — even when the latter is "getting information" or "enforcing the law" rather than maintaining order — is likely to be at best incomplete and at worst inaccurate. Furthermore, the citizen will observe that when the patrolman is not handling the citizen's momentary emergency, he is standing on a street corner, walking along the sidewalk, or driving a patrol car — apparently "doing nothing." What he *is* doing, of course, is waiting to be called to cope with someone else's emergency, and if he were not "doing nothing" he would not be immediately available. The citizen, forgetting this, is likely to wonder why he isn't out "looking for the man who stole my car," or whatever.

When the patrolman is working, not in a middle-class area where crime is comparatively infrequent and has mostly to do with stolen property, but in a lower-class area where it is frequent and has more to do with violence, then there is an even greater likelihood that the citizen and the patrolman will form an unfavorable impression of each other. About 70 per cent of all the victims of crimes against the person uncovered in the Crime Commission's household survey had incomes under $6,000 per year (over 55 per cent of the victims of crimes against property had incomes *over* $6,000).[13] Because most crimes against the person involve parties known or related to each other, a patrolman entering a low-income area, espe-

13. Ennis, *Criminal Victimization*, p. 32.

cially in response to a call about a crime of violence, is likely to be suspicious of the victim's story and is likely to communicate, consciously or unconsciously, that suspicion to the victim.

Thus, the tendency of the patrolman to be and act suspicious arises not simply from the danger inherent in his function but from his doubts as to the "legitimacy" of the victim. Middle-class victims who have suffered a street attack (a mugging, for example) are generally considered most legitimate; middle-class victims of burglary are seen as somewhat less legitimate (it *could* be an effort to make a fraudulent insurance claim); lower-class victims of theft are still less legitimate (they may have stolen the item in the first place); lower-class victims of assaults are the least legitimate (they probably brought it on themselves). A legitimate victim treated as illegitimate may become annoyed or even angered, and rightly so. But however much we may sympathize with him, we must bear in mind that it is essential for the police role to make judgments about victim legitimacy and that such judgments are in many cases based on quite reasonable empirical generalizations.

The working environment of the police is not only charged with emotion and suspicion, it is often, in the eyes of the police, hostile and uncooperative. A majority of Chicago police sergeants who completed a questionnaire in 1960 and again in 1965 felt that civilians generally did not cooperate with the police in their work, that the department did not have the respect of most Chicago citizens, that their civilian friends would criticize the department to their faces, and that most people obey the law only from fear of getting caught.[14] This view of citizens as hostile or uncooperative

14. James Q. Wilson, "Police Morale, Reform, and Citizen Respect: The Chicago Case," in David J. Bordua, ed., *The Police* (New York: John Wiley & Sons, 1967), p. 17. See also Skolnick, *Justice Without Trial*, pp. 9–65, and John P. Clark, "Isolation of the Police: A Comparison of the British and American Situations," *Journal of Criminal Law, Criminology and Police Science*, 56 (1965), pp. 307–319. But compare Banton, *The Policeman in the Community*, pp. 215–224. Banton's findings may result from having studied a small, fairly homogeneous American community; my study and Skolnick's were of large, heterogeneous cities. A theory relating police ethos to the conditions of community life is offered in James Q. Wilson, "The Police and Their Problems: A Theory," *Public Policy*, 12 (1963), pp. 189–216. A similar view is suggested in Jacob Chwast, "Value Conflicts in Law Enforcement," *Crime and Delinquency*, 11 (1965), pp. 151–161.

persisted during a period when the officers believed their department had improved greatly in quality (over half thought it poorly run in 1960; less than a fifth thought so in 1965 after five years of reform under Superintendent Orlando W. Wilson). The belief that citizens were hostile was independent of the officer's age, duty assignment, or ethnicity.[15] Finally, a majority of the respondents felt it was important that a police officer be liked by those citizens with whom he comes in contact but, as citizen respect did not rise along with departmental quality, the proportion of sergeants attaching importance to being liked fell from 79 per cent in 1960 to 59 per cent in 1965.[16]

In general, the police probably exaggerate the extent of citizen hostility. National opinion polls have shown that the vast majority of citizens have favorable attitudes toward the police.[17] Though Negroes are more critical of the police than whites, and higher-income Negroes more critical than lower-income ones, with few exceptions both races and all classes generally approve of the police. Among men, over three fourths of the whites at all income levels and over 60 per cent of the Negroes at all income levels but the highest think the police are doing a "very good" or "pretty good" job in giving protection to the people in their neighborhood;[18] over 90 per cent of the whites at all income levels and over three fourths of the Negroes at all income levels but the highest think the police are "very good" or "pretty good" at being respectful to people like the respondent.[19]

But most police contacts are not with the general public and thus general public opinion is not most relevant. Furthermore, opinions expressed to an interviewer in a moment of calm may be quite at

15. Wilson, "Police Morale," p. 150.
16. *Ibid.*, p. 147.
17. Ennis, *Criminal Victimization*, p. 53.
18. Ibid., p. 55. This finding is borne out by another study in which a sample of Negro adults living in major cities was asked how they thought the police in their city treated Negroes. The percentage answering "very well" or "fairly well" was 56 per cent in New York, 64 per cent in Chicago, 53 per cent in Atlanta, but only 31 per cent in Birmingham. Gary T. Marx, *Protest and Prejudice* (New York: Harper & Row, 1967), p. 36.
19. Ennis, *Criminal Victimization*, p. 56.

odds with behavior displayed in a moment of crisis; the police probably draw their conclusions about citizen attitudes from the behavior of those who are victims, suspects, or onlookers at the scene of a crime or disorder. Finally, what *is* true about public opinion is less important than what the police *think* is true because a misinterpretation of personal experience is harder to correct than a misreading of an opinion poll. But in any case it is not clear that the police *are* in error: if half the victims of crime do not even notify the police, if most of those who fail to notify them give as their reason a belief that police will do nothing or a desire to protect a friend or keep the matter "private," and if the police increasingly find themselves in pitched battles with rioters and looters, then they might be pardoned for concluding that citizens are at best "uncooperative" and at worst hostile.[20]

Occupations whose members exercise, as do the police, wide discretion alone and with respect to matters of the greatest importance are typically "professions" — the medical profession, for example. The right to handle emergency situations, to be privy to "guilty information," and to make decisions involving questions of life and death or honor and dishonor is usually, as with a doctor or priest, conferred by an organized profession. The profession certifies that the member has acquired by education certain information and by apprenticeship certain arts and skills that render him competent to

20. We can only speculate on the psychological costs to the patrolman entailed by his role. One study of ninety-three police suicides in New York City between 1934 and 1940 showed that two thirds occurred among patrolmen; only three occurred among plainclothes detectives. That the latter group should experience only 3 per cent of all the suicides may suggest that their role, defined by more consistent expectations, creates fewer psychological strains. Furthermore, a large number — 40 per cent — of all the suicides occurred among men who had joined between 1925 and 1927, the heyday of Tammany Hall influence in the department. Dr. Friedman conjectures that the new reform policies of Mayor Fiorella La Guardia, who came to power in 1934, produced great insecurity among these men, some of whom were unstable personalities to begin with and who got onto the force through political influence. During the Tammany era, these officers felt they were "backed up" — if not by their nominal superiors then by their political "rabbis" or protectors. During the La Guardia era, they lost that sense of support. See Paul Friedman, "Suicide Among Police" in Edwin Schneidman, ed., *Essays in Self-Destruction* (New York: Science House, 1967). After the Detroit riot of 1967, the head of the police medical division reported a growing number of "nervous and emotional problems" among the officers. See *Detroit News,* Nov. 9 and 12, 1967.

perform these functions and that he is willing to subject himself to the code of ethics and sense of duty of his colleagues (or, in the case of the priest, to the laws and punishments of God). Failure to perform his duties properly will, if detected, be dealt with by professional sanctions — primarily, loss of respect. Members of professions tend to govern themselves through collegial bodies, to restrict the authority of their nominal superiors, to take seriously their reputation among fellow professionals, and to encourage some of their kind to devote themselves to adding systematically to the knowledge of the profession through writing and research. The police are not in any of these senses professionals. They acquire most of their knowledge and skill on the job, not in separate academies; they are emphatically subject to the authority of their superiors; they have no serious professional society, only a union-like bargaining agent; and they do not produce, in systematic written form, new knowledge about their craft.[21]

In sum, the order-maintenance function of the patrolman defines his role and that role, which is unlike that of any other occupation, can be described as one in which *sub-professionals, working alone, exercise wide discretion in matters of utmost importance (life and death, honor and dishonor) in an environment that is apprehensive and perhaps hostile.*[22] The agents of various other governmental organizations may display one or two of these characteristics, but none or almost none display all in combination. The doctor has wide discretion over matters of life and death, but he is a professional working in a supportive environment. The teacher works alone and has considerable discretion, but he may be a professional and in any case education, though important, is not a matter of life or death. A welfare worker, though working alone among apprehensive clients, has relatively little discretion — the laws define rather precisely what payments he can authorize to a client and supervisors review his written reports and proposed family budgets.

21. Cf. Banton, *The Policeman in the Community*, pp. 105–110.

22. I can think of only one other occupation that has the special characteristics I impute to the patrolman: that of attendant in a mental hospital. See Charles Perrow, "Hospitals: Technology, Structure, and Goals," in James G. March, ed., *Handbook of Organizations* (Chicago: Rand McNally & Co., 1965).

This role places the patrolman in a special relationship to the law, a relationship that is obscured by describing what he does as "enforcing the law." To the patrolman, the law is one resource among many that he may use to deal with disorder, but it is not the only one or even the most important; beyond that, the law is a constraint that tells him what he must *not* do but that is peculiarly unhelpful in telling him what he *should* do. Thus, he approaches incidents that threaten order *not in terms of enforcing the law but in terms of "handling the situation."* The officer is expected, by colleagues as well as superiors, to "handle his beat."[23] This means keeping things under control so that there are no complaints that he is doing nothing or that he is doing too much. To handle his beat, the law provides one resource, the possibility of arrest, and a set of constraints, *but it does not supply to the patrolman a set of legal rules to be applied.* A phrase heard by interviewers countless times is "You can't go by what the book says."

This view of police work may be traced to the historical circumstances surrounding the creation of American municipal police forces. Police officers were originally "watchmen" whose task it was to walk their rounds and maintain order in the streets. To maintain order meant everything from removing obstructions on streets and keeping pigs from running loose to chasing footpads and quelling riots. Watchmen were not officers of the court charged with bringing to the bar of justice persons who had broken a law; that task was performed by constables, for a fee, and only on the basis of sworn warrants. These watchmen and later the police handled many situations that had nothing to do with enforcing the law or getting evidence and as a result they often acted under vague laws or no laws at all; a city council would later set down as written law rules that common practice had already established as binding. Throughout the nineteenth century, the fear of riot and popular uprising was

23. See Arthur Niederhofer, *Behind the Shield: The Police in Urban Society* (Garden City: Doubleday & Co., 1967), p. 60, and President's Commission, *The Police*, p. 179: "Typically, an officer is expected to maintain order on the street, to keep a 'clean beat,' to disperse mobs, to remove 'undesirables,' whether or not legal tools for accomplishing these results are available."

usually the reason for enlarging, professionalizing, and ultimately arming the police.[24]

This role gives the patrolman an orientation quite different from that obtaining in a courtroom or assumed by the authors of legal codes. To the judge, the defense attorney, and the legal scholar, the issue is whether a given individual was legally culpable as defined by a written rule. The individualistic, rule-oriented perspective of the courtroom is at variance with the situational, order maintenance perspective of the patrolman.[25] The patrolman senses this conflict without quite understanding it and this contributes to his unease at having his judgment tested in a courtroom.

Thus the patrolman describes his activity as "playing it by ear" and "taking each case as they come," *not* in terms of "enforcing the law" or "making exceptions to the law." Egon Bittner gives the example of a patrolman finding four men getting drunk in public; to control the situation — to prevent a disturbance that will bring a complaint, to break up the gathering, to forestall someone passing out and getting robbed — the patrolman may arrest one of the four and, having broken up the party, send the other three on their way. To him, *which* one gets arrested is not so important. To the judge, it is all-important.

To handle his beat and the situations and disputes that develop on it, the patrolman must assert his authority. To him, this means asserting his *personal* authority. As Banton points out, in a heterogeneous society where different views of proper conduct are held by various classes and subcultures, a uniform and a badge may be insufficient symbols of authority.[26] By authority the patrolman means the right to ask questions, get information, and have his orders

24. Selden D. Bacon, "The Early Development of American Municipal Police," unpublished Ph.D. dissertation, Yale University (1939), esp. pp. 735–787, and Roger Lane, *Policing the City: Boston, 1822–1885* (Cambridge, Mass.: Harvard University Press, 1967), pp. 58, 94, 221.

25. Egon Bittner makes the same point with respect to police handling of derelicts. See his "The Police in Skid-Row: A Study of Peace Keeping" and also Egon Bittner, "Police Discretion in Emergency Apprehensions of Mentally-Ill Persons," *Social Problems*, 14 (Winter, 1967), pp. 278–292.

26. Banton, *The Policeman in the Community*, p. 168.

obeyed. In a disputatious incident, the authority he personifies will not ordinarily influence the outcome unless he gets involved. To believe that a patrolman should be wholly impersonal and correct is to believe that he can control a situation by his mere presence or command; this may be true in some cases, but patrolmen do not assume it will be true in any given case. In entering a situation, he tests the participants — who is the "tough guy," who has the beef, who is blustering, who is dangerous? And he in turn is tested: how far can the policeman be used to obtain one's ends, how far can he be pushed before he responds, is he "cool" or is he unsure of himself? The patrolmen observed for this study almost always acted, and said later that they had acted, in such a way as to show immediately "who was boss." For some, their size alone was sufficient; for others, an assured and firm tone of voice was adequate; for others, shouting and pushing and cursing seemed required. (The latter were not highly regarded by their fellows as a rule, though they were rarely told to take it easy.)[27]

The felt need to "handle the situation," rather than "enforce the law" and to assert authority or "take charge" leads the officer to get involved, but "getting involved" is the antithesis of the ideal — that is, being impersonal and "correct." Patrolmen often equate being "impersonal" with being ineffective, for to be impersonal is to assume that embodying legal authority is sufficient and, in their experience, it rarely is. To get involved means to display one's personal qualities, and these qualities differ greatly among individual patrolmen. In many communities police officers are of working-class backgrounds (that is, from lower and lower-middle income families in blue-collar occupations); this means they bring to the job some of the focal concerns of working-class men — a preoccupation with

27. Bittner quotes a patrolman on skid row: "You see, there is always a risk that the man is testing you and you must let him know what is what. The best among us can usually keep the upper hand in such situations without making arrests. But when it comes down to the wire then you can't let them get away with it." Bittner, "The Police in Skid-Row," p. 711. See also Niederhofer, *Behind the Shield,* p. 53, and William A. Westley, "The Police: A Sociological Study of Law, Custom, and Morality (unpublished Ph.D. dissertation, Department of Sociology, University of Chicago, 1951), p. 112.

maintaining self-respect, proving one's masculinity, "not taking any crap," and not being "taken in." [28] Having to rely on personal qualities rather than on formal routines (in sociological terms, approved role behaviors) means the officer's behavior will depend crucially on how much deference he is shown, on how manageable the situation seems to be, and on what the participants in it seem to "deserve."

Many situations *are* manageable with little difficulty. On skid row, drunks frequently act as if they expect the officer to take charge, search or pat down the man stopped, and arrest or not depending on what the situation seems to warrant. Some quarreling husbands and wives welcome the arrival of the police because it ends the fight without either having to carry out threats that no one wants to carry out — neither side has its bluff called. The experienced officer senses this and plays the role expected of him — arbiter, keeper of the peace, source of ultimate authority, and so on. But if the participants are hostile or the bystanders unsympathetic, if danger is sensed, or if someone involved is suspected of having criminal tendencies (if he is a "bad actor" and not just a "hothead" or "liquored up"), then the patrolman will often become suspicious, defensive, tough, harsh.

Justice as a Constraint

Because of their function, patrolmen face in a special way the problem of justice. Justice — by which I mean, provisionally, fairness, or treating equals equally — is a constraint on the conduct of any organization, especially any public bureaucracy.[29] We expect teachers, tax collectors, welfare workers, and draft board members to be

28. Cf. Walter Miller, "Lower Class Culture as a Generating Milieu of Gang Delinquency," *Journal of Social Issues,* 14 (1958), pp. 5–19.

29. See John Rawls, "Justice as Fairness," *The Philosophical Review,* 67 (1958), pp. 164–194, reprinted in Frederick A. Olafson, *Justice and Social Policy* (Englewood Cliffs: Prentice-Hall, 1961), pp. 80–107; H. L. A. Hart, *The Concept of Law* (Oxford: Oxford University Press, 1961), pp. 153–163; Chaim Perelman, *The Idea of Justice* (London: Routledge and Kegan Paul, 1963), pp. 11–29.

"fair," by which we mean, usually, that we expect them to treat clients on the basis of clear rules, known in advance, and uniformly applied to all persons without "favoritism," that is, without making "unreasonable" or "irrelevant" distinctions. We are often more sensitive to the requirements of justice when we think of the police because their actions seem to have more serious consequences (honor or dishonor, freedom or imprisonment, life or death) and because the police, unlike teachers, are in theory supposed to be purely ministerial agents of the law, who leave all questions of culpability and consequences to judges and juries who have the "right" to decide these matters.

The detective's role is likely to be consistent with these assumptions. He is exposing the man he arrests to potentially serious consequences and is, in a sense, functioning in a ministerial capacity — a crime has been committed, a suspect identified, an arrest made, and in time an indictment, an arraignment, and a formal disposition will be forthcoming. The tests we apply to this process, and to the detective's role in it, are primarily procedural: Was the evidence sufficient? Were the rights of the suspect protected? Was he given the opportunity to remain silent, to secure an attorney, and to post bond? Was he brought without delay before a magistrate?

The patrolman, though he is subject to the same procedural constraints, faces in addition more substantive ones. Since he must "keep the peace," make arrests on his own authority, and handle disputes, he disposes of cases on the street, so to speak, in ways that either do not invoke the formal processes of the law (for example, when he arbitrates a quarrel without making an arrest) or that invoke them in a purely mechanistic and, to the suspect, irrelevant sense. Hardly anyone who gets a traffic ticket or is arrested as a drunk expects that his "trial" will amount to more than clerical procedure: appearing before a judge, or sometimes only a clerk, to pay a fine on the assumption that all matters of evidence and guilt were settled when the officer decided to make the arrest and prefer the charge. To those whom the patrolman confronts, there is no forthcoming procedure that can be judged as fair or unfair, there is only an immediate and substantive *outcome* that is either "right" or "not right." If justice consists of equals being treated equally, then what a patrolman *does* is the "treatment" and how *he* assesses the interests and claims of the parties is an implicit judgment of who is "equal" to whom and in what sense. The members of a quarrelling family or the participants in a juvenile brawl — and indeed the policeman himself — judge the officer's actions as an "outcome" rather than a procedure, and that outcome in turn is evaluated by some principles (which may or may not be shared) as to what is desirable, satisfactory, useful, convenient, and right.[30]

The implicit conception of justice the patrolman brings to his task is quite different from that assumed to operate in "the administration of criminal justice" or "law enforcement." Treating equals equally in a courtroom means to assume that all who enter there are equal before the law. Because such persons are by then meek in demeanor and correct in speech, the assumption seems plausible. The patrolman, however, sees these people when they are dirty, angry, rowdy, obscene, dazed, savage, or bloodied. To him, they are not in these circumstances "equal," they are *different*. What they deserve depends on what they *are*. "Decent people" and "bums" are not equal; "studs" and "working stiffs" are not equal; victims and suspects are not equal, except in some ultimate and, at the moment, irrelevant sense. To be just to these people means to give each what he deserves and to judge what he deserves by how he acts and talks. This is close to the ancient conception of "distributive" justice, which holds that things and honors should be divided among persons according to merit or so that inequality in person is reflected by a proportional inequality in treatment.[31] George C. Homans has restated this in sociological categories and finds it to lie at the basis of the behavior of many small groups, the members of which find justice to consist in the view "that if one man ranks higher than another in one respect, he should rank higher in others

30. Compare the distinction made in John W. Chapman, "Justice and Fairness," in Carl J. Friedrich and John W. Chapman, eds., *Nomos VI: Justice* (New York: Atherton Press, 1963), pp. 147–169.

31. Aristotle, *Nichomachean Ethics*, V, 3.

too." [32] Other sociologists have given the name "status congruence" to this notion.[33]

A "wise guy" deserves less than a "good guy," a man who does not accept police authority, and thus legal authority, deserves less than a man who does. The courts, however, view such situations, not in terms of distributive justice, but in terms of assigning guilt and correcting, by appropriate penalties, a specific and individual departure from a condition of initial equality. Again, the judge and the patrolman see things differently and consequently view each other with chronic suspicion and sometimes active dislike.

The problem is, of course, exacerbated when the participants in an incident are of radically different subcultures — white officers and Negro citizens, for example. The officer, less familiar with what is "normal" behavior, may make imputations of virtue and just deserts along racial lines, overlooking important (and, among white persons, obvious) individual differences. And the citizens may believe the patrolman *is* making such arbitrary imputations, whether or not he is, and by acting on that belief, resist or challenge his authority in such a way as to intensify the conflict between them.

Officers who are not called regularly to the scene of lower-class misbehavior — who work in communities or areas with no skid row, no rowdy saloons, no juvenile gangs, and no publicly quarrelling lovers — escape many of these difficulties. Middle-class families are often criticized by patrolmen for overprotecting or overindulging their children, or for trying to use influence to control the police, but these are *general* criticisms. In the *particular* case they are seen as at least courteous and deferential to authority and often as "co-operative." This makes police intervention less "messy" and therefore easier. Accordingly, we should find many middle-class communities where the police treat common offenses more formally,

32. George C. Homans, *Social Behavior: Its Elementary Forms* (New York: Harcourt, Brace & World, 1961), p. 245. Bertrand de Jouvenel states it this way: "What men find just is to preserve between themselves, as regards whatever is in question, the same relations that exist between them as regards something else." *De la souveraineté* (Paris, 1955), p. 195, quoted in Homans, p. 245.

33. See Gerhard Lenski, "Status Crystallization," *American Sociological Review*, 19 (154), pp. 405–413, and S. N. Adams, "Status Congruence as a Variable in Small Group Performance," *Social Forces*, 32 (1953–54), pp. 16–22.

and thus more seriously, than they do in working-class communities. In later chapters a modest effort will be made to test this hypothesis.

The patrolman's substantive and distributive conception of justice influences both his decision *whether* to intervene in a potentially disorderly or law-violative situation and his decision *how* to intervene. In both cases he must necessarily act in ways that deviate from the strict or procedural conception of justice that applies, in principle, in the courtroom. This is because officers are routinely called upon to "prejudge" persons by making quick decisions about what their behavior has been in the past or is likely to be in the future. The line between prejudging them purely on the basis of police experience and prejudging them on the basis of personal opinion (showing "prejudice") is often very thin.

The decision to intervene will in the narrow sense be just if the police act against only those persons, and all such persons, whose known or probable behavior is proscribed by law and act against them only in the way provided by the law. Acting in a manner not provided by the law, or acting against some law violators but not others, or acting on the basis of a person's attributes — his class, race, appearance, influence, kinship, status, or the like — rather than his behavior is, strictly speaking, unjust.[34] To the patrolman, such a test is unworkable and, in many cases, self-defeating. In preventing crime, the police must make rapid judgments about the probable behavior of a person that often, and necessarily, rest as much on appearance as on past behavior. No one would accuse the police of acting unjustly if they stopped and questioned a man wearing a mask and carrying a sack of burglar tools near a bank at three o'clock in the morning. Even though he might be entirely innocent — say, a reveler on his way home from a costume party — our instinct, formed by experience, suggests a high probability of felonious intent. But suppose the man were a poorly dressed Negro walking the back alleys of a wealthy white residential area at three o'clock in the morning. Again, he might be perfectly innocent — a

34. See the discussion of the elements of justice in David Matza, *Delinquency and Drift* (New York: John Wiley & Sons, 1964), pp. 106 ff.

domestic servant on his way home from his place of employment. But the reasonable instinct of the police is that he may well be a burglar; he will be stopped. The reason we are more concerned about the propriety of police action in the second case than in the first is that we know Negroes must wear black faces whether innocent or not, while revelers walking near banks in the wee hours of the morning can — and are well advised to — leave their masks and tools at home. Nonetheless, the statistical probability of a crime being intended may reasonably be the same in both cases. To add a final complication, suppose the police see a flashily dressed Negro woman walking late at night with a nervous white man. Many women have flamboyant clothes and nervous husbands, and no laws have yet been passed against either. But the police are likely to believe that the woman is a prostitute and the man her customer; statistically they may be right, though in any given case they may be wrong. Our concern about police intervention in this case arises not simply from the possibility that the police may be in error but from the additional fact that many of us are not likely to regard prostitution as a "serious" crime (or, to say the same thing in other words, many of us find it easy to imagine being the nervous white man) and some of us may suspect that, whatever the statistical probabilities, the police "like" to harass interracial couples out of personal prejudice.

The patrolman confronting a citizen is especially alert to two kinds of cues: those that signal *danger* and those that signal *impropriety*. A badly dressed, rough-talking person, especially one accompanied by friends and in his own neighborhood, is quickly seen as a potential threat — he may, out of his own hot temper or because of the need to "prove himself" in front of his buddies, pull a knife or throw a punch. A teenager hanging out on a street corner late at night, especially one dressed in an eccentric manner, a Negro wearing a "conk rag" (a piece of cloth tied around the head to hold flat hair being "processed" — that is, straightened), girls in short skirts and boys in long hair parked in a flashy car talking loudly to friends on the curb, or interracial couples — all of these are seen by many police officers as persons displaying unconventional and improper behavior. The patrolman is alerted to laws they might be breaking or might be about to break; he is also alerted to means of "handling" the situation, even if no law is broken, in a way that reasserts community values, indicates disapproval of their flouting of those values, and reduces the probability that these persons will in fact break a law. It is often remarked that the average police officer is a very conservative person, and so he is, but he also believes that most people share his disapproval of public impropriety and "wise guys" and agree with his judgment that a person who publicly flouts community mores is more likely than one who does not to break community laws. The patrolman believes with considerable justification that teenagers, Negroes, and lower-income persons commit a disproportionate share of all reported crimes; being in those population categories at all makes one, statistically, more suspect than other persons; but to be in those categories *and* to behave unconventionally is to make oneself a prime suspect.[35] Patrolmen

35. One might suppose that criminologists would long since have satisfied themselves that lower-income people commit more common crimes, omitting so-called "white collar" or business crime, than middle- or upper-income persons. I find to my surprise (and irritation) that this is not the case. Most of the research has been on juvenile rather than adult offenders, and has been of three sorts: studies of who is arrested or imprisoned, interviews of sample populations to discover what offenses they will admit to having committed whether or not arrested, and observations of juvenile, especially gang, activity by field workers. The data in the first category are quite clear; of those convicted and imprisoned, a disproportionally high percentage are from low-income, poorly educated, often broken families living in central city areas. President's Commission on Law Enforcement and Administration of Justice, *Crime and Its Impact — An Assessment* (Washington: Government Printing Office, 1967), pp. 78–79; Belton Fleisher, *The Economics of Delinquency* (Chicago: Quadrangle Books, 1966); Clifford R. Shaw and Henry D. McKay, *Social Factors in Juvenile Delinquency* (Washington, D.C.: National Commission on Law Observance and Enforcement, 1931), No. 13, Vol. 2. Such findings have been criticized on the grounds that the police may disproportionally arrest lower-income persons because of class bias, the vulnerable status of the poor, or the like. To learn the "real" incidence of law-violative behavior in the populace, certain scholars have collected self-administered questionnaires from samples of juveniles, usually in a schoolroom situation. These studies typically asked the persons whether they had ever committed any one of a list of common offenses and if so, how often. Surprisingly, there was no significant relationship between the admission of having committed the act and the socioeconomic class of the youth, variously measured. F. Ivan Nye, James F. Short, Jr., and Virgil J. Olson, "Socioeconomic Status and Delinquent Behavior," *American Journal of Sociology,* 63 (January, 1958), pp. 381–389; Robert Dentler and Lawrence J. Monroe, "Early Adolescent Theft," *American Sociological Review,* 26 (October 1961), pp. 733–743; John P. Clark and Eugene P. Wenninger, "Socio-Economic

believe they would be derelict in their duty if they did not treat such persons with suspicion, routinely question them on the street, and detain them for longer questioning if a crime has occurred in the area. To the objection of some middle-class observers that this is arbitrary or discriminatory, the police are likely to answer: "Have *you* ever been stopped or searched? Of course not. We can tell the difference; we have to tell the difference in order to do our job. What are you complaining about?"

People whose characteristics place them in this high-risk population see things a bit differently. An innocent teenager or Negro questioned on the street or told to move along is likely to feel harassed and perhaps the victim of prejudice. Police "handling of situations" often means, to those who are handled, police license

---

Class and Area as Correlates of Illegal Behavior Among Juveniles," *American Sociological Review,* 27 (December 1962), pp. 826–834. The Clark–Wenninger study did find higher reported rates of illegal behavior in predominantly lower-status *areas* but no higher rates attributable to lower-status individuals within those areas.

Other scholars have criticized the self-administered questionnaire on various grounds: it gives great latitude for boys to boast about imaginary or exaggerated exploits and it does not measure carefully the *rate,* that is, offenses per period of time, very accurately. When personal interviews are used and supplemented with other checks on the veracity of the reported behavior, results are obtained indicating that lower-status youngsters commit more frequent and more serious delinquencies. Martin Gold, "Undetected Delinquent Behavior," *Journal of Research on Crime and Delinquency,* 3 (January, 1966), pp. 27–46.

In my view the best studies are those few that have actually observed the behavior of juveniles at various status levels and recorded illegal acts. The most elaborate of these is that carried out over a period of several years by Walter B. Miller, only part of which has been reported in published sources. Miller divided five intensively observed gangs of lower-class boys into "upper-lower" and "lower-lower" status levels and found that, with respect to assaults, the "lower-lower" boys, white and Negro, were about *four times* as likely to commit an assault as "upper-lower" boys. Walter B. Miller, "Violent Crimes in City Gangs," *Annals of the American Academy,* 364 (March 1966), pp. 96–112. Another approach, only recently tried, is to survey populations to discover the extent of victimization; these suggest that lower-income persons are disproportionally the victims of the most serious crimes (except homicide). It is hard to believe that the rich steal (in that way, at least) from the poor; even if they are larcenous, they are certainly not stupid. President's Commission, *Crime and Its Impact,* p. 80.

In sum, my opinion, based, I confess, as much on the experience of living in lower-class as well as rich areas as on the fragmentary participant-observation studies, is that assaults and at least minor thefts are much more likely to be committed in lower-status areas and by lower-status persons. Scholars who believe otherwise are, in my view, either still suffering from a romantic or Marxist illusion that the proletariat was untouched by original sin or else they were raised in a glass jar.

to speak harshly or discourteously, to search without cause, and to behave in a patronizing manner. And in the extreme case, to be "handled" means to be physically handled — grabbed, pushed, slapped, or beaten. The resentment produced by such experiences is especially keen among young men, particularly those of lower- or working-class origins, to whom "street life" is the principal way of life and for whom establishing and maintaining their personal autonomy is very important. As Werthman and Piliavin point out, the street for many young lower-class males is a living room whose walls, though invisible, are real, defined by a sense of territory and maintained by custom and sanctions.[36] In this space, a young man must constantly prove himself by behaving in accordance with the expectations of his gang — staying "cool," not "taking any crap," and being "in the know." The patrolmen are intruders into this living area, partly because they are outsiders, partly because they act on the complaints of persons, usually older residents or passers-by, who dislike the real or imagined intimidation they must suffer in what to them should be a *public* place, and partly because the police often act on their own initiative to reassert community norms defining conventional behavior and to investigate suspicious activity or gather information. In some departments, these interventions are informal — "rousts," searches, questioning, lectures — designed to establish police authority in the area, to show who is in charge; in other departments, more formal procedures are used — "field contact reports" are filled out listing the names, descriptions, and associates of persons who are behaving suspiciously but who have not been seen to break a law or against whom no complaint rests. The gang members resent the invasion of their privacy and retaliate by refusing to cooperate in police efforts to get information or to submit to police attempts to assert authority. To all this they add cyni-

36. Carl Werthman and Irving Piliavin, "Gang Members and the Police," in David J. Bordua, ed., *The Police* (New York: John Wiley & Sons, 1967), pp. 56–98. See also Walter B. Miller, "Lower-Class Culture as a Generating Milieu of Gang Delinquency," *Journal of Social Issues*, 31 (December 1957), pp. 5–19; Leon F. Fannin and Marshall B. Clinard, "Differences in the Conceptions of Self as a Male among Lower and Middle Class Delinquents," *Social Problems*, 13 (Fall, 1965), pp. 205–214.

cism — a belief that the police in fact do not embody legitimate authority because, in gang eyes, they often tolerate, probably out of corrupt motives, illegal activities in the neighborhood.

Though the police may accept such an interpretation as the reason for the behavior of lower-class young men, they do not accept it as an excuse. The street is a public place; gangs have no right, in police eyes, to act as if they owned it. Many, if not most, of the members will have police records, proving that they cannot be trusted to obey the law. Good police work demands their constant surveillance; if they have not committed a particular crime, they are likely to know who did. Gang life, to the police, is carried on in an atmosphere of potential violence that can easily erupt and endanger the "decent people" in the neighborhood. And the police especially resent the rejection of police — which is to say public — authority by the gang's refusal to give information, by its surly and uncooperative attitude, and by the insults and occasional missiles that are hurled at officers. One particularly thoughtful and experienced senior officer explained the police problem to an interviewer this way: "[The police have to] associate with lower-class people, slobs, drunks, criminals, riff-raff of the worst sort. Most of those . . . now in [this city] are Negroes. The police officer sees these people through middle-class or lower-middle-class eyeballs. But even if he saw them through highly sophisticated eyeballs, he can't go on the street . . . and take this night after night. When some Negro criminal says to you a few times, 'You white motherfucker, take that badge off and I'll shove it up your ass,' well, it's bound to affect you after a while. Pretty soon you decide they're all just niggers and they'll never be anything else but niggers. It would take not just an average man to resist this feeling, it would take an extraordinary man to resist it, and there are very few ways by which the police department can attract extraordinary men to join it."

To handle the common situations involving young lower-class males, especially Negroes, in a way that maintains public order, keeps secure legal authority, and wins the respect of the gang is exceptionally difficult. "A patrolman," Werthman and Piliavin conclude, "can therefore compromise his legitimacy . . . in one of two ways: either by visibly betraying his obligation to enforce *some* rules of law or by fulfilling these obligations in ways that conflict with the moral standards of the local population. . . . A 'good cop' is thus a man who can successfully handle a subtle and narrowly defined moral challenge." [37]

Once the patrolman has decided to intervene in a situation, *how* he intervenes will also be judged by competing standards of justice. The kind of intervention that has attracted the most attention is the use of force — "police brutality," in the opinion of some. Officers are empowered to use "necessary and proper" force to make an arrest, subdue an unruly person, or protect themselves. What degree of force is "necessary and proper" will be a matter of dispute even when the purpose for which that force is applied — preventing the flight of a suspect, for example — is not questioned. But if the patrolman's function is to maintain or reestablish order, and if he believes that to accomplish this he must assert his personal authority, then the use or threat of force will be especially controversial because the goal is in doubt or disputed. For example, if a patrolman has arrived at the scene of a disorder and a crowd has gathered, he will ask them to "stand back" or "move on." But how far is "back" or "on"? And what comments may this impromptu gallery appropriately make about the scene they are witnessing? Many departments believe that the proper way to avoid escalating such an incident into a serious disturbance is to take the suspect out of the area as quickly as possible. But to do this, the suspect must be willing to come or proper grounds for a lawful arrest must be present. If they are not — if the officer is trying to decide whether a crime has been committed or if an arrest is warranted — he must remain there; either that, or publicly "back down." If his partner is with him, he is tempted to keep command of the situation by pushing back citizens who do not move back when ordered to do so. But one good push can lead to another and, because citizens (under

37. Werthman and Piliavin, "Gang Members and the Police," p. 66. See also William F. Whyte, *Street Corner Society* (Chicago: University of Chicago Press, 1943), pp. 136–139.

New York law) can use "limited" and "proper" force to resist an unlawful arrest or to prevent "an offense against their person where police officers exceed their authority,"[38] they may strictly speaking be within their rights to push back. The police, on their part, are alert to the possibility of an assault on themselves. In Nassau County, a low-crime suburban community, 124 persons were arrested in 1965 for assaults on police officers; even if in some or many of these cases the citizen was in fact innocent, such an arrest figure is likely to put the police on their guard to expect and perhaps thus precipitate the worst.

In fact, unnecessarily violent police interventions are, so far as we know, comparatively rare. Though charges of "police brutality" make the headlines, most surveys of public attitudes about the police and the relatively few systematic studies of police-citizen contacts suggest that it is more often the language and manner of the officer that is in dispute. The surveys reported by the President's Commission on Law Enforcement and Administration of Justice show that the poor, the young, and the nonwhite are much more likely than others to be critical of the police (who enjoy a good deal of support among American citizens as a whole), precisely as one would expect given their vulnerable position.[39] Yet when asked what police misconduct they had experienced rather than simply believed to exist, they most commonly complained of disrespect and stops and searches without cause rather than unnecessary force. In a 1966 poll taken in the Watts area of Los Angeles after the riot, about one fourth of all respondents and about one half of all male respondents under the age of thirty-five reported having undergone such experiences; only 7 per cent of all respondents, but 22 per cent of males under thirty-five, reported being subjected to "unnecessary force" when an arrest was made.[40] In another survey made in Washington,

38. New York, *Penal Law,* sec. 246(3), as interpreted by *People v. Daniels,* 163 N.Y.S. 2d 597 (1955) and *People v. Tinston* 163 N.Y.S. 2d 552 (1957).

39. President's Commission, *The Police,* pp. 146–149, 180–183.

40. *Ibid.,* p. 147, referring to Walter J. Raine, "Los Angeles Riot Study: The Perception of Police Brutality in South Central Los Angeles Following the Revolt of August, 1965" (University of California at Los Angeles, 1966, mimeo).

D.C., the same year, 60 per cent of the Negro males believed the police discriminated but only 10 per cent claimed to have seen unjustified police violence.[41]

Observations of police behavior by researchers hired by the President's Commission also suggest that unnecessary force occurs in but a tiny fraction of police-citizen contacts, that discourtesy is more common, and — most important — that such incidents seem to be provoked more by *class* than racial differences and by unconventional or bizarre behavior on the part of the suspect. In 5,339 observed police-citizen contacts in three major cities, there were 20 (about three tenths of one per cent of all cases) clearly involving excessive or unnecessary police force; more than half of those subjected to such force were white. Almost all appeared to be poor, most of whom had said something that seemed to challenge police authority; many were drunks, sexual deviates, or juveniles.[42] Data collected by the same observers show that, of all police-citizen contacts that resulted in police questioning on the street or in the home, in 66 per cent of the cases the interrogation was begun with no introductory remarks at all; the remainder were divided about evenly between those preceded by a polite or impersonal request (14 per cent) and those preceded by a "brusque or nasty command" (15 per cent).[43]

When physical force *is* used, it is sometimes justified by officers, as one study found, in terms of dealing with "disrespect for the police."[44] This, as will be suggested later, is typical of certain kinds of departments but not all; however, in any department an officer handling a street situation is alert to the potential for violence and concerned that the symbols of his authority — badge and uniform — may not be enough to avert it. Furthermore, in the experience of

41. President's Commission, *The Police*, p. 147.

42. *Ibid.*, pp. 164, 182.

43. *Ibid.*, p. 180. The report does not explain why the percentages fail to add to one hundred.

44. William A. Westley, "Violence and the Police," *American Journal of Sociology*, 59 (July 1953), p. 38. Of the 73 officers answering the question, "When do you think a policeman is justified in roughing a man up?", 37 per cent said, "When he shows disrespect for the police." See also Westley, "The Escalation of Violence Through Legitimation," *Annals*, 364 (March 1966), pp. 120–126.

many officers, conditions that threaten violence are normally, in many nonpolice situations, handled by forceful and preemptive action: a parent physically punishes an errant child; a boyhood quarrel is settled with a flurry of punches; a wise guy is put in his place with a shove. Many officers see professionally approved police doctrine — to use only the minimum necessary force to effect an arrest — as an invitation to victimization, especially when no arrest seems justified or appropriate. An officer in a department that recruits working-class men is likely to come from a background in which force is one legitimate means among many to achieve certain ends; he will be puzzled by the assumption among upper-middle-class observers of police action, or action of any sort, that violence is *never* appropriate except as a last resort and in self-defense.[45] The officer will feel he is being expected to act abnormally — that is, to show undue and self-defeating restraint. In these cases he distinguishes "normal" force from "sadistic" force (which, he admits, certain patrolmen practice).

Force used by police officers in these circumstances should be distinguished from that employed in getting confessions. The latter kind — the "third degree" — was once the form of violence most commonly referred to in both popular and serious studies of police

45. Working- and lower-class families from which many policemen come apparently rely on physical punishment in child rearing more than do middle-class families, though the evidence is not altogether consistent. See Donald G. McKinley, *Social Class and Family Life* (New York: Free Press, 1964), pp. 78, 80, 83; Arnold W. Green, "The Middle-Class Male Child and Neurosis," in Rheinhard Bendix and Seymour Martin Lipset, eds., *Class, Status and Power* (New York: Free Press, 1953), pp. 292–300; Herbert J. Gans, *The Urban Villagers* (New York: Free Press, 1962), pp. 55–60. Leonard Reissman, *Class in American Society* (New York: Free Press, 1959), pp. 237–239, contains a useful review of several of the major empirical studies.

It is also possible that Catholics attending parochial schools experience more socially approved violence in the form of corporal punishment than do persons attending public schools; on this, I have as yet found no evidence, however. I would conjecture that the principal critics of police practices, who overlap in significant degree with those who criticize the use of force in the conduct of American foreign relations, come disproportionally from a background (higher-status families, Jewish families, Quaker families) where force is at a minimum. On the class origins of the police, see Niederhofer, p. 37. Over three fourths of the officers questioned in his study had as fathers men who were skilled, semi-skilled, or unskilled workers or men in service trades.

work. The Wickersham Commission report dwelt at length on the use of the third degree, which it found to be widespread, and early Supreme Court decisions that began to bring under judicial control the prearraignment stages of the administration of criminal justice were typically aimed at ending the use or threat of force in obtaining statements.[46] Violence of this sort was intended to solve crimes, was carried out by detectives, and was related to the idealized conception of the police role — making "good pinches" on "real criminals." By contrast, the reports of the President's Commission on Law Enforcement and Administration of Justice in 1967 hardly refer to the third degree at all, and many contributors to that study believe it is no longer a serious problem in most jurisdictions. Precisely because it *was* part of the crime-solving function of the police, it was relatively easy to bring under judicial control by various appellate decisions. Instead, the President's Commission focused on the abuse and violence that occur in the course of "police field practices" — that is, in the course of handling street situations where the object is the maintenance of order rather than the solving of a crime.[47]

Some Organizational Consequences

The patrolman's conception of the police role will vary to some extent with the character of the community and with the duty assignment of the officer, but the general features of the patrol problem — coping with disorder by exercising wide discretion over vital matters in an apprehensive environment — tend to impart to the police department as a whole its special character. Perhaps because patrolmen are the most numerous rank, perhaps because all officers of whatever duty or rank must first serve in patrol, the police organization develops its special ethos: defensiveness, a sense of not being

46. Zechariah Chafee, Jr., Walter H. Pollak, and Carl S. Stern, *The Third Degree* (Washington, D.C.: National Commission on Law Observance and Enforcement, 1931), No. 11, pp. 13–261, esp. at p. 153. The United States Supreme Court shortly thereafter took the matter up in *Brown v. Mississippi,* 297 U.S. 278 (1936), *Chambers v. Florida,* 309 U.S. 227 (1940), and *White v. Texas,* 310 U.S. 530 (1940), holding that coerced confessions were inadmissible in state trials.

47. President's Commission, *The Police,* pp. 178–193.

supported by the community, and a distrust of outsiders. Most officers adjust to this by adopting the habit of "minding your own business" and "keeping your mouth shut." The young patrolman is taught "not to stick his neck out" and to "keep his nose clean." Penalties fall on the man who violates departmental procedures or who rushes into difficult situations; survival and security await the man who on procedural matters is "clean" and who on substantive issues plays it cool.

The most important consequence of this state of affairs is that, with respect to routine police matters, *the normal tendency of the police is to underenforce the law.*[48] By "underenforce" is meant making substantially fewer arrests than observed citizen behavior in theory warrants and, on those arrests actually made, preferring the lesser rather than the maximum charges. This hypothesis will be tested in later chapters. The extent of underenforcement will, it is conjectured, vary depending on the offense. Major crimes will produce arrests whenever the legal opportunity affords; departmental policy as well as the officer's conception of his own role reward such acts. The level of enforcement on minor police-invoked rules — traffic laws, for example — will depend on departmental policy almost entirely, for here the department can measure performance "objectively" and a patrolman's personal disinclination to give tickets will not cause him great difficulty if the department wants tickets written. In between, with respect to minor thefts, drunkenness, disturbances, assaults, and malicious mischief, only very strong departmental measures can counteract the tendency to handle these matters by means short of an arrest.

There may be explanations other than those derived from a consideration of the police role that account for underenforcement. Few men, especially few poorly paid men, want to work any harder than they have to. "Rate-busters" are no more appreciated by fellow workers on police forces than they are in factories. These factors may contribute to the outcome here described, and perhaps

48. Cf. Banton, *The Policeman in the Community*, pp. 127–136, and Wayne R. LaFave, *Arrest* (Boston: Little, Brown & Co., 1965), Chaps. 3–6, for similar conclusions.

more so in some cities than in others, but this study can shed little light on the extent of that contribution.[49]

The police tendency to underenforce laws against minor and especially ambiguous offenses further worsens relations between patrolman and judge, already strained by the conflict between the situation-handling orientation of the former and the rule-application orientation of the latter.[50] The police make an arrest for a minor offense when other ways of handling the situation have been exhausted or seem precluded or when police authority (and to the patrolman, *legitimate* authority) has been challenged. He takes into court those who "don't deserve a break" or who have already had a break. The judge, of course, may see this person for the first time. Strictly speaking, he is not supposed to know if he has been arrested before (though often a judge, especially in lower courts, will see the man's record before deciding the case) and certainly he is not likely to know if the man has previously had a "run in" with the police that did not result in an arrest. The judge decides the case *de novo*. Usually there is no question of guilt to decide, because most defendants will plead guilty, often on the advice of defense counsel, prosecutor, or the police. There is a question of penalty, however. The officer, if he has gone to the trouble of making an arrest and if the man is guilty, wants a fine or jail sentence imposed. On misdemeanors and offenses, he rarely gets it. For example, the Syracuse City Court in 1965 disposed of 4,182 misdemeanants and lesser offenders. Only 24 per cent were fined or jailed; 38 per cent were acquitted or had the charges dismissed and another 38 per cent received probation or a suspended sentence.[51] Of the 229 persons charged with disorderly conduct or

49. There may be other factors that help explain this aspect of police behavior (and especially variations among the police in this regard); they might include ethnicity, religion, region, age, and the like. This study can offer no data on such possibilities.

50. The Chicago survey showed that in 1961 and again in 1965, 84.8 per cent of the sergeants believed that the courts are "too lenient" and, in 1965, 67.5 per cent agreed that it is discouraging to be a policeman because the courts let so many people off with little or no punishment.

51. Calculated from Returns *B* and *E* made by the local courts to the New York State Department of Corrections for 1965.

vagrancy 15 (7 per cent) went to jail and 51 (22 per cent) were fined; the rest were dismissed, acquitted, placed on probation, or given a suspended sentence. Over 75 per cent of the 172 persons charged with assault in the third degree had their cases dismissed or acquitted — often because the victim decided not to press charges. But of the 39 persons against whom charges stuck, half got a suspended sentence. Syracuse is mentioned only because it is fairly typical and its judges are reputed to be competent and honest men.

Ironically, the person arrested for the *least* serious offense is more likely to suffer a penalty than one arrested for a more serious offense. Of the approximately 9,000 traffic summonses heard in court in Syracuse in 1965, about 70 per cent resulted in a fine being levied; only 17 per cent resulted in a finding of not guilty or dismissed.[52]

The traffic violator is, of course, the easiest offender for the patrolman to apprehend and he can be apprehended in large numbers if departmental policies require it. He is also, by police standards, the most trivial offender — except in rare accident cases, he has not "hurt anyone" — whereas a barroom brawler, a street fighter, or a shoplifter has hurt or deprived somebody. Yet the latter are, in police eyes, given only a "slap on the wrist." Of course, to the defendant, a suspended sentence or probation may indeed be punishment — he has acquired a record and the social stigma that accompanies it. The judge may see it that way also, or believe there is a chance for rehabilitation. But the patrolman attaches little significance to stigma when the offender is a "troublemaker" from a lower-class neighborhood where an arrest record is at best a fact of life and at worst a badge of honor; as far as rehabilitation goes, the patrolman believes that there is little prospect of it unless it is induced by a fear of punishment. After all, the patrolman may already have given the man a break and that produced no reform; the break the judge has given him is not likely to do better.

52. Summonses in Syracuse are issued only for the more serious moving violations and they must be heard in court. Excluded from this figure are 131,422 traffic "notices" — mostly for parking — for which people paid a fine to the clerk in the traffic violations bureau. Excluded also are summonses for persons who could not be located because they were from out of state or had moved. If all these violators were included, the proportion being penalized would be much higher.

This oft-remarked conflict between police officers and judges is sometimes described as the difference between the "punitive" police and the "lenient" or "rehabilitative" judges. This may occasionally be accurate, but as a rule it misstates the problem. The police themselves, except in the rare case when departmental norms against leniency can be enforced, are themselves "lenient," at least when no challenge either to police authority or important community interests is involved. The real source of the conflict is the effort by both the police and the judges to assert and defend their autonomy, their right to make independent judgments of what a situation requires. It is *because* the police are so often lenient that the trouble arises — they see the judge as a man failing to support the police officer when the latter has decided, with first-hand awareness of the situation, that leniency is not deserved. The judge, by contrast, feels that it is up to him to screen the guilty from the innocent and the deserving from the undeserving; in addition, he often sees a contrite and sober defendant and he may believe that a fine or jail sentence would only hurt the man's innocent family. Furthermore, the rule of law must be observed and this can be done most easily by dealing with like-minded and congenial lawyers, both prosecution and defense, who understand the law and the necessity of keeping the system going and getting the cases decided expeditiously. A negotiated plea and a suspended sentence meet both the formal requirements of due process and the more urgent requirements of getting through the calendar. To the judge, the police officer "doesn't know the law" and, worse, doesn't understand the need to decide quickly. Because the judge must decide quickly, he reduces the chance of injustice by relying on dismissals and suspended sentences. To the patrolman, however, it appears that *he* and not the defendant is on trial.

One important consequence of the special character of patrol work is that many officers try very hard to avoid it. In Chicago, with the second largest department in the United States, only one fifth of the officers who completed a questionnaire in 1961 and less than a third who did so in 1965 wanted to be assigned to the patrol division; most wanted to be either a detective or assigned to headquarters in some specialized capacity.[53] There are many reasons for preferring other duty assignments: detectives have higher prestige and usually higher pay, and specialized bureaus (the vice or juvenile squads, for example) offer to some men more interesting work with less routine, better hours, and greater freedom. But a major reason arises out of a fundamental advantage of nonpatrol duty assignments — *the officer has a better sense of what is expected of him.*[54] He has clearer, less ambiguous objectives, he need not "get involved" in family fights or other hard-to-manage situations, and he need not make hard-to-defend judgments about what people deserve. Detectives look for "real" criminals. The traffic bureau passes out traffic tickets to motorists whose behavior can be easily compared to an unequivocal written standard. A patrolman working traffic in Syracuse told an interviewer:

> I was in patrol for nine years, and as far as I'm concerned you can have it. You've got all those messy details; you're called in on cheatings and stabbings, family fights and quarrels; you're chasing kids. You never know what's going to happen next, and not all of it is very pleasant. When you get in a traffic enforcement unit you know exactly what's expected of you, and what you have to do; then you can do your work and that's it.

Similar observations were made by traffic men in Oakland, which had a list of men waiting to get in the bureau. This attitude in Syracuse and Oakland is of special interest because in both cities traffic men are expected to "produce" — a quota, or something very like it, exists. Some men resent the quotas, others dislike stopping "nice guys" and giving them tickets, all are aware that riding a motorcycle is dangerous, and yet to the outside observer the morale in these traffic units is higher than in patrol work and it is generally regarded as "good duty." The reason, it will be argued here, is that in traffic

53. Self-administered questionnaires were completed by all the sergeants serving in 1961 and by one half of those serving in 1965 on the Chicago Police Department; 19.8 per cent of the 818 responding in 1961 and 30.3 per cent of the 551 responding in 1965 preferred patrol work. Nearly half were in fact then in the patrol division.

54. Skolnick observes that in the police, as in all work organizations, "The worker always tried to perform *according to his most concrete and specific understanding of the control system*" (italics in original). *Justice without Trial*, p. 180.

work the idealized conception and the courtroom conception of law enforcement operates: the law is impersonally applied to easily ascertained infractions under circumstances such that the norms of individual culpability and equality can be observed.

To ensure that traffic enforcement has this ministerial quality and does not acquire the conflict-mediating aspects of regular patrol work, the traffic officers observed during the course of this study — especially those operating in cities where they were expected to "produce" a large number of tickets — developed various defensive strategies. In both Syracuse and Oakland, several officers described to interviewers in almost identical terms how they worked. First, give the driver a little leeway; make sure you can tell him you caught him doing ten miles over the speed limit, not just two or three miles. Second, get in and get out — spend as little time as possible with the driver and say as little as possible. What you don't say can't hurt you, and if you linger around the car, some onlooker may think there is some funny business going on. Third, try to make him thank you for the ticket by making him feel you are "giving him a break." One Syracuse patrolman described a technique many officers used: "The trick is to give him a ticket and make him say 'thank you.' Lots of times you'll stop a guy doing 35 miles per hour through a red light and [when you stop him for running the light] you'll tell him he was also speeding. Then when you give him the ticket just for the red light he actually thanks you."

Even traffic enforcement may involve some conflict over what the constraint of justice requires. A traffic "stop" serves purposes other than enforcing the traffic laws, and these other purposes place the traffic officer in the role of a patrolman deciding whether he has grounds for intervening in a situation that may be more serious than merely speeding or running a red light. Stopping the car gives the officer a chance to glance inside where he may notice "suspicious" people or merchandise (an uncrated television set, for example, or some opened bottles of whiskey). When the officer is suspicious, he will often detain the car long enough to radio in its license number (to see if it is stolen) and a description of its driver or occupants (to see if they are wanted on warrants). Though a computer in the Oakland communications center can search stolen auto and fugitive files very quickly, it still takes time, mostly waiting for "air time" to get the message out and back on the very busy police radio, and it creates an adversary relationship — the officer is questioning the driver about his identity, his business, where he is going and where he is coming from, and looking through the car. If he suspects the presence of contraband (narcotics, stolen merchandise, or hidden weapons) he may want to search the car. This raises some delicate legal issues and creates a situation that may lead the citizen to complain. A suspect may be searched if he is arrested. But detention for questioning is not an arrest, though it may lead to one. The officer must have "reasonable cause" to detain a person. In California a person detained on reasonable cause may be "patted down" or "frisked," that is, the clothing felt from the outside to detect the presence of weapons, but not searched.[55] Contraband observed through a car window may be seized. To search a car without arresting a person, however, the officer must usually get the permission of the driver, though the law is hardly clear on any of these matters. "Getting permission" is an ambiguous procedure, involving perhaps the difference between saying "Open the trunk" and "Would you open the trunk?" And if the officer senses danger, or the suspect is uncooperative, polite forms of address may be abandoned rather quickly by both parties. If the case ever

55. California law, no clearer than most on the subject of "street stops," is analyzed in Larry Waddington, "Stopping and Questioning by Police Officers on Public Streets," *Journal of California Law Enforcement,* 1 (October 1966). The general issues are considered in Wayne R. LaFave, "Detention for Investigation by the Police: An Analysis of Current Practices," *Washington University Law Quarterly* (1962), pp. 331–399, and in Lawrence P. Tiffany, et al., *Detection of Crime* (Boston: Little, Brown, 1967), Part I. The Uniform Arrest Act would allow brief street stops to permit the police to identify suspicious persons; it has been adopted in three states (Delaware, New Hampshire, and Rhode Island). So also would the Model Code of Pre-Arraignment Procedure in the March 1966 draft prepared for the American Law Institute, sec. 2.02. In New York, the so-called "stop and frisk" law was passed in 1964. It provides that: "A police officer may stop any person abroad in a public place whom he reasonably suspects is committing, has committed or is about to commit a felony [or certain other crimes], and may demand of him his name, address, and an explanation of his actions. When a police officer has stopped a person for questioning pursuant to this section and reasonably suspects that he is in danger of life or limb, he may search such person for a dangerous weapon." (New York, *Code of Criminal Procedure,* sec. 180-a, 1965).

comes to trial, however, the judge and jury will, under defense counsel leadership, show a detailed interest in just such niceties in deciding whether a reasonable search was made. These are the cases that raise for the patrolman on traffic duty many of the problems typical of patrol duty, especially when the motorist involved is a Negro who believes that he is being detained because he is a Negro.

Three The Police Administrator

The police administrator — variously called chief, superintendent, commissioner, or captain — has in common with all other executives, especially those of governmental organizations, responsibility for the policies of his agency. In principle, he is supposed to "set policy" and, having set it, to obtain resources (money, manpower, public support) from the community in order to carry it out. Ideally, performing this function requires that the administrator have sufficient knowledge about and control over the rank-and-file members of his organization — especially the patrolmen — so that he can show what the police are doing and how well they are doing it, alter more or less precisely their behavior to accord with such policies as the community may agree to, and evaluate a particular officer's actions in the light of a specific citizen complaint. With respect to some members of his organization, and with respect to some aspects of the work of all members, the administrator does have knowledge and control. He knows, or can find out, whether his officers are tolerating the operation of a brothel and how many traffic tickets they are issuing. But with respect to how well they are preventing crime, catching criminals, and maintaining order, he has very little information.

The police share with most other public agencies — the schools, foreign ministries, antipoverty organizations — an inability to assess accurately the effectiveness of their operations. Indeed, some writers, like Anthony Downs, have made the absence of an output that can be priced on a market, or otherwise given an objective, continuous evaluation, a defining characteristic of bureaucracy.[1] However they choose to interpret such measures, automobile dealers know how

1. Anthony Downs, *Inside Bureaucracy* (Boston: Little, Brown, 1967), Chap. III.

many cars their salesmen have sold, television producers know what audience ratings their programs have earned, and baseball managers know their clubs' standing and the batting averages of their players. But just as the school superintendent has only the most approximate measures of how well his schools are educating children, partly because "education" is so hard to define and measure, partly because the school's contribution to education however measured is so hard to estimate,[2] so also the police chief has only the most rudimentary knowledge of how well his patrolmen are preventing crime, apprehending criminals, and maintaining order. No police department, however competently led or organized, can know how much crime and disorder a community produces, or how much would be produced if the police functioned differently (or not at all).

Most crime becomes known to the police through citizen reports, but the citizens are likely to underreport many kinds of crime for reasons of self-interest that the police and the community cannot easily change. The true rates for rape, robbery, assault, burglary, and larceny are many times higher than the reported rates; though some of the difference is due to police error or malpractice, most of it is due to the failure of citizens to notify the police. A third to a half of the assaults in one survey went unreported; because most assaults occur among people known, or even related, to each other, it is not surprising that half the victims who did not report these offenses gave as their reason that they felt "it was a private matter" or that they did not want to get the offender into trouble.[3] Between 40 and 60 per cent of all thefts and cases of malicious mischief were unreported; because these are largely crimes of stealth, they are rarely solved by the police. Thus, it is not surprising that well over half the victims who did not report them gave as their reason that the police could not do anything. The two crimes most accurately

2. Coleman, et al., *Equality of Educational Opportunity* (Washington: Government Printing Office, 1966), Chap. III.

3. President's Commission on Law Enforcement and Administration of Justice, *The Challenge of Crime in a Free Society* (Washington: Government Printing Office, 1967), pp. 21–22.

reported are murder, presumably because it is so serious and because most murderers *are* caught, and auto theft, presumably because insurance companies require such a report and because most stolen cars are recovered by the police.

If the self-interest of the citizen causes him to underreport certain crimes, it may cause him to overreport others. A false report of a theft may be filed in order to make an insurance claim; disorderly conduct may be charged against a neighbor with whom one has a grudge to settle or against teenage boys whose rowdy (but non-criminal) behavior one wants curbed. And ignorance may cause other distortions — a stolen purse may be presumed lost, an unmarried couple caught in a motel may be thought of as having violated a moral but not a legal code.

Even when the police have accurate information, it is often difficult or impossible to devise a strategy that would make the occurrence of a crime less likely. Many serious crimes — murder, forcible rape — are of this character: though they are often reported with minimum distortion or delay, they occur, in many cases, in private places, among people who know each other, and in the heat of an emotional moment. A police department may assign an officer to each street corner, but inside the buildings on those corners, a drunken husband may still maul or murder his wife's lover as though the police were a hundred miles away.

Crimes that occur in public places are more easily suppressed by police patrol, but the police can never know whether a crime suppressed in one neighborhood reappears in another, less closely patrolled neighborhood, or in another community served by a different police department, or within the same neighborhood but in a different form. Stealing cars parked along the curb may be reduced by intensive patrol, but car thieves may then go elsewhere to steal or, abandoning the streets to the police, burglarize stores by entering them from the alley.

The rate of certain crimes is determined to a significant but unknown degree by factors over which the police have little control. Street crimes are affected by the weather, crimes against property by the prevailing economic conditions, crimes against the person by the racial and class composition of the community, delinquency by the nature and strength of family and peer group controls. The police know these things — or think they know them — but they cannot estimate the magnitude of such factors, or distinguish their effect from that of police tactics, or bring these factors under police control.[4]

Though he may talk publicly a good deal about crime rates, the police administrator knows or senses that he cannot get really reliable figures and that if he could get them he would not be able to show that police work makes a visibly dramatic difference in them. He will tell a visitor that "the police don't cause crime" and the "police alone can't stop it," and of course he is right. If the apparent crime rate goes down, he will not object if the newspapers give him credit; if it goes up, he will point, perhaps with ample justification, to reasons over which the police have no control.

As a result, few police administrators show much interest in "planning" the deployment of their manpower and equipment. There is no information — and in the nature of the case, there can never be sufficient information — on the effects of alternative police strategies on the several kinds of crime. Some problems could be dealt with by rational analysis, however. The Task Force on Science and Technology of the President's Commission on Law Enforcement and Administration of Justice showed that the probability of apprehending a suspect increased as the response time of the police

4. In addition, of course, police departments vary considerably in the accuracy with which they report such crimes as are known to them. See Ronald H. Beattie, "Problems of Criminal Statistics in the United States," *Journal of Criminal Law, Criminology, and Police Science,* 66 (July–August 1955), pp. 178–186; Marvin E. Wolfgang, "Uniform Crime Reports: A Critical Appraisal," *University of Pennsylvania Law Review,* 109 (April 1963), pp. 708–738; President's Commission, *The Challenge of Crime,* pp. 25–27; James E. Price, "A Test of the Accuracy of Crime Statistics," *Social Problems,* 14 (Fall, 1966), pp. 214–221; James Q. Wilson, "Crime in the Streets," *The Public Interest* (Fall, 1966), pp. 26–35. The President's Commission found that crime reports are significantly affected by local police reporting systems. For eleven large cities that recently changed their system, the increase in major (so-called "Index") offenses *in one year* ranged from 26.6 per cent in Miami to 202.0 per cent in Kansas City, Missouri. The cities that have made such significant changes in their reporting systems since 1959 account for *nearly 25 per cent* of all reported index crimes against the person committed in the United States.

decreased.[5] Operations research techniques are available to show how response time can be reduced most economically in a given department. Controlled experiments could be performed to assess the effect on citizen reports of crime by systematically altering the number of patrolmen and the frequency of patrol in an area.[6]

But few police administrators take even those steps that might lead to modest gains in optimal resource allocation. No department visited for this study, for example, tried systematically to measure response time and the consequences of its variations. Some departments have experimented with varying the forces assigned to particular beats, or even the dimensions of these beats, in accordance with reported crimes and calls for service, but they are the exception.[7] It is even rare for a department to keep careful and long-term records on the effect of "saturation patrol" (by a tactical squad or the like) in one or more neighborhoods.

Adequate information is, of course, not all that would be needed for a "rational" allocation of police protection. Even if the administrator had perfect knowledge of the outcome of various police deployment strategies, he would also have to have a decision rule that would tell him which outcome to prefer. There are at least two such rules and they are in conflict. One is the "crime minimization"

5. President's Commission on Law Enforcement and Administration of Justice, *Task Force Report: Science and Technology* (Washington: Government Printing Office, 1967), pp. 92, 93.

6. Such experiments are likely to have two weaknesses, however. One is that it is often difficult to know the effect of altering patrol practices on crime reports in parts of the city outside the experimental area. The other is the "Hawthorne effect" — citizens may report more crimes in experimental areas because they see more policemen about, or because they are aware they are part of an experiment, even though the actual rate of crimes has not changed; conversely, they may report fewer because they feel more secure.

7. The procedures used to allocate patrol forces in Los Angeles, Oakland, and Cincinnati are described in Frank E. Walton, "Selective Distribution of Police Patrol Force," *Journal of Criminal Law, Criminology, and Police Science,* 49 (1958), pp. 165–171. The few such efforts as are made to allocate patrol forces rationally are critically evaluated in "Program Budgeting for Police Departments," *Yale Law Journal,* 76 (March 1967), pp. 822–838. The Boston Police Department authorized a study that used operations research techniques to find ways of reducing response time. See Richard C. Larson, *Operational Study of the Police Response System,* Technical Report No. 26 of the Operations Research Center of the Massachusetts Institute of Technology (December 1967).

criterion: allocate patrolmen so that the last one assigned would deter an equal amount of crime no matter where in the city he was placed. This criterion would produce the smallest total amount of crime in the city, but because the deterrence value of a patrolman varies by type of neighborhood, some neighborhoods would have more crime than others. The other rule is the "crime equalization" one: allocate patrolmen so that the probability of being victimized is the same in all parts of the city. This might well leave the total amount of crime high in the city as a whole — equalizing victimization rates may be achieved by concentrating police in the most crime-prone areas to drive down those rates while allowing the rates in relatively crime-free areas to rise. In short, the police administrator — like all administrators — must make decisions about equity as well as about efficiency.[8]

Even if he had a decision rule, a police administrator would rarely have the funds, the information, the extra manpower, or the professionally competent assistants to make its systematic application possible. But most police administrators show little interest in such projects — partly perhaps because they have not been trained to think in these terms, but partly because they see these things as largely irrelevant. The administrator does not believe he and his organization are judged by the public in these terms, nor does he believe they should be: no statistics can be devised that would fairly measure what the police and the public take to be the true worth or failure of police work. Repeatedly, interviewers for this study were told, "You can't go by the statistics," or "You have to use judgment and you've either got it or you don't." Even those departments with the most modern technologies — including IBM machines, punched cards, computer tabulations, and the like — were administered by men who by and large used the numbers thus produced merely to compile annual reports, satisfy the FBI's need for data, and keep track of payrolls and operating expenses. Most departments gather data the way the telephone company gathers phone

8. Carl S. Shoup, "Standards for Distributing a Free Governmental Service: Crime Prevention," *Public Finance,* Vol. 19, No. 4 (1964), pp. 383–392.

numbers — individual by individual, to be filed alphabetically and consulted only when somebody needs to "look something up."

The police administrator must nevertheless deal from time to time with a public hue and cry about "rising crime rates" or the "lack of police protection." If he knew how to prevent crime, of course he would, but he is in the unhappy position of being responsible for an organization that lacks a proven technology for achieving its purpose. (In this, he is somewhat like the superintendent of a mental hospital: he too must deal with a problem of great importance for which there is no generally effective cure.) What he can do about rising crime rates, of course, is to hire more men (although the productivity of the marginal officer is impossible to measure, it is generally assumed that more men will not make matters worse and may make them better) and to use the ones he has "more aggressively." "Aggressive" police practice means gathering more information about people who may be about to commit, or recently have committed, a crime. Because he cannot, except by due process of law, put people in private places under surveillance (and the opportunities for eavesdropping or wiretapping are being restricted by court decision to the point where *any* surveillance in a private place may soon be impossible), he must gather the information in public places by stopping and questioning "suspicious" persons, checking cars, searching (where possible) people and vehicles for contraband, and keeping an eye on those locales — street corners or taverns in rowdy neighborhoods, for example — where criminal acts often occur.

In short, "doing something" about rising crime rates means putting more patrolmen on the street and ordering them to be more alert. This, of course, increases the likelihood of the patrolmen coming into an adversary relationship with citizens — innocent people, to say nothing of guilty ones, usually do not like being stopped, questioned, or frisked. Furthermore, the patrolman cannot stop everyone, and in deciding who "ought" to be stopped he will rely on whatever clues he can. Persons who appear to be lower class are more likely than others to commit crimes; Negroes are more likely than whites to commit the crimes of violence about which the public is most concerned; young men are more likely than older ones to steal automobiles. Intensifying surveillance will be experienced by people in these categories as "harassment"; failure to intensify surveillance will be regarded by people not in these categories as being "soft" on crime.[9]

Even assuming that there are substantial benefits from aggressive patrol (as there may be), these may be offset by increased citizen irritation. Today, more citizens are aware of their rights, more organizations are prepared to articulate and defend those rights, and the local political system is more vulnerable to (that is, finds it harder to ignore) complaints about the violation of rights. Those people who are most likely to believe, rightly or wrongly, that they are being "harassed" — Negroes, young adults, lower-income persons — are increasing as a proportion of many cities' population, and thus it will be more difficult than ever for the police administrator to carry out a crime prevention program based on aggressive patrol.

Managing Discretion

For these and other reasons, the administrator will have difficulty specifying in advance the circumstances under which a patrolman should intervene. To get the patrolman to do "the right thing" when he is making "street stops" in order to question persons, the administrator must first be able to tell him what the right thing is. This is seldom possible. It is difficult to describe what constitutes a "suspicious person" or a "suspicious circumstance," and some things that might have to enter into such a description cannot safely be put in

9. In 1967 the liberal mayor of Detroit, Jerome P. Cavanagh, faced a campaign led by certain white groups to recall him from office on the grounds that he had not done enough to halt the growing crime rate. He had first been elected mayor in part by Negro voters, who felt they were being harassed by a police crackdown on crime led by the previous administration. *The New York Times*, May 7, 1967, p. 66. Nor are Negroes the only group who complain of street stops. A Yale law professor wrote an article expressing his dislike at being stopped on his late evening or early morning walks or while driving and, what was worse, at being called "Charlie." Charles A. Reich, "Police Questioning of Law Abiding Citizens," *Yale Law Journal*, 75 (1966), pp. 1161–1172.

writing or made official. A poorly dressed Negro alone at night in a wealthy white neighborhood may be a suspicious person in a suspicious circumstance, but one can imagine what reaction a police administrator would get from various civic groups, to say nothing of the courts, if he instructed his men to stop all such persons and question them. One list that was made of persons who should be subject to "field interrogations" yields plenty of illustrations of the problem. Some of its items were reasonable enough ("person who fits description of wanted suspect," "narcotics users," "persons who loiter about places where children play") but most of them either gave the officer very little guidance or else made almost anybody subject to interrogation ("person wearing a coat on a hot day," the driver of a "car with mismatched hub caps," persons who are "visibly rattled when near the policeman," "unescorted women or young girls in public places," and so on.)[10]

With respect to his preventive patrol function, the patrolman can be given a clear statement about *how* to intervene even if not about *whether* to intervene. He can be taught how to approach a suspect, what to say, what kind of identification to ask for, what other questions to put, and how to check the name by radio to see if the person is wanted.

But with respect to his order maintenance function, guidance on *how* to intervene is especially lacking. Some rules, of course, can be formulated, particularly ones stating what *not* to do (don't use a racial epithet, don't hit a man except in self-defense, don't arrest without a warrant unless you have seen the misdemeanor), but no very useful — certainly no complete — set of instructions can be devised as to what the officer *should* do with, say, quarrelling lovers. Defining a policy in such matters is difficult, not because the police have not given much thought to the matters or because they do not know how they should be handled, but because so much depends on the particular circumstances of time, place, event, and personality. Psychiatrists do not use "how to do it" manuals, and

10. Thomas F. Adams, "Field Interrogation," *Police* (March–April 1963), p. 28, quoted in Jerome H. Skolnick, *Justice without Trial* (New York: John Wiley & Sons, 1966), p. 46.

they have the advantage of dealing with people at leisure, over protracted periods of time, and in periods of relative calm.

Law enforcement situations, once the intervention has occurred, can often be handled by rule; order maintenance situations usually cannot. Some rules may be prescribed for order maintenance situations but they will be either *ambiguous* (that is, open to various interpretations and, especially, failing to specify the circumstances under which they are operative) or *equivocal* (that is, combining inconsistent or competing values, presumably because the rule maker cannot decide which value he prefers).

To say that discretion inevitably exists and thus cannot be reduced to rule is not to say that the police administrator does not know what he wishes done. Often, perhaps always, he will believe that there is a right and a wrong way to handle the situation and that if he were on the spot he would know what to do. And he may in some sense be right. He may have the judgment and experience necessary to place a correct interpretation on the event, predict accurately the future behavior of the participants as a consequence of alternative courses of action open to him, and select which outcome will be optimal for the occasion. Many of his patrolmen, especially the more experienced ones, may have the same skills. But because he cannot in advance predict what the circumstances are likely to be or what courses of action are most appropriate — because, in short, he cannot be there himself — he cannot in advance formulate a policy that will "guide" the patrolman's discretion by, in effect, eliminating it.[11]

If the police administrator persists in formulating ambiguous or equivocal policies, the patrolman is likely to perceive them as "unrealistic" or irrelevant. "You can't go by what the book says" is

11. When they get the chance, the administrators often prefer to do things themselves. Gardiner reports that until recently the vast majority of police chiefs in Massachusetts instructed their patrolmen to write an account of a traffic infraction but not to issue a ticket; the chief, after reading the account, would himself decide whether to issue a ticket. The chiefs also lobbied against a bill to require that the patrolman write out the ticket at the scene of the infraction and hand it to the motorist. John A. Gardiner, "Traffic Law Enforcement in Massachusetts," unpublished Ph.D. dissertation, Department of Government, Harvard University (1965), Chap. 2.

one of the remarks an interviewer most often hears from a patrolman and that a rookie patrolman most often hears from the "old hands."[12] In this respect, too, the police administrator is in the same position as the school superintendent, the hospital director, or the secretary of state. But unlike these others, he must deal with the problem of wide discretion being exercised by sub-professionals who work alone (and thus cannot be constrained by professional norms) and in situations where, both because the stakes are high and the environment apprehensive or hostile, the potential for conflict and violence is great.

In response to this state of affairs, the police administrator tries to define his organization's mission as much as possible as one of law enforcement rather than of order maintenance (except for the special case of large public disorders, such as riots or demonstrations). For several reasons, he deals with the community at large in terms of the "crime problem," not the "order problem." First, crime, especially crime tabulated by the FBI in its annual "Crime Index," is thought by the public to be "more serious" than disorder. In this, of course, the public may be quite mistaken. Many of the most serious crimes (murder, for example) cannot be prevented by the police no matter what they do and in any case the kind of killing that is most frightening — a respectable person being killed by a stranger — is relatively rare.[13] Also, many of the more common "Index" crimes (larceny or burglary) are less serious than some of the consequences of family quarrels or juvenile disturbances. Second, "enforcing the law" is less controversial than "maintaining

12. Arthur Niederhofer, *Behind the Shield: The Police in Urban Society* (Garden City: Doubleday & Co., 1967), pp. 44, 60.

13. For example, there were 205 homicides in Philadelphia in 1965, for a rate of about 10 per 100,000 population. Wolfgang's study of murder in that city, the findings of which are generally supported by FBI and other data, showed that between 1948 and 1952, only 12.2 per cent of all murders were committed by a stranger; the rest were committed by relatives or acquaintances. Marvin E. Wolfgang, *Patterns of Criminal Homicide* (Philadelphia: University of Pennsylvania Press, 1958). This means that only slightly more than one person in every hundred thousand was murdered by a stranger and, since many of these were lower income persons, the chances of a middle-class person being the victim of a homicidal stranger were even lower. For other crimes of violence, especially robbery, the chances of being victimized are much higher (in Philadelphia, perhaps 140 times greater) but, again, the great majority of victims are lower-income persons.

order," though certain methods of enforcing laws against street crime (aggressive patrol, for example) are quite controversial. Third and most important, when "enforcing the law" the police can act more frequently within the legal fiction, as ministerial agents applying unambiguous, unequivocal rules to clear-cut cases.[14]

Many a patrolman wishes his job could be in fact what it is in theory — enforcing the law. After answering a series of calls that require him to fill out forms, provide non law enforcement services, or handle domestic disturbances, a patrolman will frequently tell an interviewer that "This isn't *real* police work" and he will grumble about all the "dull" or "messy" jobs he is given. To him, "real" police work is catching "real" criminals — making a "good pinch" on a felon, preferably while the felony is in progress. But good pinches are rare, and when the patrolman uncovers a felony from which the suspect has fled, the case is turned over to the detectives who, if they find the culprit, get all the credit.[15] The patrolman may believe that if he were left alone to handle things his own way, he could improve on the law enforcement record of the department. On his own, he might spend his time watching a liquor store where there have been several armed robberies, questioning certain people in an area where a known criminal is believed to be hiding, keeping an eye on a car that doesn't belong in the neighborhood, or picking up information by casual conversation with people hanging around on street corners.

But to do these things the patrolman requires time, freedom, and the right to assert his authority. Time is scarce because so much of it is consumed by "service" or "information" calls that "don't amount to anything" and by whatever demands his superiors put on him to issue traffic tickets or pick up drunks. Freedom is limited by supervisors (sergeants, lieutenants, detectives) who arrive on the scene whenever anything "big" develops. And authority is hard to assert because, in the patrolman's eyes, so many citizens have lost their

14. Except with respect to "unpopular" laws governing private conduct among consenting parties. Both police and public recognize that discretion is exercised with respect to "friendly" gambling, seduction, adultery, or the like.

15. Niederhofer, *Behind the Shield*, p. 58.

respect for the police, refuse to cooperate with them, and complain to the department about the least little thing.

Because of the law enforcement orientation of the administrator, or because of what he believes to be the orientation of the public, the department will be organized around law enforcement rather than order maintenance specialties. If order were the central mission of the department, there might be a "family disturbance squad," a "drunk and derelict squad," a "riot control squad," and a "juvenile squad"; law enforcement matters would be left to a "felony squad." Instead, there is a detective division organized, in the larger departments, into units specializing in homicide, burglary, auto theft, narcotics, vice, robbery, and the like. The undifferentiated patrol division gets everything else. Only juveniles tend to be treated by specialized units under both schemes, partly because the law requires or encourages such specialization. The law enforcement orientation of most departments means that new specialized units are created for every offense about which the public expresses concern or for which some special technology is required. The patrolman, who once had a chance to perform some detective functions, sees his scope of activity steadily narrowed by specialization until what remains for him is clerical work, service work, and, of course, order maintenance.

Because most crimes cannot be solved and because a comprehensive policy for order maintenance is impossible to develop, the police administrator acquires, in addition to his law enforcement orientation, a *particularistic* concern for the behavior of his men. That is to say, what preoccupies him — other than the over-all level of crime — is not how patrolmen *generally* behave but how they behave in a *particular case*. Police chiefs do not as a rule lose their jobs because crime rates go up; indeed, rising crime rates may make it easier for them to get more money and manpower from city councils. But they often get into trouble and sometimes lose their jobs because a particular officer takes a bribe, steals from a store, associates with a gangster, or abuses a citizen who is capable of doing something about it.

The administrator becomes attuned to complaints. What constitutes a "significant" citizen demand will, of course, vary from city to city. In some places, a political party will tell the police whom to take seriously and whom to ignore; in other places, organized community groups will amplify some demands and drown out others; in still other places, the police themselves will have to decide whose voices to heed and how to heed them. Whatever the filtering mechanism, the police administrator ignores at his peril those demands that are passed through. The typical demand is for *more* police protection — a patrolman to stand on a particular corner, a car to stop speeding on a certain street, a "crackdown" to curb teenage rowdies or drunks sleeping on steps or thieves preying on liquor stores. Other demands are for services not strictly "police" in nature — taking people to the hospital, for example. Every department studied had more or less elaborate ways of making sure that the chief would not have to admit that, in response to a citizen call, nothing was done. Incoming telephone messages and outgoing radio dispatches are logged; in many larger departments, they are also tape recorded automatically. Each patrolman must keep a daily log or a memo book and, in important matters, file a report. Most such cases end inconclusively — there is little the police can do. The reporting system is not designed to ensure that the problem will be solved (often it cannot be) but to protect the department against a charge that it "did nothing."

One police administrator was asked how he allocated patrolmen to the various beats. He said there were two systems: one called for leaving the same man in the same beat for a long period in order that he might become familiar with the neighborhood and its people; the other for rotating men around so as to minimize the time it would take the police to respond to a given call. Under the latter system, if one officer is busy with a call, another from an adjoining beat would fill in for him; on a busy night, the entire city may become one large beat, with everybody covering everywhere. Good arguments could be made for both systems, he said, but only the latter was used.

> If you want to develop a knowledge of the area, you would delay a call, unless it's an emergency, until the beat man concerned is free. [But] if you look around the country . . . you would find, I would guess, that 99 per cent of [the departments] are geared to response time because it's response time . . . that produces citizen complaints . . . Developing knowledge of your beat may in the long run be a better objective, but it's hard to measure and it's not reinforced by citizen complaints.

If the police administrator is more threatened by complaints over the particular behavior of his officers than over crime rates or general police strategy and if he cannot make and enforce policies that prescribe how the officer ought to "handle situations," then the kind of system the administrator develops to defend his organization and to discipline the individual officer will be oriented toward particular kinds of behavior (not general strategies) and toward those elements of police behavior that can be subject to rule. In addition, the defense and control system will confer substantial discretionary power on the administrator to decide whether or not a particular behavior was a violation of a departmental policy even though—indeed, precisely because—that policy is itself ambiguous or equivocal. A departmental rule book will contain, among other things, a set of quite specific and unambiguous rules the violation of which can be easily verified (failing to answer a radio call, failing to proceed as directed to the scene of an incident, failing to report periodically on one's whereabouts, failing to keep a log) and a set of general policies that are either ambiguous (use only necessary and proper force in effecting an arrest) or impossible of realization (enforce all laws at all times).

Easily verified violations of specific and unambiguous rules are often the source of disciplinary proceedings, especially in larger departments. Violations of more general, more ambiguous, or more unrealistic "rules" are much less often the cause of disciplinary action. As will be suggested in later chapters, police departments vary considerably in this respect, but on the whole the average officer is not likely to experience the frequent invocation of rules intended to ensure "full enforcement" of the law or to prevent him from acting "improperly" in an order maintenance situation. Being ambiguous, it would be hard to enforce such rules in any case, and the police administrator — himself once a patrolman — knows this. But occasionally they are enforced, or at least complaints from citizens that invoke such rules are taken seriously because the citizen is a "somebody" (rather than a nobody), or an organization makes a political issue of the matter, or the administrator feels that the officer's behavior discredited the whole department or was clearly beyond the bounds of tolerance.[16]

The patrolman experiences such a defense and control system as irrelevant or capricious. He sees the police administrator as the person who insists that every call be answered, however silly; that a report be taken on everything, however trivial; that the patrolman's time be accounted for, however useless the information. It is the administrator who sends in the brass or the detectives to take over the interesting cases and who breathes down his neck in the difficult situations. And, above all, it is the chief who makes him answer for citizen complaints, justify actions he can barely remember in accordance with vague or unknown standards, and explain why he did not follow the legal and official conception of his duty (either enforce the law by making an arrest or do nothing) when the legal and official conception is irrelevant and when the police administrator knows, privately, that it is irrelevant.

No employee of any organization, of course, is likely to agree with the disciplinary decisions of his superior, but the police officer, because of the nature of his role, and especially with respect to those general rules that are supposed to guide his performance of the order maintenance function, is particularly inclined to regard such acts as unwise or unfair. Because he works alone his superior can never know exactly what happened and must take either his word or the complainant's. The patrolman necessarily exercises wide discretion, but the police administrator is obliged publicly to deny that there is much discretion in police work and may have to act out that denial by deciding complaints about police behavior as if no discretion

16. Wayne R. LaFave, *Arrest* (Boston: Little, Brown & Co., 1965), p. 427.

existed. The patrolman is dealing with matters of great importance, and thus the complainant is likely to be excited and even impassioned; the latter's story may appear more dramatic, more "human" than the story of the officer for whom, public opinion may suppose, the stakes are not so high. The patrolman is not a professional, and thus the opinion of a professional colleague cannot be sought to justify his actions (the way doctors may justify each other's actions as in accord with "approved medical practice").

It is not that the patrolman is frequently punished for misusing his discretionary powers but that such punishment as occurs (being based on ambiguous rules applied after the fact in situations where the citizen's word is taken as against the officer's) is experienced by him as arbitrary or the result of "political influence." Where the requirements of justice — treating equals equally and on the basis of clear rules, known in advance — do not appear to be followed, then the only explanation, in the eyes of the patrolman, is favoritism, pressure, or caprice.[17]

One reason for the oft-noted tendency of patrolmen to form cliques, factions, and fraternal associations[18] is not so much to celebrate the virtues of ethnic solidarity, though the organizations tend to be along ethnic lines, but to defend officers against what is to them arbitrary authority and "outside influence." The power of the administrator is to be checked because the administrator, if he is a strong man, is "out to get us" and, if he is a weak one, is "giving way before outside pressure."

The problem is exacerbated in some departments by restrictive civil service regulations. Originally intended to prevent political influence in the department, they often hedge with so many restric-

17. My survey of Chicago police sergeants showed that in 1961, before the reforms of O. W. Wilson, 58.8 per cent felt that discipline was not strict enough and 47.1 per cent believed that politicians had much influence over promotions. In 1965 the sergeants felt the discipline problem had been solved — 65.9 per cent thought it was "about right" — but nearly as many as before (38.3 per cent) believed that politicians had much influence over promotions and 33.9 per cent believed they had much influence over duty assignments.

18. See Tom Brooks, "New York's Finest," *Commentary* (August 1965), pp. 29–36; Nathan Glazer and Daniel P. Moynihan, *Beyond the Melting Pot* (Cambridge: MIT Press, 1964), p. 261; and Niederhofer, *Behind the Shield*, p. 135.

tions the administrator's power to suspend, demote, or dismiss that, to do anything at all, he must necessarily harass the men — giving them poor duty assignments, transferring them to unpleasant beats, or verbally upbraiding them.[19] The patrolmen tend to use these regulations as protective devices in order to enjoin superiors from disciplining them. But what appears to be a defense against a problem is often one cause of the problem: the more restrictively enforced the constraining regulations, the more the administrator must use harassment to achieve his ends or, if he chooses to give up, the more he may ignore obvious guilt. Both responses are frequently experienced by patrolmen as unjust.

The administrator is aware, of course, that he is responsible for the morale of his men and that heavy demands are always being made on that morale by the nature of the police role. The administrator and the patrolman both know that the "true" facts of the incident — whether it involved abusiveness or unnecessary force or discourtesy — can rarely be established and that the standards governing the use of "necessary" force or "firm" language are inevitably vague, if indeed they exist at all. In these matters, the administrator would like to take the side of the patrolman, and often does, but not without misgivings. As the Task Force on the Police wrote: "The police administrator finds himself caught in a conflict between his desire to be responsive to a citizen who has reason to complain about a policeman's behavior and his fear of the reaction of his force to seemingly arbitrary discipline where there is no clear breach of a pre-announced standard of proper conduct."[20]

The administrator is caught in the middle — without clear standards, adequate rules, reliable information, or sufficient resources.

19. In New York State, the civil service law requires the local administrator to grant a person against whom disciplinary action is proposed written notice of the charges, a hearing on the charges, and (if requested) the right to counsel and to summon witnesses. If the penalty assessed involves dismissal, demotion, a fine of over fifty dollars, or suspension without pay for more than ten days, the employee may appeal the decision to the state or local civil service commission or to the courts (Chapter 790, *Laws of 1958 of the State of New York*, sections 75, 76).

20. President's Commission on Law Enforcement and the Administration of Justice, *Task Force Report: The Police* (Washington: Government Printing Office, 1967), p. 20.

It is because he feels caught that he is more likely to make imprudent public statements about this matter than any other. Some chiefs try to identify with their men by attacking (and enraging) those who fail to "support the police" and who "stir up trouble"; others try to soothe the community, and thus enrage their own men, by promising that they can "live" with a civilian review board. Most chiefs, indeed, tend to develop two views, one public and one private.

Under these circumstances, the relationship between patrolman and administrator is defined for the former primarily by the extent to which he feels himself "backed up" by the latter. If discretion is inevitable, then the administrator ought to "back up his men" in their exercise of it and give them "authority equal to their responsibilities." (Apparently the issue of support also defines to a great extent the relationship between classroom teacher and principal in the school's dealings with parents.)[21] The desire to be backed up, and the constant suspicion that he will not be, is intensified by circumstances that lead the officer to conclude that the citizenry is indifferent or hostile to the police function. When facing hostility or a lack of cooperation, the patrolman believes he should get *more* backing from his superiors. Instead, he fears he may get less because under these circumstances the administrator must deal with more complaints and take such complaints as he gets more seriously as a result of the activities of organized pressure groups, especially civil rights and civil liberties groups, which "put the heat" on politicians who in turn are too timid to face them down. The absence of agreed-upon standards for how the police should behave makes it hard for the patrolman, in his opinion, to do his job properly; the presence of many procedural rules makes it easy to penalize him for doing it, in somebody's opinion, improperly.[22]

21. Howard S. Becker, "The Teacher in the Authority System of the Public School," *Journal of Educational Sociology*, 27 (1953), pp. 128–141, and Bidwell, "The School as a Formal Organization," in James G. March, *Handbook of Organizations* (Chicago: Rand McNally & Co., 1965), p. 1004.

22. McNamara argues that a police department has the characteristics of what Gouldner calls a "punishment-centered bureaucracy" in that "the use of negative sanctions and the threat or fear of their use pervades the day-to-day operation" of (in this case) the New York City department. John H. McNamara, "Uncertainties

Not all the rules of the department are either procedural or ambiguous. On some matters, police administrators may develop quite explicit police strategies and obtain exact compliance from their patrolmen. But only some of the things police officers do are amenable to such policies — generally speaking, questions of law enforcement where the absence of compliance by officers is easily verified. Orders to close down a brothel can be enforced by checking to see if the establishment is still open for business. Orders to issue traffic tickets in large numbers can be checked by examining the ticket production records of individual officers on the assumption that there are always motoring infractions to be found and only lazy or indifferent officers will not find them. And in cities with drunks in public places, orders to arrest people on public intoxication charges can be enforced by noting the officers' arrest records.

These offenses all have in common the fact that it is the police officer rather than the citizen who invokes the law and becomes the complaining witness. To be sure, citizens may complain of the existence of a brothel, or of drivers speeding on a certain street, or of drunks annoying shoppers in front of department stores, but the arrest, if there is one, is on the authority of the officer. (An arrest for larceny or assault, by contrast, would often have to be on the sworn complaint of the victim unless, as rarely happens, the officer was a witness to the event.) Some of these arrests may even be relevant to the order maintenance function of the police. Arresting a drunk is one way of breaking up a fight or ending a disorder. But this is at the discretion of the patrolman; to the extent his superiors order him to arrest drunks, he must go out and find drunks above and beyond what he might arrest as a way of managing disorder. In studying drunk arrest figures, therefore, we want to be especially careful to distinguish between those made incidental to the management of disorder or the handling of a dispute and those made "on

---

in Police Work: The Relevance of Police Recruits' Backgrounds and Training," in David J. Bordua, ed., *The Police* (New York: John Wiley & Sons, 1967), pp. 177, 179. See also President's Commission, *The Police*, pp. 16–17, which notes "the absence of carefully developed policies to guide police officers in handling the wide variety of situations which they confront" in sharp contrast to "the efforts taken to provide detailed guidance for other aspects of police work."

view" in pursuance of a departmental order to "pick up the drunks."

The vigorous enforcement of police-invoked laws occurs in some departments but not in others. In those that follow this policy, the administrator often points to the statistics thereby produced as evidence of "police efficiency" or "police effectiveness." These efforts may lead to attaining goals generally regarded as desirable — closing down the brothels or putting drunks in jail may reduce the moral or physical annoyances suffered by citizens, though in what sense they are ultimately desirable policies is another and more complicated matter. Ticketing motorists may be justified in terms of increased auto safety, but the evidence on this is far from conclusive. A recent review of all published studies of highway safety led the staff of Arthur D. Little, Inc. to conclude:

At present there is no firm evidence to indicate the degree to which enforcement contributes to traffic accident prevention. The objective investigation of optimum methods of police supervision of traffic is just beginning . . . The limited amount of investigation now underway concerns principally rural roads and particularly the Interstate system. Specific study of the quite different problems of urban traffic supervision would seem to be in order.[23]

The police administrator can also emphasize the service aspects of police work by requiring better education, a neater appearance, and a more courteous manner of his patrolmen; by purchasing and prominently displaying modern equipment and vehicles; by moving into a new building through which public tours are conducted; and by developing a public relations program. The point here is not that these changes are mistaken (it will be argued later that they may be quite desirable) or done simply for their image value (the chief will genuinely believe that such changes aid law enforcement) but that these are, for the most part, the only matters over which the police administrator has much control. If he could control directly the exercise of discretion over substantive police matters —

23. Arthur D. Little, Inc., *The State of the Art of Traffic Safety: A Critical Review and Analysis of the Technical Information on Factors Affecting Traffic Safety* (June 1966), p. 251.

if he could act as the idealized conception of law enforcement requires so that his leadership results in more criminals being caught and more crime prevented — things might be very different.

Critical Events

Though the police administrator and the patrolman see things somewhat differently in their day-to-day affairs, on some matters they are in agreement. Indeed, to the outsider, they often seem to present a united front: critical of the community for not having clear and agreed-upon law enforcement objectives; resentful of the criticism the police receive when, by default, they must handle awkward situations which the community and not the police have created; angry at the "leniency" of the courts and the "sensationalism" or hostility of the newspapers; and distressed at the attention given groups which, in police eyes, urge others to disobey the law and which resist legitimate authority by reflexive charges of "police brutality." These common views and the defensiveness with which they are so often expressed may lead the outsider to believe that "all police are alike" or that the patrolman and the police administrator think and act as though animated by a single will. Though there is widespread agreement in most departments about *general* law enforcement issues and widespread concern about the perceived low status of the police officer, in their day-to-day behavior and their handling of particular cases the patrolman and the administrator have, as this chapter has tried to show, somewhat different perspectives that lead to conflicts and tensions.

Under some circumstances, however, these differences in perspective are set aside and both patrolman and administrator function as part of a centrally led organization with a common goal. A "hot call" — a robbery in progress or a chase of a suspect on foot or in a car — will mobilize large numbers of officers and bring them under central direction. A civil commotion — a big parade, a disaster, a large fire, a riot, a mass demonstration — also converts the organization into a quasi-military force in which the activities of large numbers of men are centrally coordinated, usually by senior officers who go out onto the street with mobile communications units. These critical events alter the roles of both patrolman and administrator. The former becomes, as his idealized conception holds he should be, a defender of the peace and an agent of some deliberately chosen community goal (in the case of a demonstration, that goal can be to stop the demonstration, harass the demonstrators, or protect the demonstrators — the important thing is that *somebody* in authority has decided which it shall be and the somebody will have to take the consequences). The latter becomes a leader deploying men, not a paper-shuffler fretting over budgets, maintenance, and citizen complaints.

That some departments may handle critical events poorly should not obscure the significance of the change in organizational climate and strategy occasioned by such events. Problems may arise, but they arise out of circumstances quite different from those governing the normal patrol function. The community may choose the wrong goal (for example, blocking a march rather than regulating it) or select the wrong means (mass arrests rather than individual arrests); the officers may be unprepared for the event, or badly led, or simply confused and undisciplined. The problems of handling the critical event, in short, are precisely the kinds of problems that are amenable to solution through quasi-military training and discipline; the best evidence of this is that, on the whole, regular Army units have been able to perform creditably under very difficult circumstances despite their lack of any prior experience in urban law enforcement.[24]

24. Bruce Smith, Sr., an experienced police consultant, wrote in *Police Systems in the United States,* 2d ed., rev. (New York: Harper and Brothers, 1960), pp. 136–137, that the "disciplinary requirements of a quasi-military body" such as the police are greater than for most organizations because the nature of the work tends to make infractions of rules "a matter of more frequent occurrence and of more serious moment"; thus, the disciplinary powers of the police administrator "need to be kept in good working order because there is likely to be frequent need for their exercise." No doubt the opportunities for corruption, shirking, and brutality are such as to require more discipline in a police than a nonpolice organization. But the analogy to the military is misleading, for in the latter case, the most important kind of discipline — discipline under fire — is maintained, not by formal sanctions, but by the norms of the small unit, the desire to live up to the expectations of buddies, and the direct supervision of commissioned and noncommissioned officers. See S. L. A. Marshall, *Men Against Fire* (New York: William Morrow & Co., 1947), Chap. 9,

In discharging their routine order maintenance and law enforcement functions, the police do not operate at all as a military or quasi-military organization, and analogies drawn between the two kinds of organizations — including those drawn by some police administrators — are quite misleading. The patrolman normally works alone or with a partner, not in a unit as does, say, an army platoon or company, and thus the police administrator is not really a "commander" at all. Police communications are organized so as to bypass administrators. Incoming telephone calls from citizens go in most cases directly to a clerk, usually a patrolman, who decides whether a police service is necessary and who either radios it personally and directly to the man on that beat or hands it to a radio dispatcher (another patrolman) seated near him. Police communications, unlike military communications, tend to cut across rather than work through the chain of command; the police equivalent of operational intelligence is not only gathered by the lowest-ranking personnel but is evaluated and disseminated by them as well. Senior officers may and do listen in on radio calls (they usually have no way of listening in on the telephone messages) and sergeants particularly may "cover in on" (that is, go to the scene of) important or unusual incidents, but such information as they obtain in this way is incomplete and mostly after the fact.

Those police departments that have, by their actions, exacerbated tensions or failed to maintain order might be said to be those that have failed to recognize the radical difference between their normal duties and those they are called upon to perform in critical events. The desire of an individual officer to assert his personal authority may be inevitable and perhaps desirable in patrol situations; it can be disastrous in a mass deployment of police when discipline and concerted action are necessary. This is especially true when television cameras and newspaper photographers are recording what happens — the normal police assumption that the mass media will

---

and Edward A. Shils and Morris Janowitz, "Cohesion and Disintegration in the Wehrmacht in World War II," *Public Opinion Quarterly,* 12 (Summer, 1948), pp. 280–315. No such sanctions or supervision exist for the lone patrolman.

treat them unfairly[25] in any case can provoke them to great anger when they are "on camera" every moment and know that journalists will show or print only those pictures that are "dramatic" and thus tend to show the police in the worst possible light. Finally, officers not trained to know what to expect from their colleagues (they have, after all, rarely worked together in units larger than two) can, when outnumbered by demonstrators or rioters, easily come to feel insecure and threatened. It should be remembered that a police department in even a large city can field only a few men at one time. A city of 200,000 population will have perhaps 400 officers; only about 240 or 250 will be assigned to the uniformed forces (patrol and traffic); of these, only a fourth will be in a single platoon and thus on duty at a given time of day, and some of these will be sick or on leave. Thus, perhaps 50 or 60 men are available on short notice to handle whatever disorder a city of 200,000 can produce. Small wonder that an unexpected riot can lead the police to become initially overwhelmed.

Many countries recognize this problem by having a special riot police or civil guard barracked in local garrisons to supplement the ordinary constabulary. The United States, perhaps unwisely, has expected the municipal police with occasional assistance from state troopers and national guardsmen to handle these matters as part of the regular police function.[26] Many police departments — especially

25. In 1961, when the newspapers were very critical of corruption in the Chicago Police Department, 78.6 per cent of the sergeants felt the newspapers were "too critical." But in 1965, when the newspapers were, on the whole, praising the police for their successful reformation, 65.3 per cent of the sergeants *still* felt the newspapers were too critical. The police respond to newspaper coverage of particular cases as much or more than they do to generalized newspaper attitudes toward law enforcement.

26. The response of American cities in the nineteenth century to riots and demonstrations was to attempt to change the casual watchmen into a police force rather than to garrison the city with a military force. Perhaps the recollection of British garrisons was still too fresh in their minds. In any case, though riot and the fear of riot, rather than crime, led cities such as Boston to the creation of professional police departments (see Roger Lane, *Policing the City: Boston, 1822–1885*, Cambridge, Mass.: Harvard University Press, 1967, Chap. 3), the combining of crime control and order maintenance functions in one agency brought problems. To control crime, the force had to be dispersed in beats; to suppress disorder, it had to be concentrated. The incompatibility of these two strategies was never resolved and American police departments today suffer from that legacy.

those in cities that have experienced disorder — have recognized the new problem and have begun to devise plans, train men, and obtain equipment that will permit the police to handle crowds, disperse mobs, and provide mutual self-defense.

However successful a department may be in meeting this challenge, it will not necessarily have altered its manner of handling the normal patrol function, for each has a quite different logic. How the critical event is handled may have indirect effects, however. Successfully restoring order during a riot may lead the community at large to have a reawakened interest in, and manifest their support of, the police; this support in turn could help police morale and police acquisition of more resources. Or possibly such disorders will only confirm in the eyes of the police the lawlessness of the central city population and especially its young people and minority groups and thus intensify the suspicions and defensiveness of the police in handling routine patrol functions.

Four Police Discretion

Though the legal and organizational constraints under which the police work are everywhere the same or nearly so, police behavior differs from community to community. First, the conduct with which the police must cope varies from place to place. Both crime and disorder are more common in low-income areas than in high-income ones. How frequently the police intervene in a situation, and whether they intervene by making an arrest, will depend in part on the number and seriousness of the demands the city places on them. Second, some police behavior will be affected by the tastes, interests, and style of the police administrator. Finally, the administrator's views of both particular problems and the general level and vigor of enforcement may be influenced, intentionally or unintentionally, by local politics.

In this chapter, the extent to which police behavior varies among eight American communities will be considered, especially the degree to which that variation is in accord with the intentions of the administrator. In the next three chapters, these differences will be grouped into three archetypal police strategies or styles, and the departmental policies and organizational codes, implicit and explicit, that seem to animate and sustain those strategies will be discussed, along with the consequences of such strategies for various groups in the community, especially, but not exclusively, for Negroes and community notables. Succeeding chapters will deal with the extent to which these strategies are, or can be, influenced by specific political decisions or by the general distribution of power within the community.

The Determinants of Discretion

The patrolman's decision whether and how to intervene in a situation depends on his evaluation of the costs and benefits of various kinds of action. Though the substantive criminal law seems to imply a mandate, based on duty or morality, that the law be applied wherever and whenever its injunctions have been violated, in fact for most officers there are considerations of utility that equal or exceed in importance those of duty or morality, especially for the more common and less serious laws. Though the officer may tell a person he is arresting that he is "only doing his duty," such a statement is intended mostly to reduce any personal antagonism (that is, psychic costs to the officer incurred by being thought a bad fellow). Whatever he may say, however, his actual decision whether and how to intervene involves such questions as these: Has anyone been hurt or deprived? Will anyone be hurt or deprived if I do nothing? Will an arrest improve the situation or only make matters worse? Is a complaint more likely if there is *no* arrest, or if there *is* an arrest? What does the sergeant expect of me? Am I getting near the end of my tour of duty? Will I have to go to court on my day off? If I do appear in court, will the charge stand up or will it be withdrawn or dismissed by the prosecutor? Will my partner think that an arrest shows I can handle things or that I can't handle things? What will the guy do if I let him go?

The decision to arrest, or to intervene in any other way, results from a comparison, different perhaps for each officer, of the net gain and loss to the suspect, the neighborhood, and the officer himself of various courses of action. Under certain circumstances, the policy of his department may set the terms of trade among these various considerations or alter the scales on which these values are measured. Such policies may in some cases make arrest (or no arrest) so desirable that, for all practical purposes, the patrolman has no discretion: he is doing what the department wants done. In other cases departmental policies may have little or no effect, and thus such discretion as is exercised is almost entirely the officer's and not the department's.

To explain fully the uses of discretion many factors would have to be considered. For simplicity, two major determinants (major in the sense that they explain "enough" of the variation) suffice: whether the situation is primarily one of *law enforcement* or one of *order maintenance* and whether the police response is *police-invoked* or *citizen-invoked*. To repeat the difference between law enforcement and order maintenance, the former involves a violation of a law in which only guilt need be assessed; the latter, though it often entails a legal infraction, involves in addition a dispute in which the law must be interpreted, standards of right conduct determined, and blame assigned. A police-invoked response is one in which the officer acts on his own authority, rather than as the agent of a citizen who has made a specific verbal or sworn complaint (though citizens "in general" may have complained about "the situation"); a citizen-invoked response is one in which the officer acts on the particular complaint or warrant of the citizen. Although some situations cannot be neatly placed in any category, enough can, I hope, so that we can imagine four kinds of situations in which discretion is exercised, as illustrated by the figure below.

Figure 1. Four kinds of discretionary situations

		Basis of police response	
		Police-invoked action	Citizen-invoked action
Nature of situation	Law enforcement	I	II
	Order maintenance	III	IV

Each case offers a different degree of discretion for the patrolman, the department, or both.

Case I: Police-Invoked Law Enforcement

In this situation the police themselves initiate the action in the specific instance, though sometimes in response to a general public concern over the problem, and whatever action they take is on their own authority. If there is an arrest, the officer is the complaining witness. Many crimes handled in this way are "crimes without victims" — that is, no citizen has been deprived and thus no citizen has called the police. Such calls as the police may get are from "busybodies"—persons who dislike "what is going on" but who themselves are not participants. Enforcement of laws dealing with vice, gambling, and traffic offenses are of this character. The rate and form of police interventions in these situations can be strongly influenced by the policy of the administrator. He can apply a performance measure to his subordinates, though (to introduce a further distinction) that measure differs with the particular offense. With respect to certain forms of vice and gambling, his measure will be whether a brothel or a bookie operates; if they do, his men are "not performing" and the administrator, if he is so inclined, will urge them to greater efforts. His performance measure is *goal-oriented*—that is, it is based on his observation of whether the substantive law enforcement goal has been attained. Accordingly, not only does the administrator have substantial control over his officers, but the community (the mayor, the city council, the newspapers), being able to make the same observations, has substantial opportunity to control the administrator. With regard to traffic enforcement, however, the administrator's measure will be how many traffic tickets the officers have written, not how safe the streets are or how smoothly traffic flows. He cannot judge his men, except perhaps in the extreme case, on these substantive grounds because he knows that writing traffic tickets has only a small effect on actual traffic conditions. Accordingly, his performance measure will be *means-oriented,* and as a result, the community will be less able to hold him responsible for traffic conditions. Should they accuse him, which is unlikely, of letting the accident rate rise, he can reply reasonably that, unlike police attitudes toward brothels, police attitudes toward traffic law enforcement are not the sole or even the major determinant of whether there will be accidents.

Case II: Citizen-Invoked Law Enforcement

Here a citizen is the victim of a crime and he or she complains to the police. The vast majority of crimes with victims are those against property—larceny, auto theft, and burglary—and the vast majority of these are crimes of stealth for which the suspect is unknown. As a result, only a small percentage are solved by an arrest. The patrolman in these circumstances functions primarily as a report taker and information gatherer except when the suspect is still on the scene or has been caught by the victim or an onlooker. This is often the case, for example, with shoplifting. Here the patrolman must decide whether to make an arrest, to tell the citizen that it is up to him to handle the matter by getting a complaint and taking the suspect to court himself, or to encourage him to effect a citizen's arrest on the spot. The police department in turn may insist that prosecutions once started, either by an officer or a citizen, may not be dropped; conversely, it may make it easy for the arresting party to change his mind and forget the whole thing. The patrolman's attitude and departmental policy are amenable to some control by the administrator, especially since a majority of the suspects are likely to be juveniles.[1] The police are formally and legally vested with considerable discretion over juveniles (any person in New York under the age of sixteen and in California and Illinois under the age of eighteen). They can decide, if not *whether* to intervene (that is decided for them by the citizen who invokes the law), at least *how* to intervene (to arrest, take into temporary cus-

1. Property crimes — burglary, larceny of items valued over $50, and auto theft — accounted in 1965 for 82 per cent of the major crimes ("Index Crimes") reported to the FBI and 84 per cent of the causes of victimization reported by respondents in the Crime Commission household survey. About 21 per cent of these three crimes were, according to police reports to the FBI, "cleared by arrest." About 57 per cent of those arrested for these offenses (and those arrested, of course, may not be a representative sample of those who committed the crimes) were under the age of eighteen. See President's Commission on Law Enforcement and Administration of Justice, *Crime and Its Impact — An Assessment* (Washington: Government Printing Office, 1967), p. 17; and Federal Bureau of Investigation, *Uniform Crime Reports, 1965* (Washington: Government Printing Office, 1965), pp. 97, 112. A study by the Oakland Police Department in 1963 showed that 74.6 per cent of all persons processed by the police for shoplifting were juveniles, that is, under the age of eighteen. Most of these cases came from retail stores with security guards and only a few stores accounted for most of the arrests. Between January 1962 and October 1963, 2,394 shoplifting cases were reported by 453 stores; over half came from 57 stores, 29 per cent came from only 4 stores, and 10 per cent came from just one store. Oakland Police Department, "An Analysis of the Shoplifting Problem in Oakland, 1962 and 1963," (mimeograph, November 1963). See also Walter B. Miller, "Theft Behavior in City Gangs," in Malcolm W. Klein, *Juvenile Gangs in Context* (Englewood Cliffs: Prentice-Hall, 1967), pp. 25–37.

tody, warn and release, and so forth). The police administrator can influence the use of that discretion significantly, not, as with Case I, by observing substantive outcomes or by measuring the output of individual officers, but by setting guidelines on how such cases will be handled and by devoting, or failing to devote, specialized resources (in the form of juvenile officers, for example) to these matters.

Case III: Police-Invoked Order Maintenance

In this instance the police on their own authority and initiative intervene in situations of actual or potential disorder. The most common charges are drunkenness, disorderly conduct, or breach of the peace. Not all drunk or disorderly arrests, of course, result from a police-invoked response — some, to be discussed below, are police ways of handling disorderly situations to which the police have been called by the citizen. Because the police invoke the law, the administrator has some control over patrolmen's discretion. He can urge them to "keep things quiet" but he cannot, as in traffic enforcement, judge each officer's "production" by how many arrests he makes on the assumption that there is an almost inexhaustible supply of disturbances to go around. Nor can he insist, as he might with cases of shoplifting, that an arrest is always the best way to handle the situation. In short, discretion in these cases is more under the control of the patrolman and can be modified only by general incentives to be "more vigorous" or to "take it easy." The administrator can boost drunk arrests but only by ordering his officers to treat drunks as problems of law enforcement rather than order maintenance: arrest on sight a man intoxicated in a public place even if he is bothering no one. In this case, a drunk arrest falls under Case I and accordingly is subject to the same relatively high degree of control.

Case IV: Citizen-Invoked Order Maintenance

In this last case, a citizen calls for police assistance because of a public or private disorder. But for the reasons given in Chapter 2, being of assistance is often not an easy matter. In almost every department, such a citizen call must be followed by a police response to avoid the charge of "doing nothing"; however, the way the patrolman handles these situations will depend on his assessment of them and on the extent to which the participants are inclined to be tractable and victims prepared to sign a formal complaint. Thus, although the handling of these situations will vary considerably, that variation will depend more on the personal characteristics of the officer and the citizen participants than on departmental policies. Young college-educated patrolmen in a pleasant suburb may handle these matters in one way; older, working-class officers in a racially mixed central city may handle them in another.

In sum, in Cases I and IV the patrolman has great discretion, but in the former instance it can be brought under departmental control and in the latter it cannot. In Case II the patrolman has the least discretion except when the suspects are juveniles and then the discretion is substantial and can be affected by general departmental policies and organization. Case III is intermediate in both the degree of discretion and the possibility of departmental control. In the remainder of this chapter, such evidence as exists will be introduced to indicate the extent to which departments differ in handling these four police situations and the degree to which those differences are intended by the administrator. Because the amount of police activity and the way that police discretion is used will depend in part on the character of the community, it is first necessary to describe the eight communities in which the observations were made.

The Eight Communities

Five of the communities in this study are industrial, working-class cities with a median family income that is below the state average, a declining downtown business district, and a population that is at least one fourth of foreign stock; four of the five (Albany, Newburgh, Oakland, and Syracuse) have in addition a large and growing Negro population. The fifth, Amsterdam, was bypassed by the northward migration of Negroes and, because the city has lost much of its industrial base and thus many of its low-skill jobs, Negroes are not likely to start arriving. The other three communities are well-to-do suburban areas; one, Brighton, is a town near Rochester; a second, Highland Park, is a city near Chicago; and a third, Nassau, is an urbanized county adjacent to New York City. These suburbs have all experienced rapid population growth in the last decade or two. There are virtually no Negroes in Brighton or Highland Park; only about 4 per cent of the Nassau population is nonwhite. Statistical profiles of the eight communities are contained in Table 2.

The table conceals many important differences, of course. In New York State, "foreign stock" means primarily white European Catholics; in Oakland, the same term refers mainly to Mexican-Americans. And the foreign stock of the industrial cities of New York tend to live in old, fairly stable, ethnically homogeneous neighborhoods; though such neighborhoods have existed in Oakland, they are not conspicuous today. Rapid population movements, the heavy influx of Negroes (and Indians and Mexicans), and the weakness of institutional (for example, church) ties to a particular place have made Oakland's white population rather heterogeneous or, perhaps, "assimilated." The economic base of the communities differs as well. Albany, besides being industrial, is also a capital city where the three largest employers are the city and county of Albany and the state of New York. One fourth the work force in 1960 was employed in public administration, public utilities, and public education. Employment is thus more stable and, in addition, the city is flooded with politicians and lobbyists when the legislature is in session. In all three suburban communities, a large fraction of the work force is employed in the nearby central city, but in Nassau there is also a good deal of indigenous economic activity — an aircraft plant, several very large shopping centers, and an assortment of industrial and commercial enterprises. Albany, Amsterdam, and Newburgh are all river cities and Syracuse is on the site of the old Erie Canal, but shipping to or through these places is no longer substantial. Oakland, by contrast, is a bustling port city where sailors from both merchant and naval vessels regularly come ashore seeking entertainment. (Not

Table 2. A statistical profile of the eight communities.

Community characteristics	Four high-crime cities				Four low-crime communities			
	Albany	Newburgh	Oakland	Syracuse	Amsterdam	Brighton	Highland Park	Nassau County
1960 population	129,726	30,979	367,548	216,038	28,772	27,849	25,532	1,300,171
Per cent Negro, 1960	8.5	16.6	22.8	5.7	0.6	0.2	2.2	3.2
Estimated 1965 Negro population (as per cent of estimated 1965 total population)	11.7	25.0	30.2	8.3	insignificant	insignificant	insignificant	4.0
Per cent foreign stock	27.9	30.1	28.2	32.4	48.8	31.0	34.9	39.0
Median family income, 1959	5,778	5,363	6,303	6,247	5,501	11,109	13,007	8,500
Per cent under $3,000	17.5	19.7	17.3	13.9	18.0	4.3	4.3	5.5
Per cent $10,000 and over	15.9	11.8	19.7	18.0	10.0	54.3	62.6	37.6
Median school years completed, 1960	10.9	9.4	11.4	11.1	9.1	13.2	13.0	12.2
Per cent employed in manufacturing jobs	14.3	37.3	20.5	31.3	48.2	31.5	19.8	24.9
Per cent employed in white collar jobs	51.3	34.9	45.0	48.9	39.1	39.4	66.7	58.7
Population change 1950–1960	−3.9	−3.1	−4.5	−2.1	−10.8	54.4	51.9	93.3
Number of uniformed full-time police officers, 1960	241	60	647	369	42	30	37	1,952
Police officers per 1,000 population, 1960	1.8	1.9	1.7	1.7	1.4	1.1	1.4	1.5
Police expenditures, 1961	1,524,211	412,675	6,510,818	2,786,599	230,723	221,987	277,172	17,366,321
Police expenditures per capita, 1961	11.72	13.31	17.71	12.90	7.95	8.22	10.85	13.35

Sources: U.S. Bureau of the Census, *County and City Data Book,* 1962; International City Managers' Association, *The Municipal Year Book,* 1961 and 1962. 1965 total and Negro population based on estimates by local planning agencies.

finding much, most of them promptly cross the bay to San Francisco.)

Table 3. Rates of murder and auto theft reported by the police in eight communities, 1965, by population size.

Community by population	Murder and nonnegligent manslaughter rate	Auto theft rate
Places over 1,000,000 population		
National average	9.6	585.6
Nassau County[a]	1.5	205.2
Places 250,000 to 500,000 population		
National average	7.2	468.2*
Oakland	8.7	615.8
Places 100,000 to 250,000 population		
National average	6.4	353.1
Albany	2.5	565.0
Syracuse	2.8	325.1
Places 25,000 to 50,000 population		
National average	3.1	212.4
Amsterdam	0	57.1
Brighton	0	63.3
Highland Park	0	121.3
Newburgh	10.0	220.0

* *Sources:* For communities, reports of local police departments to the FBI, 1965; for national averages, FBI *Uniform Crime Reports,* 1965, pp. 94–95. Rates for communities based on 1965 population estimate by local planning agency; rates for national averages based on 1965 population estimated by the U.S. Bureau of the Census. Rates are per 100,000 population.

[a] Crimes and crime rates for Nassau County are only for those sections of the county served by the Nassau County Police Department; the rates are based on population estimates for 1965 for NCPD-served areas.

All eight places have their own police departments. Though Nassau is a county, its department is not a sheriff's office but a large agency supplying regular municipal police services to about 80 per cent of the county's population (the remainder is served by twenty-odd city and village departments). Obviously, the magnitude and character of the problems confronting the police vary a good deal among the eight communities. In this analysis I shall from time to time speak of "high crime" and "low crime" cities. Table 3 indicates how this distinction is made. Albany, Newburgh, Oakland, and Syracuse all have reported rates of murder and auto theft, the two crimes about which police reports are generally most accurate,[2] one or both of which are at or near the national average for cities of their size and much higher than the rates for the other four communities. Oakland has the highest rates, followed by Albany, Newburgh, and Syracuse; Amsterdam and Brighton have the lowest, followed by Nassau and Highland Park. The reported rates for many crimes have risen in all four high-crime cities — spectacularly in the case of Syracuse, partly because that police department was reorganized in 1963–64 in a way that led to more accurate, and thus more numerous, reports of offenses known to the police.

There are three reasons for making this distinction. First, a high rate of serious crime may incline the police to devote their resources to preventing, insofar as they can, such offenses and apprehending the perpetrators, to the neglect of such "minor" offenses as traffic violations, juvenile misconduct, and various adult misdemeanors. And even where there is no such emphasis, the police might claim there is in order to justify a lax attitude toward "small stuff." Second, a higher-than-normal crime rate is often associated with the presence of a larger-than-normal Negro population in the city. The four high-crime cities have the highest proportions of Negroes. Some studies have found that the nonwhite percentage of a city's population is strongly correlated with rates of murder and assault.[3]

2. See Chapter 2 above and President's Commission on Law Enforcement and Administration of Justice, *The Challenge of Crime in a Free Society* (Washington: Government Printing Office, 1967), p. 21. There is no pejorative implication in the term "high-crime city"; it is simply a convenient label to distinguish one group of cities from the other. There are, in fact, many American cities with far higher crime rates than those discussed in this study.

3. See Karl Schuessler, "Components of Variation in City Crime Rates," *Social Problems*, 9 (November 1962), pp. 314–323. The Schuessler study is marred by a too uncritical acceptance of the validity of reported crime rates, but his finding of an association between the murder rate — the most reliable statistic — and the proportion nonwhite is probably valid. The high Negro murder rate has been inde-

The extent to which this is true — and if true, the reasons for it — are questions that need not concern us here.[4]

What does concern us is the fact that the presence of large numbers of Negroes raises in especially acute form the potential problem of unequal police treatment of citizens. Though the police in a community with no Negroes might treat the rich or politically powerful one way and everybody else another, it would be very hard to prove — the rich and powerful are not likely to admit it and everybody else may be unaware of their different treatment or,

---

pendently verified by analyzing the causes of death by race. Negroes are murdered about ten times as often as whites and, because other studies have shown that the vast majority of Negro victims are killed by Negro murderers (and the vast majority of white victims by white murderers), there appears to be little doubt of the abnormal Negro homicide rate. See National Office of Vital Statistics, *Death Rates for Selected Causes by Age, Color, and Sex: United States and Each State, 1949–1951* (Washington: Government Printing Office, 1959) and Thomas F. Pettigrew, *A Profile of the Negro American* (Princeton: D. Van Nostrand Co., 1964), p. 142.

4. There is some evidence that the primary factor is economic. See Belton M. Fleisher, "The Effect of Income on Delinquency," *American Economic Review*, 56 (March 1966), pp. 118–137. Using as data the number of juveniles arrested or appearing in court (somewhat suspect because it leaves out of account the much larger number of juveniles handled informally by the police) for 101 American cities over 25,000 and for 45 Chicago suburbs, Fleisher concludes that "a 1 per cent increase in incomes may well cause a 2.5 per cent decrease in the rate of delinquency" (p. 134) and that "the addition of a racial variable adds almost nothing to the explanatory power of the regression model in any of the samples" (p. 133).

Whether Negro and white crime rates would be similar if Negroes had income, occupational, and educational levels comparable to those of whites has been almost impossible to prove. One study tried to compare crime rates in two Negro neighborhoods with those in two white neighborhoods of similar socioeconomic and demographic characteristics, but the conclusions are marred by the fact that the white areas turned out, in several possibly important respects, to be less disadvantaged than the Negro areas. Earl R. Moses, "Differentials in Crime Rates between Negroes and Whites, Based on Comparisons of Four Socio-Economically Equated Areas," *American Sociological Review*, 12 (August 1947), pp. 411–420. The incidence of broken homes — which has been shown to be strongly associated with delinquent behavior — is higher among Negroes than whites and we cannot as yet be confident that this contributing factor will disappear if Negro incomes rise to white levels. See Thomas P. Monahan, "Family Status and the Delinquent Child: A Reappraisal and Some New Findings," *Social Forces*, 35 (March 1957), pp. 251–258. Thus, though I believe that the Negro-white differential in crime rates would be substantially reduced if socioeconomic conditions were equalized, I find no hard evidence to support the conclusion of the Task Force on Crime of the President's Commission that "if conditions of equal *opportunity* [my italics] prevailed, the large differences now found between the Negro and white arrest rates would disappear." President's Commission, *Crime and Its Impact*, p. 78.

if aware of it, lacking in a sense of group identity or the organizational capacity with which to express their feelings in the matter. Negroes, on the other hand, being marked by color, are perhaps more likely to be singled out for special treatment if the police have any such tendency, are more likely to *believe* they get special treatment because they are Negroes, and are likely to have organizations and leaders ready to express such views. Third, in cities with higher-than-average crime rates, crime is more likely to become a political issue. This has been the case in every one of the four high-crime cities here described. By contrast, the low-crime cities — except for Nassau, where there has been some political concern over juvenile delinquency, narcotics, and residential burglaries — have not had a public debate over "crime in the streets."

The Uses of Discretion

Case I: Police-Invoked Law Enforcement

The rate at which traffic tickets are issued varies enormously among the eight police departments and this variation is primarily the result of the policies of the administrator, not the characteristics of the community. Table 4 shows the rate per thousand population at

Table 4. Tickets issued for moving traffic violations, and rates per thousand population, 1965.[a]

City	Tickets for moving violations	
	Number	Rate per 1,000
Albany	1,368	11.4
Amsterdam	460	16.4
Newburgh	1,226	40.9
Brighton	1,829	61.0
Nassau County	68,375	61.0
Highland Park	2,933	97.8
Syracuse	23,465	109.1
Oakland	90,917	247.7

[a] Ticket rate based on 1965 population estimates.

which tickets were issued in 1965. In Syracuse, the rate was ten times that in Albany, though the social composition and street pattern of the two cities are quite similar. Highland Park's police department issued half again as many tickets as the department in Brighton, though the two communities are almost identical upper-status suburbs. Both Oakland and Nassau County are criss-crossed with major high-speed highways connecting large cities to their suburbs, yet the Oakland police issued four times as many tickets as the Nassau police.

These findings are in every respect similar to those of Gardiner, who in his studies of the cities and towns of Massachusetts and of over five hundred cities in all parts of the country found that only a small part of the great differences in traffic enforcement levels could be explained by differences in the character of the community (income, education, ethnic composition, population mobility, or the like) but could be explained by the policies of the chief.[5]

The chief may influence traffic law enforcement by creating specialized units for that purpose, or by inducing officers in or out of that unit to "produce" tickets, or both. In Amsterdam and Newburgh, specialization occurred but without strong inducements to produce. In 1964, both departments purchased a radar speed detector and trained officers in its use. Because of the new technology and the fact that during its use the cars and men assigned did nothing else, traffic ticket rates in both cities more than doubled in one year. In Amsterdam, however, the equipment is used only sporadically, and hence traffic ticket production varies erratically. In a recent year, only six tickets were issued in February and seven in November, but eighty-eight were issued in April and one hundred and five in May. Newburgh has two units rather than one and uses its radar more regularly; thus its ticketing rate is not only twice that of Amsterdam's, but more constant from month to month.

With or without specialization, the chief has various means of inducing officers to "produce." One is the quota system. Almost no

5. John A. Gardiner, "Police Enforcement of Traffic Laws: A Comparative Analysis," in James Q. Wilson, ed., *City Politics and Public Policy* (New York: John Wiley & Sons, 1968). Of all the demographic variables, only population mobility was correlated with ticket rates.

police administrator will admit he sets a traffic ticket quota (the one who came closest insisted on calling it a "norm"), but several use devices that are quotas in everything but name. In Brighton the chief expects all his men (there is no specialized traffic unit) to write at least two tickets per man per week, and in 1966 fourteen of his twenty-one full-time patrolmen did. In Oakland, the members of the traffic division are expected to write two tickets per man *per hour*. For a six-week period selected at random, the thirteen men assigned to one shift worked 1,266 hours and wrote 2,505 tickets for a rate of 1.97 per man per hour and ten of the thirteen men came within plus or minus 0.3 tickets per hour of the standard rate of 2.0 — striking testimony to a large organization's ability to achieve uniform behavior among its members when the objectives are clear and quantitative performance criteria are available.

Syracuse and Highland Park have not had exact numerical quotas, but careful records have been kept of each man's performance and superiors have examined these records regularly to let the men know if they were "falling behind." A senior officer in the Syracuse traffic division described how he ran his unit:

> Nobody likes to talk quotas, but that's what is in the back of everybody's mind. We don't tell the men they have any quota, but the deputy chief is always onto me about enforcement, enforcement, enforcement, and I'm always onto the lieutenant about the same thing, and he gets to the sergeant and the sergeant gets to the men. We have a daily report on how many tickets each man writes, how many tickets each platoon writes, and how many tickets are written for each of the various moving offenses. This is put on my desk and on the chief's desk every day. We can glance down here and see how the men are doing . . . if somebody is falling off, we can go around and talk to him and ask him why he isn't pulling his share of the load.

Additional evidence of the ability of the administrator to determine policy in this area can be adduced from the changes some have achieved. When a "reform" police chief came to Syracuse in 1963, he announced that he expected all officers — in and out of the traffic division — to enforce traffic laws. By the end of 1964, ticket production had increased 58 per cent and between 1964 and 1965 it increased another 18 per cent. After a new chief arrived in Highland Park in the mid-1950's, the number of tickets issued tripled during his first two years in office.[6] Though no quota existed, any officer who "was below the average" for a particular month was called in by the chief and, according to one lieutenant, "had to explain why."

Indeed, pressure more than specialization seems to account for the very high rates of some departments. The Nassau police, for example, have a large traffic division that operates sixteen cars (two equipped with radar) and twelve two-wheel motorcycles, but they write tickets at a rate no greater than that in Brighton — largely because there is no quota for traffic officers and no strong pressure for nontraffic patrolmen to write tickets at all. Albany also has a specialized traffic unit with forty-five men and fifteen vehicles assigned to it but the men are used primarily to direct traffic at intersections and the vehicles to aid in enforcing parking regulations (over thirty thousand parking tickets but only a few hundred moving violation tickets were issued in the first half of 1966).

The combined effects of specialization and pressure can be seen in

Figure 2. The influence of specialization and administrative norms on traffic ticket rates in eight communities, 1965

		Use of pressure or norms		
		None	Traffic unit only	Department-wide
Specialized traffic unit	No	Amsterdam (16.4)	—	Brighton (61.0) Highland Park[a] (97.3)
	Yes	Albany (11.4)	Newburgh (40.9) Nassau (61.0)	Oakland (247.7) Syracuse (109.1)

[a] Highland Park traffic enforcement policy changed after 1964.

Figure 2, which suggests that pressure is more important than specialization: the four departments in the right hand column (expe-

6. Data before 1956 are very scanty; the threefold increase is an estimate based on magistrate's records.

riencing strong pressure from the chief) are as high or higher than any other department in ticketing rates, but are evenly divided between those that are specialized and those that are not.

Police policies towards gambling and vice are also strongly subject to the control of the police administrator, but unlike traffic law enforcement these policies are also constrained by community characteristics. The social composition of the city is one determinant both of the potential market for illicit services and of the degree to which public opinion will tolerate activities that serve that market. In almost all cities with a substantial lower class and in almost all large cities whatever their class composition, there will be a demand for vice and gambling that will be served by those residents who find such enterprises profitable. In small, upper-status communities, on the other hand, whatever demand exists will be served, if at all, only with great difficulty. Being small, any activity that requires the regular coming and going of customers can be easily detected; being upper-income, not many residents are likely to find the money profits of prostitution and gambling worth the social costs and most potential customers would probably prefer to avail themselves of such services more anonymously in the nearby central city. Finally, in any city other agencies of law enforcement in addition to the police must act before vice and gambling can be curtailed. Prosecutors must prosecute, judges must convict, and sentences must be imposed that are severe enough to raise the cost of doing business above what the market for such services will support.

In short, the widespread opinion that gambling and prostitution could not exist in a city unless the police tolerated them is not generally or simply true. The level of vice depends on the character of the community and the legal resources available to the police (primarily the ability to impose certain and severe sanctions) as well as on police competence and honesty. To impose such sanctions, the police must have evidence. Unlike a traffic infraction, an act of prostitution or gambling is not easily detected; moreover, gathering evidence admissible in court — by actually placing a bet, or seizing betting slips, or having a girl accept money to commit an act of prostitution — is difficult, especially when professional gamblers and prostitutes know police vice officers by sight. Under prevailing rules of evidence, judges are not easily convinced and even when they are they tend to impose penalties that are modest in proportion to the earnings of the gambler. Nassau County, with 1.4 million persons, has gamblers partly because the cost of being arrested for gambling is not high. In 1965, 104 cases involving gambling were disposed of by the Nassau District Court. In 14 per cent of them the charge was dismissed or the defendant was acquitted; in another 19 per cent the defendant received a suspended sentence. Half the defendants were fined, the typical fine being $250; only 15 per cent of the defendants went to jail, most for less than 45 days.[7] A $250 fine, even if imposed twice a year, is a small fee to pay for a lucrative business — less than what it would cost in taxes and fees to own a liquor store legally. A prostitution conviction is rarely more serious.

Arrest and prosecution are not the only ways the police can deal with vice, of course. They can follow a strategy of harassment whereby buyers or sellers or both are kept under obvious surveillance, picked up for frequent interrogations, and arrested on lesser charges (public intoxication, disorderly conduct, breach of the peace, or the like). Certain forms of illegal commerce are more vulnerable than others to such methods. Brothels, for example, can be put out of business by periodic raids or even by merely stationing a police officer outside to take the names of customers, even though no individual prostitute is seriously penalized. Gamblers in "horse rooms" can likewise be kept under such heavy pressure that, though they may not go out of business, they must so severely restrict their clientele to friends and persons with the right introductions that it becomes, in effect, private gambling rather than a service available to anybody in the market. On the other hand, streetwalkers in a big-city slum or call girls in the downtown business district are elusive prey even for a dedicated vice squad. They operate alone without houses to be raided (hotel rooms, bars, or even parking lots

7. Calculated from the docket of the Nassau County District Court, Vols 43–48. Many gambling cases were adjourned into the next calendar year, so the totals do not correspond to police arrests in 1965.

suffice), they must (if streetwalkers) be approached in public or (if call girls) through friends and intermediaries, and they can quickly and easily disappear into the neighborhood or change their area of operations. Police activity can raise the cost of information to the potential customer to the extent that only the most persevering girl hunter will find what he wants, but it cannot put big city prostitution out of business altogether.

Thus, the relevant question is not, "Is there vice in this city?" but "Given the characteristics of the community, has or has not vice been reduced to the level one would expect from intensive police activity and prevailing judicial penalties?" Intensive police activity should produce a highly decentralized industry that utilizes least-risk communications systems and avoids fixed locations, the production of physical evidence, or dealings with strangers.

Because of these considerations, the police administrator has some ready-made excuses if he should decide for any reason to tolerate a certain amount of vice and gambling. Wherever researchers for this study found illegal enterprises, the police responded by saying that it is "small-scale stuff," that "We can't put them out of business" because "they know all our men," "You can't get evidence," "The courts won't issue search warrants or authorize wire taps," and "The judges let them off with a slap on the wrist anyway." The police claimed that such inhibitions were more constraining than in fact they were, but there was some truth in all their arguments.

In upper-income suburbs such as Brighton and Highland Park, there was no vice, at least of the sort run by professionals. The Brighton police on at least one occasion found bookies attempting to set up business in a motel on the outskirts of town but, with the cooperation of the State Police, they raided them and put them out of business. In another case, a woman complained that her husband was losing money gambling at a veteran organization's picnic; the police closed the game down. In one of the towns, the chief admitted he had been offered a large bribe by a big-city gambler eager to move in, but he turned it down (there is no reason to doubt him). If organized gambling or vice were discovered in such towns, there would be a scandal and the police know it. Residents would expect that "In a town like this" the police could "keep that element out," and they would be right.

In small industrial towns such as Amsterdam and Newburgh, it is another story. With many bars and dance spots and a working-class population, there are many opportunities for illegal businesses and little, if any, pressure from public opinion to eliminate it altogether. Unlike in Brighton and Highland Park, the gamblers would not be "outsiders" seeking to bribe or sneak their way in, but locals running local businesses for local customers. As they are members of the community, they cannot be kept out and, so long as they are reasonably discreet, they will not be harassed. In any case, as locals they know by sight every police officer and thus, should the police want to crack down, it would be hard to gather the kind of evidence (for example, actually placing a bet) that the courts increasingly require. The issue in such cities, then, is not whether there will be illegal businesses, but only on what scale they will operate.

In Amsterdam, they are small scale and confined mostly to gambling. In 1961 the State Police raided and made arrests at fourteen gambling spots, in 1964 city police made three arrests at a numbers game, apparently because of complaints the game was not honest, and in 1966 the State Police raided ten places and arrested thirteen persons. In at least the last instance, the State Police were called in by local authorities but only to "keep the situation under control" not to "end gambling in Amsterdam."

In Newburgh, on the other hand, vice is a major industry and, at least for college boys and servicemen, a principal tourist attraction. There are at least two brothels,[8] but as of 1966 there had not been a single arrest for prostitution since 1958, and that year there were only four. There have been gambling arrests almost every year — especially in 1963 and 1964, when there were some State Police raids — but rarely more than four or five, and these men usually reopen business at the same locations.[9] Prostitutes solicit openly in

8. The adage that a sociologist is a man who needs a $50,000 grant to find a whorehouse is either untrue or inapplicable to political scientists.

9. See accounts of gambling raids in the Newburgh *Evening News*, June 20 and December 8, 1963; May 4 and December 20, 1964; and March 9 and July 15, 1965.

some of the city's thirty-three bars. One girl told an interviewer how the system worked:

> A lot of these bartenders let us come in to pick up men. Sometimes if a guy is looking for a girl, the bartender will phone us and tell us to come on over, there's somebody they want us to meet. They never ask for money. Of course, they expect that we will have a few drinks in their place before leaving. It's all nice and friendly . . . We don't let outside girls come in. I was raised right here in Newburgh and I would talk to some people if any girl from New York tried to operate here . . . The police let us alone and they don't try to shake us down as long as we're quiet and don't try to rob some guy.

An important political leader in Newburgh accepted this situation matter-of-factly. He told an interviewer: "I'm too old to be interested in that sort of thing myself, but everybody says that Little Lil's place [pseudonym] down in the colored section has twenty or thirty cars parked out in front of it on Saturday night. I don't know much about it . . . but it's common gossip."

More and better-organized illegal businesses are tolerated in Newburgh than in Amsterdam. The extent to which these differences are simply the result of police policies and the extent to which they represent political decisions is partly a matter of conjecture, but interviews with Newburgh politicians suggest that they at least consent to the existence of a conspicuous vice industry. It is important to bear in mind, however, that the major difference between the two cities is in the level of prostitution and that in Newburgh most, but certainly not all, the prostitutes are Negro. There are very few lower-income Negroes in Amsterdam; if there were more, vice there might not be so very different from in Newburgh. As will be suggested in a later chapter, the police strategy in such cities is based in part on standards of public morality that vary for different racial groups.

In the larger communities, the police have more resources to devote, if they wish, to vice suppression. They have more men, they can create specialized units to deal with vice, and they can enlist as allies civic associations and newspapers that either do not exist at all in the small town or that feel their mission is to boost and defend, rather than criticize or investigate, the community. At the same time, the big city's vice industry has more resources with which to resist suppression — urban anonymity makes concealment easier and talented criminal lawyers can usually be hired to oppose prosecutors and the police.

The four large communities included in this study show almost the full range of police policies. In three of the four places, there have been significant changes in these policies since the 1940's. In Nassau County, for example, a major gambling scandal in the police department in the 1940's led to the appointment of a "reform" police commissioner, and since that time a tough policy on vice has been followed, complicated only by some rivalry between the NCPD and the District Attorney over control of the vice squad. The twenty-man squad, now part of the NCPD, conducts a vigorous program of surveillance on bookies and prostitutes; court-authorized wiretaps are used to get information on the former, undercover men to get evidence on the latter. In 1965 the police made 479 vice arrests — 115 for bookmaking, 101 for operating a policy racket, 73 for running a dice game, 42 for prostitution, 26 for distributing pornographic materials, and the rest for assorted offenses. There have been in addition, several major gambling and prostitution raids.[10] The State Police, frequently active in other New York communities, have not had occasion to intervene in Nassau County.

Syracuse has also changed, but because it is a large industrial city with a substantial Negro and other lower-income population, reducing vice and gambling to the relatively low level found in suburban Nassau is much harder. The present policy dates from the report of the Temporary Commission of Investigation of the State of New

10. In May 1966 ninety NCPD officers conducted gambling raids on twenty-eight homes in the North Shore area, arresting twenty-eight persons on bookmaking charges. *New York Post,* May 12, 1966. Earlier, a tavern owner was arrested for trying to bribe the vice squad commander in an effort to squelch a gambling investigation. And before that, Nassau County received national publicity for breaking up what was erroneously described as a "housewives prostitution ring." (In fact, it consisted, not of suburban housewives earning pin money while their husbands were away, but of professionals operating out of motels and bars.) Two Nassau County police officers were apparently involved in the ring, one of whom allegedly checked the license plate numbers of customers to make certain none was an NCPD detective.

York (popularly known as the "SIC") issued in February 1963, which condemned the Syracuse Police Department in the strongest language: "In summary, the investigation disclosed police corruption; unchecked gambling, prostitution and violations of the liquor laws; 'tip-offs' by Detectives of impending police raids; and improper police associations with criminals." [11]

The report contained excerpts from testimony and extracts from wiretaps confirming that money and "Christmas gifts" were given police officers, that leading gamblers held frequent meetings with detectives, that rookie officers who made gambling arrests without departmental approval were rebuked or given no support, that the police chief never took effective steps to initiate an anti-gambling investigation, and that high political figures intervened with the chief to help certain officers, including some close to gamblers, to win promotions.[12] At almost the same time that the report appeared, a newly elected mayor appointed a new chief and deputy chief of police. A strong effort was made by the new leadership to close down gambling and prostitution, which they discovered existed, but not as flagrantly as the SIC report had suggested. The Syracuse department in 1965 made 116 gambling arrests, producing an arrest rate five times higher than that in Albany or Newburgh. Most bookies and card game operators seem to have been put out of business or at least driven behind the closed doors of "private clubs" where they deal only with persons known to themselves. The level of prostitution is harder to evaluate, but interviewers could find no bars where open solicitation occurred nor were bartenders and the like able or, if able, willing to give the addresses of brothels.

Because resources in any police department are limited, some aspects of vice are emphasized more than others. Before the new police administration took over, there were only three men on the

11. Temporary Commission of Investigation of the State of New York, *Summary of Activities during 1962* (New York: 1963), p. 47. A 1947 grand jury report had censured the Syracuse police department for its "complete lack of police work in respect to gambling." During the period 1947–1962, state police and U.S. Internal Revenue agents made a total of twenty-seven gambling raids in the city, arresting 47 persons. After — but rarely before — each raid, the Syracuse police would also make some arrests.

12. *Ibid.*, pp. 84–90, 98–100, 102–107, 110–114.

Syracuse vice squad. As a present member of the squad told an interviewer, "Those three men had to spend their time on after-hours places and on prostitution because those were the things that got the church groups excited." The new police chief enlarged and reorganized the squad into a ten-man "organized crime division," which increased gambling arrests by more than 25 per cent during the first year of its operation. Even so, gambling continues to exist and these men know it. Of 58 gambling cases disposed of by the Syracuse City Court during 1964, over half (59 per cent) were dismissed or the defendant was acquitted; none resulted in a jail sentence. One judge told an interviewer that this happened both because of the nature of the case and because of the attitude of the judges:

> Most of the gambling cases that are brought before us are weak cases. There are very difficult technical motions on rules of evidence, search and seizure procedures, and the like that the judge must consider. But above all, I don't believe gambling constitutes a serious crime. The judge has to reflect community attitudes. What else can he do? He's a human being . . . Seventy-five per cent of the public gambles . . . I know the police chief here is death on gambling, but I can't understand why . . . It's not a great sin in my eyes. I simply cannot get too excited about it.

The police are aware of this and resent it. If they fail to arrest gamblers, the public will suspect them of being corrupt or incompetent; if they do arrest them, no serious penalty ensues and the effort seems pointless. As a result the police try to harass the gamblers. An officer in the organized crime division told an interviewer:

> We keep on these gamblers because we feel that's our job. We mug 'em, we print 'em, we book 'em. And what happens after that is not our business. We have to keep reminding ourselves of that or we would get discouraged. Basically, we are harassing the gamblers and even though all we're doing is arresting them and bringing them in here, we're hurting them plenty . . . We're at least forcing them to hire a lawyer and we're breaking up their operations and we're making life tough for their customers.

Oakland also was once a more tolerant city. Before the reform police administration came to power in the mid 1950's, gambling was widespread, including regular games in the basement of a major labor union headquarters and in the Chinese district. The churches ran bingo contests. A long-time member of the vice squad told an interviewer about the change:

The police tolerated these things because the community wanted them tolerated. Nobody complained and nobody demanded the police do anything about it. About fifteen years ago, a new chief and city manager came in and decided to close it down. They were closed down and they've been closed down tight ever since . . . There is no lottery; the labor temple has been closed down tight. We had to write a letter to all the churches . . . telling them that bingo was not going to be allowed anymore. I almost got myself excommunicated! I had to go around and see all those priests and tell them I was closing up their carnivals, but it stuck.

In a series of raids beginning in 1955, gambling was hit hard, not only at labor headquarters and among the Chinese tongs, but at churches and civic organizations.[13] Individuals and organizations with carnival-style gambling, normally immune from police action, were not exempted. The police raided a bingo game run by a seventy-year-old lady at a women's fraternal organization, a gambling carnival run for charity, it was claimed, at a local Lion's club, and a wheel-of-fortune game at two separate Catholic church bazaars.[14]

13. In October 1955 thirteen persons were arrested in a police raid on the American Federation of Labor Temple in Oakland. The police stated that gambling had been going on there for twenty-two years, producing a monthly revenue of $3,000 for the Temple. In June 1956 fifty-eight persons were arrested on gambling charges at another fraternal order. And in April 1959 fourteen persons were arrested in a raid at the Boilermakers' Union, Local 10. See *Oakland Tribune,* October 11, 1955; June 23, 1965; April 22, 1959. The organized gamblers did not give up easily. In 1959 the police arrested five Chinese, including the leader of a local tong, for attempting to bribe top Oakland police officers in order to obtain police consent to operating two gambling centers with six card tables each; every table was to pay off $50 to $90 per day, or a total of $18,000 a year, to the police. *Oakland Tribune,* March 10, 1959. In 1965 Oakland police arrested a patrolman on charges of accepting bribes to protect a poker game. Another patrolman believed to have been involved killed two men he thought were informants and then tried to commit suicide. *Oakland Tribune,* December 8, 1965.

14. *Oakland Tribune,* November 30, 1960; March 11, 1961; October 23, 1961.

(There are limits to police zeal in these matters. A member of the vice squad told an interviewer that a "friendly poker game" in a home or at a lodge or club would not be bothered unless there was evidence it was being run by professionals or the house was taking a profit from the pots.) The pressure has continued. In 1965 Oakland police made 415 gambling arrests, mostly by the eighteen-man vice control division. This arrest rate was over ten times that of Albany and Newburgh and twice that of Syracuse. Very few of the arrests are of bookies, mostly because serious bookmaking has been all but eliminated in the city.[15]

Prostitution arrests are also numerous—295 in 1965—but the industry flourishes nonetheless. The police deny there are brothels in the city, and no informant or researcher could find one, but the police do not deny—indeed, they complain about—the large number of predominantly Negro streetwalkers, especially in and around the bars on the lower-class east side. It is difficult under the law to make a good pinch that does not also involve entrapment, that is, unlawfully inducing a person to commit an illegal act.[16] Men, mostly white, drive slowly through the Negro area on East Seventh Street; girls hail them and they negotiate through the open car window; if a bargain is struck, the girl gets in the car and directs the driver to a rendezvous—sometimes in a hotel room, sometimes in a parking lot. The practice is called "trolling." To stop it, the Oakland vice squad officers—often using new recruits or others as undercover "special employees"—troll also and spar verbally with the girls until one takes the step that makes a legal arrest on a prostitution charge possible: offering on her own initiative to commit an act of prostitution for a stated sum of money. Prostitutes are still easily found because, in the opinion of the police, the courts "do nothing" with the girls after they are arrested. One vice squad officer told an interviewer:

15. The market for certain forms of gambling in Oakland may be reduced, and therefore the pressure on the police eased, by the fact that draw poker casinos are legal in the neighboring city of Emeryville.

16. Jerome H. Skolnick, *Justice without Trial* (New York: John Wiley & Sons, 1966), pp. 96–106, has an interesting account of prostitution arrests in a California city.

There are lots of whores here. They come in from Los Angeles, San Francisco, Fresno, from all over. They come in because the heat's on in these other places. Down in Los Angeles, judges have been giving 30, 45, 90, and 180 day jail sentences. Over in San Francisco, the police have been rousting them — picking them up on weak holding charges and shipping them out of town . . . The reason we make so many arrests is because the girls are back out on the street before the officer can finish making out his report. We've had cases of girls being busted twice in the same night for prostitution . . . [Some] judges are just not locking these people up. They've told me flat out they don't believe prostitution is really wrong. But we have to do our job and they have to do theirs, and we just have to try to forget about what happens after we've done our job.

Albany has changed also, but not in response to a scandal or the advent of a reform administration and not with the intention of reducing the level of vice and gambling to a minimum. Rather, the changes have been made by the police and the city government to adjust the level of illegal business to new conditions of demand and public tolerance. Until the 1960's, Albany was famous for its "Gut" — several blocks of bars packed with B-girls and interspersed with brothels. One officer who used to walk that beat told an interviewer a few years later that "when things were going good" in that area "there were forty or fifty gin mills, most of them with girls hustling in them, just in the two-block area next to police headquarters." Another officer told an interviewer that when the Gut was flourishing, prostitutes paid off to party headquarters at the rate of $20 each per week but that most patrolmen were themselves forbidden to take anything but "small favors." In the spring of 1961, investigators for the State Liquor Authority (SLA) charged twenty-six Albany bars, mostly in the Gut, with a total of 140 violations of the liquor code for allegedly permitting gambling on the premises and allowing B-girls to loiter and solicit for immoral purposes.[17] The police made little effort to close down these places.

17. *Knickerbocker News,* March 15, 1961, and Albany *Times-Union,* April 20, 1961. The police chief told a reporter that such matters were the responsibility of the SLA, adding that "anytime a crime is committed in the presence of a police

Not long afterward, the Republican administration of Governor Rockefeller tore down the Gut in order to make way for a new, 100-acre state office building complex (and also, one suspects, to weaken the power and lessen the income of the Democratic administration that runs the city). With a few exceptions, the bars and brothels that were torn down never reopened. At least one well-known brothel still operates in the area (though staffed with Negro girls it is for white men only) and several girls continue to work the streets or hustle in bars, mostly in the Negro section; some of the street girls, but none of those in the brothel, are occasionally arrested. To the casual visitor, Albany is now a quiet, even dull, city. Girls are available, but one must search a bit to find them — their presence is no longer advertised by the bright lights and loud noises of honky-tonk bars — which is, one imagines, just the way the police now want it.

Gambling continues to flourish but also more circumspectly. In June 1964 agents of the U.S. Internal Revenue Service arrested twenty-nine persons in Albany on charges of failing to purchase a $50 federal wagering tax stamp.[18] The Albany police chief answered "no comment" when reporters asked whether he knew of the gambling and, if so, why he had not ended it. The Internal Revenue Service spokesman said the Albany police had not been informed of the raid and their cooperation had not been sought.[19] Most of those arrested were eventually fined sums ranging from $150 to $1,250. Two years later, the State Police raided the Albany area again, arresting twenty-six persons on gambling charges, mostly for bookmaking.[20] This time the Albany police participated in the raid but those arrested managed to escape punishment.

---

officer, an arrest is made and proper action is taken." *Times-Union,* April 25, 1961. In 1960, the year before the SLA investigation, the Albany police made thirty arrests on prostitution charges, but this had little effect on business.

18. *Knickerbocker News,* June 10, 11, 12, and 13, 1964.
19. *Ibid.,* June 11, 1964.
20. *Times-Union,* July 17, 1966.

Case II: Citizen-Invoked Law Enforcement

When a victim of a crime calls the police, the latter have little discretion *whether* to intervene (not answering a citizen call is easily made the subject of a complaint) but they may have considerable discretion regarding *how* to intervene. In the routine case, of course, there is little for the patrolman to do but fill out a report on the offense and file it at headquarters. If a suspect has been caught by the citizen or the store guard, however, the patrolman can choose whether to make an arrest, ask the victim to make a citizen's arrest and allow the officer to take the suspect into custody on the citizen's behalf, or do nothing. Doing nothing can be risky but, if the offense is a misdemeanor, and the officer did not see it committed, doing something is also risky.

That risk is greatly reduced, and accordingly the officer's discretion is considerably broadened, when the suspect is a juvenile. The law restricting the power of the police to make arrests in misdemeanors does not apply to juveniles in some states. Under California law, for example, a patrolman may "take into temporary custody" without a warrant a person under the age of eighteen if the officer "has reasonable cause for believing" that the juvenile has, among other things, violated "any law." [21] Once in custody, the juvenile may be taken before a probation officer to determine whether further detention is necessary or the police may release him, with or without some form of reprimand, or order him to appear before the probation officer at a later date.[22] Under New York law, the police have somewhat less authority. They may take into custody without a warrant a person under the age of sixteen who commits or attempts in the officer's presence a crime, who has committed a felony but not in his presence, or who the officer has reasonable cause to believe has committed a felony.[23] The police, once they have taken a child into custody, must immediately notify the parents and either release

21. California, *Welfare and Institutions Code,* secs. 602, 625.
22. *Ibid.,* secs. 626, 628.
23. New York, *Family Court Act,* sec. 721; *Code of Criminal Procedure,* sec. 177.

the child to them without bond or take the child directly to the local family court or to a reception center designated by the family court.[24]

Most citizen-invoked law enforcement deals with theft (larceny, burglary, and auto theft). If a suspect has been caught, the police will have some discretion if he is an adult and considerable discretion if he is a juvenile. The police administrator can constrain this discretion, but not, as with traffic tickets, by setting production norms or, as with vice, deciding how much crime he will tolerate. Rather, he will create, or fail to create, various procedures or specialized units for handling suspects. A detective squad is one such specialized unit used for following up on "cold" cases, that is, those in which no suspect was on the scene at the time the patrolman arrived. Not every administrator specializes even to this degree — in Highland Park, for example, there was not until fairly recently a detective squad and thus there was no organized follow-up on burglary reports. But the chief's greatest opportunity for shaping, intentionally or unintentionally, the discretion exercised by his men in this area lies in the decision to create a juvenile unit and to determine its strategy.

Of the eight communities studied, three (Nassau, Oakland, and Syracuse) had specialized juvenile divisions, three (Albany, Amsterdam, and Newburgh) had no juvenile specialists, and two (Brighton and Highland Park) had at least one officer who spent more or less full time on juveniles. The consequence of specialization is that juveniles are "taken seriously" — there are officers who devote their energies to deciding how to handle them, who follow up leads on suspected juvenile offenders, and who keep records on delinquents and suspected delinquents.

The police departments in the four high-crime cities differ substantially in the rate at which they arrest persons on charges of larceny, the most common victim-producing crime. As Table 5 shows, the arrest rate in 1965 in Albany was only half that in Syracuse and one ninth that in Oakland. The rate in Newburgh was also lower than that in Syracuse and only one fifth that in Oakland. A

24. New York, *Family Court Act*, sec. 724.

major reason for this difference is the fact that in Albany and Newburgh very few juveniles are arrested on this charge, but in Oakland and Syracuse many are. Persons under the age of sixteen accounted for about 23 per cent of the larceny arrests in Albany and 18 per

Table 5. Arrest rates for larceny, by age group, in four high-crime cities, 1965.[a]

City	Arrest rates (per 100,000 population) for larceny		
	All persons	Adults[b]	Juveniles[c]
Albany	92.5	96.6	80.6
Newburgh	163.3	186.4	105.9
Oakland	894.0	416.7	1,201.8
Syracuse	203.3	138.5	374.6

[a] All rates are calculated on the basis of estimates of the number of persons living in the city in 1965 whose ages corresponded to the age group of those arrested.

[b] Persons sixteen years of age or over in the New York cities and eighteen years of age or over in Oakland.

[c] Persons under the age of sixteen in the New York cities and under the age of eighteen in Oakland.

cent of those in Newburgh, but 48 per cent of those in Oakland and 51 per cent of those in Syracuse. In fact, because a person in California is a juvenile until he reaches the age of eighteen, an even larger proportion — over 62 per cent — of the Oakland larceny arrests that year were made under the procedures governing the handling of juveniles. If we compare only the adult arrest rates in the four cities, much of the difference disappears. As Table 3 shows, the adult arrest rate in Albany is about the same as in Syracuse and the rate in Newburgh is even higher than that in Syracuse. The Oakland rate is still high but not nearly as high as when all larceny arrests are treated together — the difference between Oakland and Albany falls from nearly ten to one to about four to one and the difference between Oakland and Newburgh drops from over five to one to a little over two to one.

If the crime committed by a juvenile is serious enough, he will be arrested in any city. To a patrolman, a felony arrest is a "good pinch" even if the felon turns out to be fifteen years old. Thus, such juvenile arrests as occur in Albany and Newburgh are primarily for major crimes. Of the 167 arrested in Albany in 1965, 114 (68 per cent) were held for robbery, aggravated assault, burglary, and auto theft. In Newburgh the same year, 74 per cent of the 31 juveniles arrested were held for these major offenses. The one juvenile arrested in Amsterdam was held for robbery. By contrast, in Syracuse, and to an even greater extent in Oakland, police officers arrest many juveniles for misdemeanors as well as felonies. In Syracuse only 31 per cent and in Oakland only 14 per cent of those formally processed by the department were charged with what, if committed by an adult, would be a felony; the rest were held for misdemeanors and offenses.

Over time the differences are even more striking. Despite a good deal of talk among patrolmen about the rising lawlessness of youth, juvenile arrests between 1960 and 1965 decreased by 20 per cent in Albany and by 22 per cent in Newburgh. In Oakland and Syracuse, by contrast, they increased by 55 and 54 per cent, respectively.[25]

The fact that juvenile arrest rates are substantially influenced by departmental policies and that such arrests account for a large part of all arrests for petty larceny may explain why arrest rates for this offense are not significantly associated with the population characteristics of cities. It is quite another story with major thefts, however. Because they are felonies, arrests can occur on the basis of probable cause; because they represent large losses or frightening events, there is likely to be a victim who takes the matter seriously; because (judging from arrest statistics) major thefts are more likely than petty ones to be committed by adults, the discretion afforded by the laws governing juveniles does not apply. As a result, arrests for these crimes — grand larceny and robbery — tend to vary with community characteristics, while arrests for petty larceny seem to be independent of such characteristics (see Table 6) but, as argued above, quite dependent on police policies.

This finding casts doubt on the view that the police in middle-class suburbs are "soft" on the kids, presumably out of regard for the political influence of their parents, whereas the police in working-

25. Here and elsewhere, the Oakland arrest figures for juveniles exclude persons charged with loitering because no similar charge is available to the police in the New York cities studied.

Table 6. Correlation between arrest rate for various thefts and community characteristics in forty-one New York communities (1962).

Community characteristic	Petty larceny	Grand larceny	Robbery
Median family income	−.03	+.43	+.22
Percentage of families earning over $10,000 a year	+.03	+.51	+.34
Percentage of population nonwhite	−.01	+.36	+.47

class communities are "tough," perhaps because such parents are lacking in influence. There is, of course, no way to know how much juvenile crime occurs in any community and therefore no way of knowing what proportion goes unreported and what proportion, though reported, is ignored by the police. But the strong impression of interviewers is that suburban police officers are intimately familiar with what is going on — in great part because, lacking much serious crime to attend to, they have the time and the inclination to keep track of minor matters. Furthermore, there are highly developed informal communications in a small town: teachers, parents, and little old ladies keeping watch on flower gardens are apt to notice any strange or objectionable behavior and they will want to "do something" about perceived threats to property.[26]

26. Though there is a good deal of talk about "suburban delinquency" or "middle class delinquency" and even some speculation that if the *true* rates of delinquency in the suburbs were known they would not be much better than those in the central cities, there is surprisingly little systematic evidence on the matter. The best study thus far made is that by Walter Miller, who concludes that, far from there being a great and rising amount of middle-class, suburban delinquency, the rate of offenses in these outlying areas is vastly lower than in the central cities and rather stable. Where "suburban" crime rates are going up, it is related in many cases to changes in the proportions of lower-, working-, and middle-class residents in the population. There is in the suburbs much less "hidden delinquency" because the police are fully informed about and take more seriously minor juvenile offenses in middle-class residential areas; in lower-class central city areas, by contrast, there is so much juvenile misconduct that much is not reported and of that which is reported the police have the resources to handle (or want to handle) only the more serious offenses. Walter B. Miller, "A Preliminary Report on Suburban Delinquency," typescript, April 1967, Joint Center for Urban Studies of M.I.T. and Harvard.

When the suburban police learn of a juvenile incident, they tend to take it seriously — again perhaps because they have little else to do or perhaps because the community wants it so. Nathan Goldman, in a study of police-juvenile contacts in four small Pennsylvania communities, found that the police were more likely to detain a juvenile in a high-status residential suburb he called Manor Heights than in a small working-class town ("Steel City") in the same county — 37.3 children per thousand (between the ages of 10 and 17) were detained in Steel City but 49.7 per thousand in Manor Heights. However, a larger proportion of the Steel City arrests were for the more serious offenses — 26.9 per cent of the Steel City juvenile arrests but only 6.7 per cent of those in Manor Heights were on charges more serious than larceny. Accordingly, a much higher percentage of the Steel City juveniles were referred to court — 46.1 per cent as compared to 8.6 per cent in Manor Heights. The Manor Heights police were thus not letting the sons of the affluent off easy — they were picking them up at a higher rate than the Steel City police were detaining the sons of blue-collar workers, and for less serious offenses. And when the Manor Heights police found a child who had committed a serious offense, they were even more likely to send him to court than the Steel City police — 96.0 per cent of all arrests on "serious" charges went to court in Manor Heights, only 80.1 per cent in Steel City.[27]

There are, in short, as many reasons to believe that a middle-class community is tough on juveniles as to believe that it is soft on them. In this study, Goldman's general findings are confirmed with the important qualification that there are significant differences among police departments in upper-middle-class suburbs. Table 7 shows the number of juveniles in the low-crime communities processed by the police for all offenses in 1965 and, of those processed, the number arrested — that is, turned over to the court for a formal hearing on delinquency charges. There is no record on how many juveniles were

27. Nathan Goldman, *The Differential Selection of Juvenile Offenders for Court Appearances* (New York: National Council on Crime and Delinquency, 1963), p. 86. See also James Q. Wilson, "The Police and the Delinquent in Two Cities," in Stanton Wheeler, ed., *Controlling Delinquents* (New York: John Wiley & Sons, 1968), pp. 9–30.

Table 7. Juveniles processed and arrested in four low-crime communities, 1965.

City	Number of juveniles processed [a]	Number of juveniles arrested [b]	Juvenile arrest rate	Per cent of those processed arrested
Amsterdam	–[c]	1	13.4	–
Brighton	133	9	93.8	6.8
Highland Park	135	30	312.5	22.2
Nassau County[d]	–	440	110.6	–

[a] By "processed" is meant that the police brought the juvenile to police headquarters for questioning on a criminal charge and completed a formal record on him.

[b] By "arrested" is meant that the police have taken the juvenile to the local juvenile or family court for formal disposition on delinquency charges.

The juvenile arrest rate is based on the number of persons estimated to be living in the community in 1965 under the age of sixteen. In Highland Park, a person is a juvenile until he reaches the age of eighteen, but for purposes of comparison only those who were under the age of sixteen are included here.

[c] Not available.

[d] The Nassau County arrest and population figures apply only to those parts of the county patrolled by the NCPD.

handled informally in Amsterdam, but it is striking that despite the working-class character of the city only *one* juvenile was formally arrested, and in that case the charge was very serious — robbery. Brighton and Highland Park, about the same size as Amsterdam but much higher in socioeconomic status, had 133 and 135 juveniles, respectively, processed by the police and of these, nine from Brighton and about thirty from Highland Park were taken to court.[28] Nassau County police took 440 juveniles to court, for an arrest rate about the same as Brighton's. Of all the persons picked up by the police on charges of larceny, *none* in Amsterdam was a juvenile but 32 per cent were in Brighton and 90 per cent were in Highland Park.

No doubt there are cases of the police protecting the children of the rich, but on the whole theft in suburbia is not treated lightly. That Brighton and Highland Park have specialized juvenile officers while Amsterdam does not may account for some of the difference.

28. The Highland Park figure is an estimate. Fifty-one persons under the age of eighteen were taken to court. There is no record as to how many of these were under sixteen, but applying age-specific arrest rates for juveniles from national figures for cities of that size, thirty seems a conservative guess.

But specialization alone does not necessarily lead the police to make more arrests. The administrator can through specialization achieve the opposite effect, as the case of Nassau County shows. Since 1963 the police there have had a Juvenile Aid Bureau, expanded in 1967 to a Youth Division, but the number of juveniles arrested has *declined* as a result. Between 1963 and 1964, they dropped by 10 per cent and between 1964 and 1965 by another 23 per cent. This change was in accordance with the intentions of the police administrators. The commissioner later told an interviewer that he had instructed the lieutenant in charge of the juvenile bureau to try to cut arrests: "I told [him] that if he didn't cut juvenile arrests by 30 per cent in two years, I would consider the JAB a failure. We're a semi-social agency. I think it's a great mistake to feel that you're dealing with the problem solely by making more arrests." By contrast, the police in neighboring Suffolk County, which also created a juvenile bureau (in 1961), decided to operate it on the opposite philosophy—to stop delinquency by increasing the number of arrests. Accordingly, between 1963 and 1964 such arrests increased by over 30 per cent.[29]

Case III: Police-Invoked Order Maintenance

The most common police-initiated intervention in a situation where disorder exists or is likely occurs in dealing with drunks. The usual police policy toward drunks is to avoid an arrest if possible. Avoiding an arrest is easiest for the patrolman when the inebriate can take care of himself and is not bothering other people or, if he is bothering them, can be persuaded to "be good" or can be put in the care of a wife or friend who will take him home. In many cases, the police will take him home themselves. Only as a last resort will an arrest be made. A senior officer explained to an interviewer the policy in Newburgh:

> If the person is properly dressed, and if the officer knows him or knows where he lives, and if he's not disturbing anyone, the officer will take him home. Sometimes, though not often, we'll let him dry out in

29. See the article in *Newsday*, September 24, 1965, p. 1C.

the station without booking him, and then we'll call his wife. But our obnoxious drunks — the tramps and the ones who get nasty — and anyone who gets rowdy in the business district or in a quiet residential area, we'll arrest.

A Syracuse patrolman described the same policy in more colorful language:

If a drunk is wandering around downtown, slobbering all over himself, you have to get him off the streets. You might get a buddy to take him home if it's close. If he's going to make a scene that will embarrass some citizen or will hurt himself, you've got to take him off the streets and put him in jail and let him sober up . . . If a guy just happens to be drunk, you call a cab.

The statistics support this interpretation. A sample of fifty-eight drunk cases taken from the files of the Newburgh City Court in 1964 shows that thirty-five (60 per cent) of the persons had no home to be taken to and thus were arrested — twenty-six were out-of-town residents and nine were homeless tramps. In Syracuse, though a "reform" police administration came to power in 1963–64 and, as a consequence, traffic tickets began being issued in floods, the number of drunk arrests did not increase; in fact, there was a slight decrease between 1960 and 1964 (from 2,424 to 1,793). In 1965 it rose again slightly to 1,952 but was still below the 1960 level. The new chief, though he devoted much time to developing and using administrative controls that would induce patrolmen to write more tickets, left the handling of drunks to the traditional practices of sergeants and patrolmen. It cannot be proved, but it may be that drunk arrests slipped slightly because the men had to spend so much time on traffic. In sum, Newburgh and Syracuse, despite very different police administrations, had comparable drunk arrest rates in 1965: 870 per hundred thousand in Newburgh, 914 per hundred thousand in Syracuse.[30]

There are several reasons why patrolmen are reluctant to arrest a person simply for being drunk. First, it is a messy business:

30. Syracuse also has a city ordinance that permits arrests for intoxication in private places. Adding such arrests to the figure given in the text would increase the arrest rate slightly to about 1,050 per hundred thousand.

derelicts are often ill-clothed, unwashed, foul-smelling men who rarely make pleasant companions on the ride back to the station. Second, drunks who are not derelicts may be important people; unless they create a disturbance, an arrest may expose the officer to complaints that he was bothering "decent citizens" over "trivial matters." But most important, though the police are sometimes accused of having a "punitive" attitude toward drunks, in fact the typical officer interviewed for this study felt that drunkenness was not "really a crime" and that society ought to provide an alternative way of coping with the chronic, lower-status alcoholic. The police would be delighted to be relieved of the burden of handling the drunk, as would anyone who has had someone vomit in the back seat of his car a few times; they would not, however, like to see the public intoxication statute abolished because it can be used for many other purposes. For over a century, police officers have tried to deal with the problem in other ways. In 1860, the Boston police arrested 17,352 persons as drunks but in addition they "lodged" (that is, gave a free bed and meal to) another 13,157 persons, many of them homeless alcoholics.[31] Early police administrators often referred to drunkenness as a social or medical problem; they disliked, and often sought to evade, the responsibility, thrust on them by a Yankee legislature, to reduce or prohibit drinking among the lower classes.[32]

31. Roger Lane, *Policing the City: Boston, 1822–1885* (Cambridge, Mass.: Harvard University Press, 1967), p. 114. In the 1870's, the Boston police provided free soup and distributed shoes and medicines to the "deserving poor." Private charities objected to this as unfair competition. *Ibid.*, pp. 191–195.

32. *Ibid.*, p. 135. Ironically, it was these early prohibition and sumptuary laws that first gave the police, at least in Boston, the right to arrest without a warrant. The descendants of those Yankee statesmen who created this situation are now among the most vocal of those who would like to curb the power of arrest. Sometimes, however, it was the Yankee reformer who caused the police to *reduce* drunkenness arrests. Perry Knapp, a reform police chief in Toledo and a disciple of Brand Whitlock, instituted the "golden rule" policy toward minor offenders, especially drunks and vagrants, whereby they were taken home instead of arrested. He also took away the policemen's clubs, much to their disgust. Similar policies were being followed in Cleveland at about the same time. The Whitlock-Knapp era may mark the period when reformers began to change from repression to rehabilitation in their efforts to improve the behavior of the lower classes. See Robert H. Bremner, "The Civic Revival in Ohio: Police, Penal and Parole Policies in Cleveland and Toledo," *American Journal of Economics and Sociology*, 14 (July 1955), pp. 387–398.

Because the patrolman views public drunkenness as a problem of potential disorder rather than one of law enforcement, most arrests on this charge are made when something more than mere drunkenness is involved — namely, when disorder has become real rather than potential. Typically, a drunk arrest is made when the patrolman sees no other way to handle a dispute in which one or more persons have been drinking. In Syracuse, for example, at least 55 per cent of a sample of persons arrested in 1965 for intoxication had been fighting, resisting or abusing a police officer, involved in a neighborhood dispute, or the like.[33] In Brighton, of eighty-three persons picked up for drunkenness over a two-year period, only sixteen (20 per cent) were taken in simply because the police saw them intoxicated. The rest were arrested for assorted disturbances, fights, arguments with the police, and the like.[34] One Albany police officer put it this way: the "public intox charge is like aspirin — it covers a multitude of ills."

As a result, only a minority of drunk arrests in most cities studied are made solely on the initiative of the officer. They are not, in police jargon, "on view" arrests. In Syracuse, only 39 per cent (of 150 intoxication arrest records studied) were on view; most of the rest were made after the police had been summoned to the scene of an incident by a citizen call. In Brighton, only fifteen (18 per cent) of the eighty-two drunk cases were "on view"; the rest resulted from a citizen report.

So long as the administrator takes the view that the patrolman should handle the drunks he sees in ways that will prevent disorder, assure the safety of the inebriate, and avoid complaints of excessive zeal, the latter will have considerable discretion as to what measures the situation requires. There are, however, two ways by which the administrator can affect the patrolman's discretion: one is to indicate, though rarely by an explicit policy statement, what level of disorder is tolerable; the other is to instruct, almost always by explicit direc-

33. See Table 8 below.

34. The Brighton figure includes persons taken into custody but released without charges being preferred as well as those arrested and taken to court. The data were extracted from reports filed by patrolmen for the period January 1, 1965, to December 31, 1966.

tive, the patrolman to treat problems of disorder as if they were problems of law enforcement.

The first strategy can be seen in the differences in drunk arrest rates in Amsterdam, Brighton, and Highland Park — all small cities with insignificant Negro populations. Amsterdam is a working-class community, which had (in 1965) 149 licenses allowing the sale of liquor in 69 bars and restaurants, 15 liquor stores, and 10 clubs and the sale of beer at 50 grocery stores.[35] Brighton, by contrast, is an upper-middle-class suburb which had, in 1965, only 29 licenses. Liquor was available at only one fourth as many stores and one sixth as many bars and restaurants as in Amsterdam. And Highland Park, also an upper-middle-class suburb, was bone dry — there was not a single liquor store or bar in town. Yet over a two-year period, the Amsterdam police arrested only ten persons on intoxication charges, and only three of these were cases in which the man was simply drunk (in the rest of the cases, the man had broken down the door to a house, set a fire, threatened a police officer, or got into a fight). In Brighton, on the other hand, eighty-three persons were picked up on intoxication charges and twenty-six of these were simply drunks — that is, the arrest record alleged no disturbance, fight, or the like. Highland Park, though dry, managed to arrest in the same two-year period forty-two people on drunk charges.

Obviously, the police in Brighton and Highland Park have less tolerance for disorder than the police in Amsterdam — the number of persons arrested on intoxication charges was four to eight times higher in the suburban cities than in the working-class city. Perhaps even more important, the straight drunk arrests — that is, those in which no serious disorder was alleged — were eight times more common in Brighton than in Amsterdam. The suburban police are more likely to use arrest as a way of coping with disorder; the Amsterdam police may dislike drunks, though there is no evidence of that, but they resort more often to informal measures to deal with them (telling them to get out of town, to go home, or the like). Perhaps the suburban police would make greater use of informal

35. Division of Alcoholic Beverage Control, State of New York, *Report of the Activities of the State Liquor Authority for 1964*, pp. 54–83.

measures if the situation permitted them, but typically it does not. Only ten of the eighty-three persons picked up by the police in Brighton on intoxication charges lived in Brighton; of the rest, sixty were from out of town. Thirteen were from the nearby county farm where persons sentenced on drunk charges serve their time. Thus, taking the drunk home was not a possibility for the Brighton police in the great majority of the cases. There is, unfortunately, no record of the place of residence of those arrested in Amsterdam.

The second way the administrator can affect the patrolman's discretion in such cases is to develop policies that lead the officer to treat the matter as if it were a problem of law enforcement — that is, to arrest drunks on view simply because they are drunk. Table 8 gives the public intoxication arrest rate and the police account of

Table 8. Arrests for public intoxication in three cities: rates and distribution by reported behavior.

Arrests	Albany	Oakland	Syracuse
Total, 1965[a]	3,226	16,532	1,965
Rate per 100,000 population (est.)	2,688.3	4,504.6	914.0
Reported behavior (per cent)[b]			
Drunk, or drunk and disturbing	82.5	71.0	44.7
Down, asleep, passed out, lying on sidewalk	11.9	17.5	24.0
Fight or assault	4.2	3.5	13.3
Resisting, abusing, or disobeying police	0.4	4.0	8.7
Other	1.1	4.0	9.3
100 per cent equals:	285	200	150

[a] Total arrests from 1965 reports of police departments.

[b] Reported behaviors from sample of arrest records. Albany sample includes all arrests from May 18 to June 15, 1967; Oakland sample includes 200 cases immediately preceding May 31, 1967; Syracuse sample includes all arrests from June 8 to June 30, 1967. The Newburgh reports did not permit tabulation.

The possible distortion from using 1965 arrest rates and 1967 arrest records should be borne in mind, though it is not likely to be great since total arrests tend to remain constant from year to year. Extracting 1965 arrest reports would have been extremely difficult in most cities, owing to haphazard filing and indexing procedures.

the behavior leading to those arrests for the three large, high-crime cities. The total intoxication arrest rate in Syracuse is only a third that in Albany and a fifth that in Oakland. The reason is apparent: the police in Albany and Oakland compared to those in Syracuse arrest a much larger percentage of persons merely for being drunk or "drunk and disturbing" (a phrase used on the reports of arresting officers to conform to the requirements of the legal code and one that is not necessarily descriptive of how much of a disturbance, if any, actually occurred).[36] Indeed, in those cases where order is clearly at issue, the arrest rates of Albany and Syracuse are almost identical. Arrests in cases where the person was endangering himself (for example, having passed out on the sidewalk) or endangering or bothering others (for example, fighting or resisting an officer) accounted for only 17.6 per cent of the total in Albany but 55.3 per cent of that in Syracuse. Applying these percentages to the total arrest rate would lower it to 475 per 100,000 in Albany and 505 per 100,000 in Syracuse — surprisingly close, considering the many imperfections in the data.

Though police administrators in Albany claim that they "leave alone" ordinary drunks seen on the street, in fact they are much

36. Some difference among these cities may well be due to differences in the number of drunks to be arrested. Estimating the actual rate of public intoxication, as opposed to the police arrest rate for intoxication, is virtually impossible. Some attempts have been made to ascertain the rate of alcoholism, as estimated from deaths attributable to cirrhosis of the liver, for states and big cities in this country as well as for foreign countries. These conclude that as of 1950 the rate per hundred thousand adults of alcoholics with complications (persons with recognizable physical or mental symptoms due to excessive drinking) in Albany was 1,200; in Oakland, 1,980; and in Syracuse, 1,060. Mark Keller and Vera Efron, "Alcoholism in the Big Cities of the United States," *Quarterly Journal of Studies on Alcoholism*, 17 (1956), pp. 63–72. Their method is based on the Jellinek estimation formula. See E. M. Jellinek in "Report" of the First session of the Alcoholism Subcommittee of the Expert Committee on Mental Health (Geneva: World Health Organization technical report, serial 42, 1951). The Jellinek formula has been criticized in Robert E. Popham, "The Jellinek Alcoholism Estimation Formula and Its Application to Canadian Data," *Quarterly Journal of Studies on Alcoholism*, 17 (1956), pp. 559–593, and in John R. Seeley, "Estimating the Prevalence of Alcoholism: A Critical Analysis of the Jellinek Formula," in *Quarterly Journal of Studies on Alcoholism*, 20 (1959), pp. 245–260; see also the reply by Jellinek in the same volume, pp. 261–269. Despite the logical arguments that can be brought against the formula, it has shown surprisingly good agreement with some rates independently derived from survey and other data. (See Popham, "The Jellinek Formula.")

more likely to arrest them than the police in Syracuse. Of the sample of drunk arrest records examined in the two cities, "on view" arrests accounted for at least 65 per cent of the total in Albany but only 38.6 per cent of the total in Syracuse. This emphasis on drunk arrests — the reasons for which will be examined in a later chapter — is made easier by the city's arrest procedures. For every nontraffic offense except public intoxication and vagrancy, the arresting officer must appear the next morning before the clerk of the police court or an assistant district attorney and state the circumstances of the arrest so that an official information or complaint can then be drawn. Few Albany officers — indeed, few police officers anywhere — are eager to be in court at ten o'clock in the morning after being on duty all night. For intoxication and vagrancy arrests, however, the officer need only bring the person into the station house where the desk sergeant fills out on the spot an information or complaint blank, which the arresting officer then signs; all such cases are prosecuted the next morning without the officer having to be present, except in the very rare case when a man pleads not guilty and asks for a trial. The law, in short, makes it easy to implement any departmental policy that seeks to have drunks handled on a law enforcement basis.

The clearest example of this strategy can be found in Oakland, where the policy toward drunks underwent a change in the mid-1950's. In 1954 the police arrested 6,887 persons for drunkenness, for a rate comparable to that in Albany today. By 1960 both the total and the rate had more than doubled. The reform police administration that came to power in the mid-1950's decided that skidrow drunks were disproportionally the victims of strongarm robberies; furthermore, drunks in and near the downtown bars disturbed the peace and annoyed citizens by disorderly behavior, panhandling, and trespassing. Accordingly, the department decided to arrest all persons who were intoxicated in a public place. Once arrested they were to be formally processed — booked and jailed — rather than allowed to "sleep it off" at headquarters. Under state law a person is eligible for release from jail the next morning without going to court and being sentenced if he is being held only for drunkenness and has not been arrested on that charge during the preceding six months. Under this policy, about one fourth — 26.7 per cent — of the more than 16,000 drunk arrests made in 1965 resulted in the person being released after a night in jail. The rest of the cases were heard in court. A sample of 670 drunk cases — the total for a one-week period, October 1–5, 1962 — heard before the Oakland Municipal Court shows that about half the cases result in suspended sentences, usually for first offenders, about a third in jail sentences, usually thirty days, and the rest in fines.

Whereas a patrolman in another city will wait until some one complains of a drunk or until he sees one creating a disturbance, an Oakland patrolman working a downtown beat will often stop and investigate any person he sees who appears to have been drinking. One such check witnessed by an interviewer was typical of many. The patrolman stopped at a downtown park, walked over to two men, one white, the other Negro, and asked them politely for their identification. They fumbled about and muttered rather incoherently; the pair clearly had been drinking. A few empty wine bottles lay nearby. The officer asked them to take a sobriety test involving standing on one foot and holding the other foot a few inches off the ground. Both failed. They were then asked to walk a straight line, heel to toe. Neither could. The patrolman patted them down and put them in the back of his car, filled out two arrest reports, and called for the wagon. The white man muttered belligerently; the Negro was quieter and kept asking to be let off, since he claimed he lived only a few blocks away. Neither had been creating a disturbance and neither was, when spotted, in any obvious danger. The patrolman explained to the interviewer:

> We have to bring them in to cut down on the strong-arms. When we picked up those two guys in the park, did you see that other guy with the hole in his head? The one with the big wound right in the middle of his hair? He had gotten himself half killed the other night and just got out of the hospital. Those drunks get rolled even when they don't have any money. We have to bag 'em to keep that sort of thing from happening.

The department claims that the crackdown on drunks has reduced strong-arm robberies but this is very difficult to prove. Between 1957 and 1959 drunk arrests increased by about 11 per cent (from 11,037 to 12,298) and the number of strong-arm robberies reported fell by 35 per cent (from 330 to 203). Over the next two-year period, however, drunk arrests increased even more (up to 14,778 in 1961, a gain of 20 per cent over 1959) but reported strong-arm robberies also increased (up to 266, a gain of 30 per cent). By 1965, drunk arrests had increased by nearly 50 per cent over 1957 but reported strong-arm robberies were back up almost (296) to the 1957 level. There is, of course, no way of knowing how many more robberies there would have been if drunk arrests in skidrow were much lower; what can be said is that the statistical record — which shows both drunk arrests and reported strong-arm robberies increasing in most years since 1960 — does not offer much encouragement. One reason may be that there are so many derelicts who drink and so much stealing going on among them that arresting more drunks deprives the thief of such a small proportion of his total target population as to have little or no effect on his operations — alternative victims are readily available. In any case, the law of property among derelicts is not highly developed, to say the least; what one "owns" he probably took from a fellow drunk and when the latter seeks to get it back, the incident could as plausibly be called private justice or a dispute over common property as a robbery.[37] And it is doubtful

37. Egon Bittner, "The Police in Skid Row: A Study of Peace Keeping," *American Sociological Review*, 32 (October 1967), pp. 699–715. The police records of a sample of chronic inebriates arrested in Monroe County (Rochester and environs, including Brighton) in New York are analyzed in David J. Pittman and C. Wayne Gordon, *Revolving Door: A Study of the Chronic Police Case Inebriate* (New York: Free Press, 1958), pp. 41–52. The Pittman-Gordon data suggest that there are three main types of drunks: one third of the sample were simply alcoholics who had never been arrested for anything but public intoxication; another third were more mischievous and had been arrested for a number of alcohol-related offenses, including disorderly conduct, vagrancy, driving while intoxicated, and assault; and a final third appeared to be serious criminals as well as inebriates, having been arrested for homicide, rape, robbery, burglary, larceny, auto theft, forgery, and other major offenses. (*Ibid.*, pp. 47–50.)

In New York, the offense of intoxication is nowhere defined by statute but it has been held by the courts to occur when in a public place a person by reason of having used alcoholic beverages attracts the attention of the public to himself. *Penal Law*, sec. 1221, as interpreted by *People v. Weaver*, 177 N.Y. 71 (1919). In California, intoxication is legally a form of disorderly conduct, a misdemeanor, and

such a loss would even be reported to the police, because few "victims" would welcome police inquiries. Thus the efficacy of the Oakland police strategy on drunks is, like most police strategies, hard to evaluate. But officers in downtown beats are still expected to produce drunk arrests, and because in this case the police are invoking the law rather than responding to a citizen complaint, the drunk arrest rate reflects as much the nature of the department as the characteristics of the population.

Because of this dual influence, the relationship between the rates for such arrests and the socioeconomic status of the city is weak. For forty-one New York communities, the simple correlation of intoxication arrest rates in 1962 with median family income was —.18 and with the nonwhite proportion of the population exactly zero. This means that although a higher status community compared to a lower status one is much less likely to have persons drunk in a public place (how many are drunk in a private place is another matter), the police in such a community are only slightly less likely to make arrests for this offense.

Case IV: Citizen-Invoked Order Maintenance

In this case the police administrator has the least influence over the discretion of the patrolman. Not only can few rules be prescribed in advance for handling disorderly situations, but there is little opportunity for inducing the patrolman to act as if it were a matter of law enforcement. Unlike police-observed situations of disorder — for example, the drunk bothering passers-by on a street — this situation often presents no grounds for making a lawful arrest. Because the citizen has initiated the police action, presumably it is the citizen who has witnessed the offense and it is upon the citizen's cooperation that the officer depends — by law in many states and by custom in all — for such arrests as may ensue.

---

is committed by a person who is "in any public place under the influence of intoxicating liquor, or any drug, . . . in such a condition that he is unable to exercise care for his own safety or the safety of others, or . . . interferes with or obstructs or prevents the free use of any street, sidewalk or other public way." *Penal Code*, sec. 647(f).

If the disturbance occurs in a public place — in a tavern or on a street corner — an officer so inclined could arrest a person for public intoxication (if the person has been drinking) or disturbing the peace. But if the disorder occurs in a private place, for example, in a family quarrel, then even these legal options are on the whole foreclosed — either a citizen makes an arrest on the spot, or swears out a complaint to permit an arrest with a warrant the next day, or there will be no arrest at all. Sometimes, of course, the patrolman will stretch a point and arrest on charges of public intoxication people who are drunk in private, or at best semi-public, places simply in order to cool the situation down.

An interviewer accompanying a Syracuse patrolman for a few nights witnessed four public intoxication arrests; three in fact involved something much more serious than simply intoxication but, because of the complexities of the situation, no more serious charge seemed appropriate. One arose because a slum mother complained her son had tried to kill her, but she was unwilling (or, in the eyes of the police, unlikely) to sign a formal complaint; she just wanted him "locked up." When the son returned, obviously drunk, he was arrested for intoxication and taken away. If the mother still wanted to charge him with assault, she could appear in court the next morning (she didn't). The second case arose because of a profane quarrel between the manager of a flop house and a young man about whether the latter had paid for his bed; when the accused took a swing at the manager in the presence of the police, he was arrested for being drunk and taken away. The third arrest was of a middle-aged man with a bloody face who had been fighting with a younger man accused of paying unwelcome attention to his daughter. A crowd had gathered, obviously hostile to the young man. But the daughter refused to say that the young man's attentions were unwelcome. The officer vainly tried to separate the men and to get everyone to calm down. When the father, who had been drinking, insisted upon launching another assault on the suitor, the officer took him away on an intoxication charge. In these three cases there were, had the officer arrested on the maximum available charges, at least one instance of attempted assault in the second degree (a felony), two assaults in the third degree and one case of defrauding an innkeeper (both misdemeanors), and disorderly conduct (an offense). The advantage of the public intoxication charge is that no warrant is necessary, the officer need not have the cooperation of a complainant, and as the offense does not technically constitute a crime it will not seriously hurt the record of the accused. Similar incidents could be described for every high-crime city visited.

There is one major exception to the generalization that the patrolman will be reluctant to make an arrest as a result of a dispute or fight he has not witnessed. This situation arises when one or the other of the quarreling parties turns on the officer and abuses, resists, or attacks him. Then the officer is likely to use a general charge, such as disorderly conduct, to make an arrest.[38] Table 9 shows for the three high-crime cities where the information was available the behavior reported by the police in a sample of arrests for disorderly conduct. Resisting, disobeying, or abusing a police officer accounted for over *half* of such arrests in Syracuse and for 40 per cent of those in Newburgh. A typical case would be the following: a man who appears to have been drinking gets into an argument with another man in front of a bar; the police arrive and tell him to calm down and move on; the man continues to argue and perhaps threatens the other man with a punch in the nose; the officer tells him that if he doesn't behave he will be arrested (at this stage the officer may intend charging only public intoxication); the argumentative gentleman then turns on the officer and tells him to mind his own business, though often in language a good deal more colorful; the officer becomes angry and perhaps shouts back; the man offers some graphic, but biologically impossible, suggestions as

38. New York courts have upheld officers who arrested on disorderly conduct charges persons who have assaulted them (*People v. Tepperman,* 273 N.Y.S. 690, 1934) or resisted them (*People v. Clark,* 12 N.Y.S. 2d 8, 1939). It is not clear, however, that a person who simply insults a police officer can be so charged. *People v. McMinn,* 189 N.Y.S. 2d 627 (1959); *People v. Lassiter,* 170 N.Y.S. 2d 702 (1958); but compare *People v. Clark,* 12 N.Y.S. 2d 8 (1939) and *People v. Franke,* 281 N.Y.S. 158 (1935). Many judges interviewed for this study were of the opinion that the "peace of a policeman cannot be disturbed" — that is, he has no legal recourse against an insult. Such views, needless to say, irritate police officers profoundly and perhaps make them more willing to defend their peace by other means.

Table 9. Arrests for disorderly conduct or disturbing the peace, by reported behavior, in three cities (by per cent).

Reported behavior	Newburgh	Oakland	Syracuse
Disturbing the peace, but no fight or assault	30.0	20.3	33.3
Fight or assault	21.4	30.5	11.1
Resisting, disobeying, or abusing a police officer	40.0	15.3	52.8
Other	7.1	10.2	2.8
Unknown	1.4	23.7	–
100 per cent equals	70	59	36

Source: Samples are drawn from arrest records of local police departments. For Newburgh, all arrest reports charging disorderly conduct for January–July 1967, were tabulated. For Oakland, fifty-nine cases counting backwards from May 31, 1967, were used. For Syracuse, all cases from May and June 1967 were used. Behaviors were classified by the most "serious" behavior reported on the arrest document. Such reports are not, of course, perfectly accurate accounts of what actually transpired, especially if the event was "routine," in which case the police normally employ conventional legal language asserting a breach of the peace. But the police have an incentive to make special note of more serious matters, partly to alert their superiors should there later be a complaint and partly to let the judge know that this is no ordinary "dis con" but in fact an assault or an (alleged) attack on a police officer. The police expect that more serious punishment will be awarded in nonroutine cases.

to what the officer should do; the officer expresses doubt that the man himself is equipped to carry out any such activity, raises some question as to the legitimacy of his birth, and calls for the wagon.

But in those cases where the patrolman manages to stay out of the fight, an arrest for assault or battery, even if the officer desires to make one, depends crucially on the cooperation of the victim, or whoever claims to be the victim. There is relatively little the police can do to induce that cooperation and thus arrests on this charge seem, statistically, least sensitive to police policies and most sensitive to the characteristics of the population: there is a very strong correlation (+.67) between the arrest rate for assault and the proportion of the population nonwhite in forty-one New York communities as of 1962. Furthermore, because a police officer who has been (in his view) assaulted is not likely to use his discretion to forgive the person, arrests for disorderliness also bear some relationship (more than in the case of drunkenness, at least, where the officer exercises wide discretion) to community characteristics: the simple correlation among the forty-one cities between arrest rates for disorderly conduct and proportion nonwhite is +.47.[39]

Accordingly, the variation in arrest rates for simple assault (or, as it is called in California, battery) among the four high-crime cities is less than the variation in arrest rates for drunkenness, traffic offenses, or petty theft (see Table 10). Because assault arrests are

Table 10. Arrest rates, by race, for simple assault in four high-crime cities, 1965.[a]

City	All assault arrests	Assault arrests of whites	Assault arrests of Negroes
Albany	116.7	82.1	371.4
Newburgh	306.7	204.4	613.3
Oakland	395.4	191.0	836.0
Syracuse	120.9	74.2	561.8

Source: Reports of local police departments to the F.B.I.
[a] All rates are calculated using 1965 population estimates for whites and Negroes supplied by local planning agencies.

apparently so sensitive to the proportion of a city's population that is nonwhite, the rates are here given separately for whites and Negroes. Once again, Oakland has the highest arrest rate, but the difference between it and other cities with respect to assault — its overall rate is about three times that in Albany or Syracuse — is much less than the very large differences in traffic ticket or juvenile arrest rates. (Compare Tables 4 and 5.) Part of this difference can be explained by the higher proportion of Negroes in Oakland. The assault arrest rate for Negroes is only about twice as high in Oakland as in Albany and only about fifty per cent higher in Oakland than in Newburgh or Syracuse.

Nonetheless, the Oakland rate *is* higher. And compared to other New York communities, so is the Newburgh rate — especially for

39. Strangely, there was almost no correlation between assault arrests and median family income (+.18) or between disorderly conduct arrests and income (+.20).

whites. Both cases can be explained by local law enforcement policies. What control the police administrator has over an officer's discretion in the handling of private disputes is to be found in the legal procedures used to charge persons with assault.

In Oakland, the police are no more eager than those elsewhere to arrest a husband who hits his wife — wives have a way of transferring their indignation from the husband to the patrolman if the latter does more than take her side verbally — but when the victim is willing to see an arrest made, the Oakland police are prepared to accommodate her or him. Because the assault typically has occurred before the officer arrives, it was not committed in his presence and thus he cannot arrest on his own authority without a warrant. In most of the New York communities studied, getting the warrant is the responsibility of the victim and this usually means a trip downtown the next morning. In Oakland, however, the police provide a printed form which permits the citizen-victim to arrest his attacker and thus become his accuser; the police officer simply takes the subject of the citizen arrest into custody.[40] The citizen must sign a statement on the arrest report that reads: "I hereby arrest the above defendant on the charge indicated and request a peace officer to take him into custody. I will appear as directed and sign a complaint against the person I have arrested."

The arresting citizen is instructed to appear the next morning at police headquarters where he meets with a patrolman assigned to the misdemeanor assault section of the criminal investigation division. The officer reviews the case and, if the facts are not strong enough to warrant prosecution, tries to discourage the citizen from proceeding. If the case is a good one or the citizen insists, then the officer takes him to the office of the prosecuting attorney in the same building to swear out a formal complaint. The patrolman handling this assignment told an interviewer that he is "not inter-

40. Citizen arrests are authorized by California *Penal Code,* secs. 837, 847. They are also permitted in New York State under a generally similar statute: *Code of Criminal Procedure,* sec. 183. It is rarely used, however. A senior Albany police officer, when asked about it, said it was possible but he could not remember a single case of its happening. The Nassau County Police Department has a small slip a complainant can sign and thus arrest a person for an assault. I have not been able to learn how commonly it is used, however.

ested in just making arrests" and that he tries to adjust many matters without completing the arrest procedure.[41] This officer's disinclination to make the maximum number of arrests is borne out by the procedure he uses with reports sent to his office from citizens who are complaining of the behavior of a neighbor or acquaintance. If the complainant is unwilling to make a citizen arrest on the spot, his complaint is filed without any follow-up investigation. If he later calls to find out what the police are doing about the matter an investigation is made, but if there is no follow-up call to headquarters the case is considered closed and the matter forgotten. The majority of all complaints made are "cleared" without an arrest.

Despite the interest of this officer in settling matters out of court, the availability of the citizen arrest procedure to the irate citizen at the moment of the assault and with a police officer standing before him telling him, in effect, to put up or shut up undoubtedly leads to more arrests for assault being made than would occur otherwise. Once the person has signed as the "arresting citizen," he has taken the officer off the hook[42] and placed himself on it. Though the arresting citizen may still change his mind and not go downtown to swear out a formal complaint to complete the arrest procedure, the suspect has meanwhile been taken into custody and booked.[43] Of the 163 battery reports examined in Oakland, an arrest was made in 46 cases (28.2 per cent). The great majority of these — 31, or 67 per cent — were citizen arrests; most of the remainder were arrests on warrants — that is, arrests made after a person has appeared downtown to swear out a complaint against an attacker who could not, because he had left the scene at the time, be arrested when the police first arrived. Only *one* arrest was made solely on

41. The officer told an interviewer: "I'd guess you'd say I'm an old-time cop. I want to see people get together." He is an older man and perhaps different in his point of view from the younger, more eager patrolmen on the street.

42. The law relieves the police officer in such cases of all civil liability provided that he had reasonable cause to believe at the time that the citizen arrest was lawful. California *Penal Code*, sec. 847.

43. The accused is brought before a judge the next day. If the arresting citizen also appears, he is allowed to plead; if not, the case is postponed for a day or two and the accused is remanded to jail or continued on bail. If at the second hearing the arresting citizen still has not appeared, the case is dismissed.

the authority of the police officer, and in this case the charge preferred was drunkenness. But of the 31 citizen arrests made at the time of the offense, 12 of the complainants later failed to appear to testify against the accused in court, and so the charges were dropped. Thus, 12 of the 46 battery arrests — over one fourth — were arrests that would not have been made at all in other jurisdictions where the citizen arrest procedure is not used.

In fact, some of the 19 citizen arrests that did stick might not have been made in other jurisdictions, either. No doubt some of the arresting citizens wished they could forget the whole matter but felt that having made the arrest they had better carry through and sign the complaint. And the Oakland police have a policy that, while only rarely enforced, may strengthen such determination. When the reform police chief came to office in the mid-1950's, he concluded that citizens (privately, he meant Negroes) were "using" the police to settle family quarrels without making arrests. The chief, after conferring with the judges and prosecutors, announced a policy of "full enforcement" in battery cases whereby the district attorney would refuse the request of an arresting citizen that charges be dropped and the judge would consider a charge of contempt of court or of making a false report against any victim who denied facts he had earlier alleged to the police.[44] The police later claimed that the proportion of misdemeanor assault cases which were "cleared" only because the victim failed to prosecute dropped from 53.4 per cent in 1956 to 15.9 per cent in the first quarter of 1959.[45] Today, this rule is rarely enforced; indeed, it is not certain it was *ever* enforced seriously. But awareness of it may affect what police officers tell arresting citizens about their duty to prosecute and in any case, as the police chief told an interviewer, "The act of signing the arrest report seems to have been enough to prevent most of the trouble we used to have."

Newburgh is a different story. Citizen arrest procedures are rarely invoked there. Indeed, if the citizen does go to the trouble

44. Joseph Goldstein, "Police Discretion Not to Invoke the Criminal Process: Low-Visibility Decisions in the Administration of Justice," *Yale Law Journal* 69 (March 1960), pp. 577–580.
45. *Ibid.*, p. 580.

of seeking a formal complaint against a citizen who has assaulted him, the assistant district attorney who serves the city as its prosecuting officer will discourage him by making it clear that he will not prosecute. A high law enforcement official described the procedure to an interviewer:

> The assistant district attorney here will not prosecute private complaints. If you charge somebody else with an assault, swear out a warrant, and get him arrested, the DA will not handle the prosecution. You can either prosecute him yourself, or you can go out and hire a lawyer to do it for you . . . I don't know why they do it, [but] it's the policy of the district attorney in Orange County.

This system of privatizing citizen disputes (with the important difference that the judicial proceedings occur under the criminal law and the fine, if any, goes to the state and not to the citizen-prosecutor) extends even to assaults that occur in semi-public places, such as saloons. If a disturbance in such a place leads the bartender or owner to call the police, they will often make an arrest only if the owner will swear out the next morning a warrant for the arrest of the suspects and will, when the matter comes to trial, undertake to provide the prosecution. Though nominally a criminal action, the matter is handled as if it were a civil action. Few bar owners are likely to go to all this trouble and expense for the dubious privilege of losing a customer and possibly having a notice sent to the State Liquor Authority that his premises are known for the unsavory conduct of the clientele. Such a notice can count against the owner when his liquor license comes up for renewal.

If Newburgh makes it so hard for a person to get himself arrested for assault, why then are there so many arrests? The evidence suggests that many of the persons who are charged with third-degree assault are in fact persons who, in the opinion of the police, have committed a first- or second-degree assault. Because assault in the first or second degree is a felony, a police officer can arrest a person if he has reasonable cause to believe that the person committed the crime even though the crime did not occur in his presence. These are typically assaults in which a weapon has been used and there has been a serious injury. The police officer or the prosecutor marks these down as third-degree assaults because most officers believe that the judge of the city court (with jurisdiction over all misdemeanors) is "tough" and can be expected to "give the maximum," whereas the judge of the county court (with jurisdiction over all felonies) is "soft" and "lets them off with a slap on the wrist." The police are not zealous about making arrests, but when they go to the trouble of making one they want to see a penalty imposed. A high law enforcement official who regularly deals with such cases told an interviewer "The police here have a habit of marking down the offenses to misdemeanors to keep them in our jurisdiction because they know that [it is] tougher than the county court." The city court judge was prepared to play his part — "If there's an injury of any kind, or if a weapon was used, such as a knife or a razor or a gun, then there must be a jail sentence." The court records bear him out.

In 1965, out of 92 persons arrested for assault in Newburgh, only 33 were disposed of in court — the rest of the cases were dropped owing to want of prosecution. But of the 33 that were heard, the sentences were much more severe than in most local courts. Only 18 per cent won dismissals or acquittals, another 18 per cent were fined, but a third were sent to jail. Of the ten imprisoned, five went for thirty days, one went for fifty days, two for six months, and two for eleven months and twenty-nine days — the maximum sentence that a city court can impose. In no other city studied was the proportion going to jail so large or were the jail sentences so long.[46]

Since many felonious assaults in Newburgh are charged and recorded as simple assaults, the rate of arrests for felonious assault, controlling for race, is significantly smaller in Newburgh than in Oakland. The white arrest rate for aggravated asault in 1965 in Newburgh was less than half that of Oakland (18 per hundred

46. The Syracuse City Court provides a useful comparison. Of the 254 persons arrested in 1964 for assault, 155 appeared in court. The loss for want of prosecution was thus about 40 per cent as compared to nearly 67 per cent in Newburgh. Of those appearing in Syracuse, 61 per cent were dismissed or acquitted, 48 per cent received suspended sentences, and only 18 per cent went to jail. None of those jailed was given the maximum sentence.

thousand compared to 38 per hundred thousand) but the white arrest rate for simple assault in Newburgh was *higher* than in Oakland (204.4 per hundred thousand compared to 191.0 per hundred thousand).

In sum, altering the manner in which police discretion over private disputes is used is possible but difficult — not only because of the nature of the offense, but because other criminal justice agencies are involved (the district attorney and the judges). Though these agencies are related one to the other in the sense that the output of one (for example, an arrested suspect) becomes the input of another (for example, a person standing trial), they are not subject to any common policy-making authority nor do they often devise common policies cooperatively. Indeed, for reasons explained in Chapter 2, the police and the courts are often in conflict. Thus, cities do not differ greatly in their handling of order maintenance situations where citizens summon the police.

The police administrator must decide what steps he will take to affect the way in which his officers use the discretion they have in the four cases described in this chapter. Though in principle one could imagine an administrator picking and choosing among the various possibilities by, for example, instructing his men to crack down on traffic tickets but to ignore brothels and to press hard for assault arrests but to ignore common drunks, it is not likely that such combinations as these will appear in practice. Partly this is because certain policies seem to embody inconsistent goals — for example, allowing the peace to be disturbed without punishment in public places, where police controls are relatively effective, but not allowing it to go unpunished in private places, where police controls are relatively ineffective. But in addition the necessities of managing a large organization are such as to make, if not necessary, then highly desirable the development of a policy that seems to "hang together" — to reflect a general underlying principle that can be inculcated in the members of the organization and that will guide their use of discretion in cases where no rule seems to apply. Controlling subordinates depends only partly on sanctions and inducements; it also requires instilling in them a shared outlook or ethos that provides for them a common definition of the situations they are likely to encounter and that to the outsider gives to the organization its distinctive character or "feel." This process of socialization is especially important in organizations like the police in which the rank-and-file members exercise very wide discretion over important matters under conditions of low visibility. In the next three chapters, three distinctive police styles or strategies will be described.

Five The Watchman Style

In some communities, the police in dealing with situations that do not involve "serious" crime act as if order maintenance rather than law enforcement were their principal function. What is the defining characteristic of the patrolman's role thus becomes the style or strategy of the department as a whole because it is reinforced by the attitudes and policies of the police administrator. I shall call this the "watchman" style, employing here for analytical purposes a term that was once — in the early nineteenth century — descriptive generally of the mission of the American municipal police.[1]

In every city, of course, all patrolmen display a watchman style, that is, a concern for the order maintenance aspect of their function, some of the time, but in a few places this style becomes the operating code of the department. To the extent the administrator can influence the discretion of his men, he does so by allowing them to ignore many common minor violations, especially traffic and juvenile offenses, to tolerate, though gradually less so, a certain amount of vice and gambling, to use the law more as a means of maintaining order than of regulating conduct, and to judge the requirements of order differently depending on the character of the group in which the infraction occurs. Juveniles are "expected" to misbehave, and

1. A social scientist reading this and the next two chapters will understand that any typology is an abstraction from reality that is employed, not to describe a particular phenomenon, but to communicate its essential or "ideal" form — in this case, the "flavor" or "style" of the organization. The lay reader should bear this in mind and guard against assuming that because two or three police departments are grouped together they are identical in all respects. They are not. Furthermore, a typology can only suggest, it cannot prove, that a particular operating style is associated with certain organizational characteristics. Finally, merely because it was found convenient in this study to group these departments together into three styles, no one should assume that these are the only police styles or that every police department in the country displays one or the other of them. I assume if enough departments were studied that one would probably learn of other styles in addition to these and that one would certainly learn that many, if not most, departments display a combination of two or more styles.

thus infractions among this group — unless they are serious or committed by a "wise guy" — are best ignored or treated informally. Negroes are thought to want, and to deserve, less law enforcement because to the police their conduct suggests a low level of public and private morality, an unwillingness to cooperate with the police or offer information, and widespread criminality. Serious crimes, of course, should be dealt with seriously; further, when Negroes offend whites, who, in the eyes of the police, have a different standard of public order, then an arrest must be made. Motorists, unless a departmental administrator wants to "make a record" by giving a few men the job of writing tickets, will often be left alone if their driving does not endanger or annoy others and if they do not resist or insult police authority. Vice and gambling are crimes only because the law says they are; they become problems only when the currently accepted standards of public order are violated (how accurately the political process measures those standards is another question). Private disputes — assaults among friends or family — are treated informally or ignored, unless the circumstances (a serious infraction, a violent person, a flouting of police authority) require an arrest. And disputes that are a normal business risk, such as getting a bad check, should be handled by civil procedures if possible. With exceptions to be noted, the watchman style is displayed in Albany, Amsterdam, and Newburgh.

The police are watchman-like not simply in emphasizing order over law enforcement but also in judging the seriousness of infractions less by what the law says about them than by their immediate and personal consequences, which will differ in importance depending on the standards of the relevant group — teenagers, Negroes, prostitutes, motorists, families, and so forth. In all cases, circumstances of person and condition are taken seriously into account — community notables are excused because they have influence and, perhaps, because their conduct is self-regulating; Negroes are either ignored or arrested, depending on the seriousness of the matter, because they have no influence and their conduct, except within broad limits, is not thought to be self-regulating. But no matter what his race, if a man's actions are "private" (gambling, for instance, or driving while intoxicated) or if they involve only another person with whom he has a dispute (an assault or a petty larceny), then, unless the offense is a "serious" one, the police tend to overlook the violation, to handle it informally (by a reprimand, for example), or to allow the two aggrieved parties to resolve it between themselves as if it were a private matter (a storekeeper getting restitution from a shoplifter or an assault victim bringing a civil action). If, on the other hand, the public peace has been breached — creating a disturbance in a restaurant, bothering passers-by on a sidewalk, insulting an officer, causing a crowd to collect, endangering others, or publicly offending current standards of propriety, then the officer is expected to restore order. If order cannot be restored or respect for authority elicited in any other way, an arrest is appropriate.

This "privatization" of the law defining misdemeanors and offenses and the emphasis on keeping order in public places is squarely within the nineteenth-century tradition of American law enforcement. As Lane notes in his history of the Boston police, the present-day force grew out of men appointed as part-time watchmen to keep the streets clear of obstructions, human and material, and to supervise a number of ordinances pertaining to health, lighting, and animals running loose. Vagabondage, raucous behavior, public lewdness, and street fights were the "criminal" matters handled by the watchmen and later by the police. *Real* crime — theft, robbery, murder, a private assault — was not in their province at all; detecting the perpetrators was essentially a private matter. If the victim could learn the identity of the thief or assailant, he applied for a warrant, which was then served, for a fee, by a constable. Later, detectives added to the force aided in the apprehension of criminals, but still on a fee-for-service basis: they were paid with a share of the recovered loot. The object of the process was not so much punishment as restitution.[2] Prostitution flourished, as did ille-

2. Roger Lane, *Policing the City: Boston, 1822–1885* (Cambridge, Mass.: Harvard University Press, 1967), pp. 7, 56, 57, 150. See also Seldon D. Bacon, "The Early Development of American Municipal Police," unpublished PhD. dissertation, Yale University (1939), p. 784. Professor Herbert Jacob suggests another way in which the law may become privatized. In his study of bankruptcy and wage garnishment

gal drinking establishments; when they became too noxious — that is to say, when their toleration became impolitic — a "descent" (in modern terms, a raid) was carried out, never to eliminate the nuisance but to contain it.[3] As late as 1863, a Boston alderman, the aristocratic Thomas Coffin Amory, objected to proposals that the police play a more aggressive role in enforcing laws, especially those against drinking, and proclaimed: "It is the duty of the police officer to serve . . . warrants, when directed to him. It is nowhere made his duty to initiate prosecutions."[4] A few years later, Alderman Jonas Fitch rejected complaints against detective procedures and argued instead for a return to purely private enterprise.[5] When a visitor to Albany or Newburgh remarks that the city appears to be still in the nineteenth century, he is making a more significant observation than he may realize.

Cities where the police follow a watchman style will not thereby have identical standards of public order and morality. The quality of law enforcement depends not simply on how the police make judgments, but also on the socioeconomic composition of the community, the law enforcement standards set, implicitly or explicitly, by the political systems, and the special interests and concerns of the police chief. A city like Amsterdam with almost no Negroes and few derelict drunks obviously cannot ignore petty Negro crime or chronic alcoholics. Whether or not a city is "wide open" with respect to vice and gambling depends as much on what the political leadership will allow as on what the police are willing to ignore. And although the police in all three cities tend to make very few misdemeanor or juvenile arrests and issue very few traffic tickets, there are exceptions — the Albany police arrest drunks in large numbers, the Newburgh police issue many more speeding tickets.

proceedings in four Wisconsin cities, he found that in some, such as Green Bay, there is relatively little inclination to invoke the legal processes to handle debts, while in others, such as Madison, there is a strong inclination. Green Bay prefers to settle such matters privately, Madison to settle them formally and publicly. Herbert Jacob, "Wage Garnishment and Bankruptcy Proceedings in Four Cities," in James Q. Wilson, ed., *City Politics and Public Policy* (New York: John Wiley & Sons, 1968).

3. Lane, *Policing the City*, pp. 115–116.
4. Quoted in *ibid.*, p. 130.
5. Quoted in *ibid.*, p. 154.

The police style in these cities is watchman-like because, with certain exceptions dictated by the chief's policies or the city's expectations, the patrolman is allowed — and even encouraged — to follow the path of least resistance in carrying out his daily, routine assignments. His desire "to keep his nose clean" is reinforced by the department's desire "not to rock the boat." The police handle the problem of an adversary relationship with the public by withdrawing from as many such relationships as possible. As in all cities, these departments are highly sensitive to complaints from the public, though they differ in their handling of them. There is no formal complaint procedure nor any internal review or inspection system; instead, the chief handles such matters personally. Depending on the kind of political system of which he is a part, he may defend the department vocally, or hush the matter up quietly, or, if an influential person or segment of opinion has been offended, "throw the man to the wolves" by suspending or discharging him. (There were cases of officers dismissed in all three cities.) The chief tries to avoid such difficulties, however, by tightly restricting the discretionary authority of his patrolmen ("don't stick your neck out" unless you can make a "good pinch") and by having them refer all doubtful matters to the sergeants, the lieutenant, or even the chief himself.

In none of the three cities did even the critics of the police allege that serious crime was overlooked, nor did anyone deny that police tolerance of vice and gambling had declined somewhat over the years. All three communities were once a good deal gaudier and there is still a lot of life left in Albany and Newburgh. But all have become, at least publicly, more decorous, and this was accomplished without any significant change in the police — it was simply understood that the politicians and the community and church leaders wanted things a bit quieter, a process aided in Albany by the fact that the governor tore down the wooliest part of the city. (As in all land clearance programs, a large proportion of small businessmen, illegitimate as well as legitimate, never survive the relocation process.)

To a watchman-like department, the penal law is a device

empowering the police to maintain order and protect others when a serious infraction has occurred; the exact charge brought against the person is not so important — or rather, it is important mostly in terms of the extent to which that particular section of the law facilitates the uncomplicated exercise of police power and increases the probability of the court sustaining the action. The charges of public intoxication and disorderly conduct are useful, and thus frequently used, in this regard — they are general, they are difficult to dispute, they carry relatively light penalties and thus are not likely to be resisted, and they are not technically, in New York, "crimes" that might hurt a man's record.

In these cities, the patrolman is expected to ignore the "little stuff" but to "be tough" where it is important. For example, the police have essentially a "familial" rather than law enforcement view of juvenile offenders. Their policy is to ignore most infractions ("kid's will be kids") and to act *in local parentis* with respect to those that cannot be ignored: administer a swift kick or a verbal rebuke, have the boy do some chores ("Tom Sawyer justice"), or turn him over to his parents for discipline. An Albany probation officer who handles many young people told an interviewer that "sometimes a cop has to do things that aren't strictly legal, like taking a kid into the back room . . . The parents should do it, but don't."

The Amsterdam police recall fondly the days when such elaborate procedures were not necessary. The officer who caught the window smasher or bicycle thief meted out curbstone justice that would instill, if not the fear of God, then at least the fear of cops. "You used to be able to take care of the whole thing yourself," one officer told an interviewer, "but if you hit a kid today, you would really get clobbered." Whatever was once the case, it is clear that the police still rely largely on informal means for controlling juveniles — lecturing them on the street corner, taking them home to their parents, or telling them to "break it up" or "move along." Such informal methods have even been institutionalized in what one department calls "Saturday morning probation." Juveniles who commit more serious, or more frequent, offenses are told to come to police headquarters every Saturday morning for a few weeks or months to report on their behavior. The parents are informed and told the alternative could be an arrest. The chief conceded to an interviewer that "It's probably not kosher," but the family court judge is aware of the system and cooperates. If the offense is not, in the eyes of the police, a "real" crime at all — as, for example, drinking under age — nothing is done. If it is a "real"crime — such as auto theft or a burglary — then an arrest is made.

Informal settlements are also the rule with minor adult offenses. In Amsterdam, for example, in cases where disorder occurs or is likely, the police commonly tell the aggrieved party to "see the judge" and the abusive party to "go home" or, if he has no home, to "get out of town." All nontraffic incidents recorded by the Amsterdam police during June 1967 were examined; there were twenty-nine. About half — fourteen — involved a fight, dispute, disturbance, or drunkenness. In three cases the persons were taken home, in five they were told to see the judge, and in four they were pacified on the scene. Only two persons were arrested; they were charged with resisting or abusing the police.

There appear to be two exceptions to the watchman style in these three cities. First, the Newburgh police issue many more traffic tickets than Albany or Amsterdam. Second, the Albany department arrests many more drunks than not only other watchman-like departments but more than almost any kind of department. Traffic, however, is that police function most easily brought under the control of the administrator — as explained in Chapter 4, his interest in ticketing, and almost nothing else, determines how many shall be issued. And in Newburgh, it was not even the chief, but his deputy who, together with the city manager, put on the pressure for ticketing. But that pressure was limited to the men assigned to traffic and never became a department-wide policy.

The high drunk arrest rate in Albany has a somewhat different explanation. There appear to be simply more drunks — especially derelicts — on the streets: Albany is a major transportation center for people moving up and down the Hudson River, east and west between Boston and Buffalo, Cleveland, and Chicago, and to and from the summer resorts in northern New York State. In the past, the city was a place where people went looking for a good time. When the famous "Gut" was flourishing, a large number of arrests for intoxication were required to maintain some semblance of order and, more important, keep the carousers from leaving the area to annoy the "decent people" elsewhere in the city. What the detectives condoned the patrol force had to cope with. Though much of the Gut is gone, the city still attracts derelicts from all over the state. Thus, part of the high arrest rate can be explained by the fact that there are not simply more drunks, there are more *homeless* drunks in Albany than in most other cities. The tendency of a watchman-style police force to go easy on local drunks cannot, obviously, operate if the drunks are not locals — not only will out-of-towners not be bound by local norms, they may become a burden on local charity. Albany, accordingly, makes proportionally seven times as many arrests for vagrancy as does Oakland. As a high law enforcement official in Albany told an interviewer:

> We're pretty tough on vagrants here. We give them summary justice and send them to jail. There, the police rough 'em up a bit and then we send them out of town. These people could work if they wanted to. There's plenty of jobs here, what with all the construction going on . . . The only reason these men don't work is that they don't want to work.

There may be other explanations as well, but they must remain conjectural.[6] What is clear is that in Albany there is not, as in Oakland, a concern for the law enforcement implications of drunkenness — its relation to strong-man robberies, for example. Drunkenness in Albany is a matter of public order; it so happens that for various reasons, drunks are more likely in that city (than in, say, Newburgh) to be seen by the police as a threat to order.

In a watchman system, little emphasis is placed on a "correct"

6. A former Albany police officer to whom this manuscript was shown offered in a letter to me an additional explanation for the high drunk arrest rate: "Many times a person will go to a police station to make a complaint. This could be anything from an auto accident, an argument, or of being rolled. The policeman on the desk will inform the person that he will look into the matter and then ask the person if they have been drinking. No matter how many or how few beers he may have had, he will be booked for public intox."

appearance or manner. Since the task of the police is to be ready for a serious crime or to restore order, neatness or courtesy are not especially important, though by the same token one does not wish to do anything that will needlessly antagonize the "respectable" element in the city, for that could cause "trouble." A watchman-like department is as interested in avoiding trouble as in minding its own business.

It would be a mistake to assume that a watchman-like department is necessarily a corrupt one, though there may be a little corruption in all such departments and a great deal in a few. The predisposition to avoid involvement — to control (not eliminate) public disorder rather than to enforce the law — depends not on corrupt motives, but on the inclinations of the men recruited into police work and the norms of the organization to which they belong. In a small town, the police may tolerate illicit businesses because no one with any influence wishes to have it otherwise; if tolerance rests on community indifference rather than police forbearance, then the police have nothing to sell and, except for small gifts, nothing to gain. Of course, if such enterprises operate on a scale larger than what public opinion would tolerate, then the police can sell their ability to "keep things quiet." In a larger city, with an organized political opposition and formal institutions (newspapers, churches, civic groups) that might wish to act as keepers of the community's conscience, tolerance is more valuable because more precarious. It may, therefore, be sold, though not necessarily by the police. A strong political party may sell "licenses" to run illegal businesses and simply order the police to respect the licenses; if there is no strong party to which they are beholden, the police may sell the licenses themselves. The Amsterdam police, for example, are not bribed to be tolerant of gambling; rather, they believe that the community expects them (and pays them) to behave as mere night watchmen, and they do.

Even in Albany, a police officer, himself very critical of the department's leadership, denied that there were large payoffs. He told an interviewer:

There's nothing of that. You'd think in most police departments . . . any cop has something going for him — the cop on the beat directing traffic picks up a few bucks here, the guy who hands out parking tickets picks up a few bucks there. In Albany . . . you can't make more than a dollar or two. A guy who picks up $50 a year on the side is doing good. This is a city in which everybody at the top has their huckle, but not the cop on the beat. Everything goes to the top . . . Most of the officers have two jobs. There's a lot of moonlighting going on. There has to be.

Why then, do they ignore so many things that technically are violations of the law? The same officer continued, referring to the patrol force:

The motto is, "don't rock the boat." Don't get the citizens upset, keep the taxes down, keep stories out of the newspapers, and keep things quiet. There's no reason and no incentive for writing a lot of traffic tickets. Nobody puts the pressure on you to write that kind of paper. The cops are low paid and they won't do it unless they are forced to do it and nobody forces them to do it.

A senior officer of the department, who would be a source of any "pressure" to produce, told an interviewer it would be a mistake to push the police into situations that were not a "police matter."

People are always expecting the police to do things. They have no idea of what we can really do and what we can't do. They want us to use our position to settle family fights. We can't do that. We can't do anything unless we see a crime committed, or we have a signed complaint if one was committed. What are we supposed to do about a lot of these things? Nothing!

An officer in the Newburgh police department admitted the force made relatively few arrests of Negroes and none of prostitutes:

Well, I guess that needs a little explaining. I don't know all the reasons. One reason, I think . . . is that the word has sort of come down from the top that we're to lay off the colored community. With all this Black Power talk, people are afraid of an incident . . . But I don't think anybody wants to make any arrests in that area unless they absolutely have to, and particularly not make any arrests when it spoils their chances for having a little fun over in the colored parts. We don't want to make them mad at us.

Because they have a watchman style, it does not follow that all three departments are identical in all respects. From the patrolmen's point of view, perhaps the most important differences are in the extent to which they feel the police chief is "on their side" and willing to "back them up." In Amsterdam, a city with little crime, almost no Negroes, and not much police zeal, a policeman rarely gets in trouble. The chief could not remember the last time somebody was dismissed, though minor penalties are imposed from time to time. One reason may be that, were a man dismissed, nobody could be found to replace him. The police in Albany and Newburgh, on the other hand, have been "on the spot" several times. The few patrolmen willing to discuss the matter seemed to feel that in Albany the chief backed up his men and in Newburgh he did not.

Newburgh officers were outspoken in their dislike of the chief. They alleged that he publicly criticized them, never praised them, and did not "stand up" for them in several fights with the city administration. The chief was seen as "close" to the city manager (and, of course, by law he is supposed to be); the difficulty was that a recent city manager had been bent on making some radical changes in the department, and the men — rightly or wrongly — saw the chief as the agent of this unwanted change. Some patrolmen had been criticized by Negroes; the chief, in the view of some, did not stand behind them as solidly as he should have.

In Albany, the chief — perhaps because his position was more secure and the local political system more congenial to his law enforcement style — was thought by many officers to be behind them. During one visit to Albany, a racial disturbance broke out in a nearby city and two officers accused of mistreating Negroes were suspended pending an investigation. An Albany detective told an interviewer that this would never happen in his city:

We feel they're behind us here. It's not like in X where the chief knuckled under and suspended two officers just to please the mob. You're either right or wrong; there's no compromise with it. And no compromise with a mob. People argue about whether politics is a good or bad thing in a police department. Well, of course, it's both. But the good side is that [here] they back you up 100 per cent. We're not afraid to do our jobs.

Such perceptions may well influence police behavior and may — there is no evidence — explain why the Albany police appear to be somewhat more willing to make arrests, especially Negro arrests, than the Newburgh police. But the differences appear to be marginal (to a particular person, of course, a marginal difference in police behavior may be all the difference in the world) and do not alter the pattern that is common to all three cities — few traffic tickets, except for those produced by the Newburgh radar car, relatively few misdemeanor arrests, except for Albany drunk arrests, informal handling of juveniles, and tolerance of discreet immorality.

The Organizational Context

Associated with these behavioral similarities are certain aspects of departmental organization and personnel. Patrolmen are locally recruited, paid low salaries, expected to have second jobs, given the very minimum in initial training and almost no in-service training, and not rewarded for having or getting higher education. As late as 1964, the chief of police in Albany was paid only $7,399; in 1967 he got $9,800. The beginning salary for patrolmen in 1966–67 was $4,800 in Albany, $5,100 in Newburgh, and $5,110 in Amsterdam.

Low pay helps make recruitment difficult. In 1964 only two candidates signed up to take the state civil service examination for policemen in all of Zone 5, which includes not only the city of Amsterdam but the six surrounding counties as well; as a result, the test was cancelled. In 1965 no one even bothered to schedule an examination. Because of a high turnover rate in the department, especially among the younger officers, the force has a high average age (only five of the 38 men were in 1965 under 30). The brighter young men often quit to join the better-paying New York Central Railroad's private police force or the Capital District police in Albany. The Albany police department is 45 men under authorized strength. But low pay does not explain all recruitment problems; high-paying cities, such as Oakland, are also under-strength.

In none of the three cities has a high school diploma been required for entrance into the force and many officers could not meet such a requirement were it imposed. Until 1959, each police department decided for itself how much training its recruits would get; most got virtually none. New York State law has since then required that a minimum number of hours of training be provided each recruit — at first 80 hours (two weeks), later increased to 120 hours (three weeks), and, since January 1967, 240 hours (six weeks).

The senior officers of some of the departments are not generally enthusiastic about these new requirements. In Albany, one said: "You can't apply book training out on the street. You have to rely on men with experience. The training is all right but you can't take it too seriously."

In Newburgh, a senior officer desirous of improving the force was nonetheless skeptical of training: "Police science courses are not necessary. You can't teach a man to be a good policeman; he must have the aptitude naturally. And there's no reason for anyone to take one on his own; they don't help you pass the sergeants' or lieutenants' exam. I've never taken one."

The three departments are composed, then, of low-paid men with high school educations or less, who were raised in or very near the town where they now serve, who have rarely lived anywhere else (except, perhaps, while on military duty), and who receive the minimum in formal training (and that is provided by local departments, not by a specialized police academy) and little or no encouragement to take additional training. The departments display in extreme form the craft-like characteristics of all police departments — that is to say, learning is by apprenticeship rather than formal training, procedures and rules are passed along by word of mouth and example rather than by written instructions or published manuals, there is comparatively little specialization of tasks (a patrolman, like a carpenter, is supposed to be able to do everything that comes his way) and a minimum of deference to a formal hierarchy. Police work in these cities is not, of course, wholly craftlike: it is done in a permanent rather than ad hoc organization, there are some written rules (for example, the penal code), and there are some people performing managerial and bureaucratic tasks (the desk sergeant, the communications personnel, the jail keeper, and the like). But in comparison to other kinds of police departments, and more important in comparison to other organizations with tasks that would appear to call for as much coordination and record keeping as police work, there are remarkably few men in staff positions in these three departments.

The absence of staff personnel and of civilian employees, who in other kinds of departments perform many staff tasks, may be partly the result of a lack of resources. A small department with a small budget, almost all of which goes for the wages and salaries of uniformed personnel, can hardly be expected to have a criminalistics laboratory or a computer. It is not even clear that such facilities would be of much value in a small city, even if they were available free of charge. Yet, as will be pointed out later in this chapter, equally small departments with a different police style have managed to achieve a rather high degree of specialization and staff service. One senior Albany officer explained why he opposed having civilians in police departments doing other than mechanical jobs, such as repairing cars: "We [the sworn officers] have all worked together a long time; this is our life. We know each other and we stick together. You get a civilian in here, to him it's just a job. He'll learn things and start blabbing them around. You get a lot of sensitive stuff in police work and you have to know how to keep your mouth shut."

Whether or not hiring civilians has that effect, it may have others. One study prepared by consultants to the President's Commission suggests a correlation exists between increases in the number of offenses known to the police and increases in a department's civilian employees. Possibly hiring more civilians makes the "crime rate" go up by having offense reports recorded by persons who, as the Albany commander suggests, are not constrained by the norms of the uniformed force.[7]

In *any* police department, accurate case records are very important whether they are kept by hand or by machine. By case records are meant records of crimes, criminals, and police actions, and not *statistical* records, which are of little value to anybody in most instances. But in a watchman-like department, records are skimpy and often incomplete — except for detectives preparing a case, producing written documents is not highly rewarded. A patrolman answering a call in these three cities rarely fills out any forms unless something very serious has happened.

How the patrolman behaves at all depends very much on who, if anyone, is supervising him. "I don't care who the police chief is," said one, "I only care who my sergeant is." Standardized procedures are neither the practice nor the ideal. A senior Albany officer explained why: "Never write things down. The written word is always there, like in a newspaper . . . If you print it, it's always there and people can look it up. I think it's a mistake to have too many things written down in a department. Anyway, you can never go by the book out in the streets. It won't work."

Related to the absence of written rules is the lack of specialization. Specialization is another way to produce what written rules tend to produce: uniform behavior. An officer given the task of handling all juveniles, for example, will develop an operating procedure, whether formal or informal, that will produce more consistent, which is not to say identical, police behavior toward juveniles than if each patrolman or detective handles the juveniles he meets on his own. The merits of specialization are not at issue here; the point is that the three departments have few specialized personnel. None has a juvenile officer, and for several reasons. It would take a man off the streets (or require hiring a new man, which the department cannot

7. Philip C. Sagi and Charles F. Wellford, "Age Composition and Patterns of Change in Criminal Statistics," paper prepared for the President's Commission on Law Enforcement and Administration of Justice (typescript, no date).

afford); it would require new procedures to coordinate patrolmen and juvenile officers involved with the same juvenile, and these would cause "headaches"; it would constrict the generalized role of the patrolman who is supposed to "handle his beat" and anything that comes up on it; and — perhaps most important — it would create an organizational pressure to "get involved" in matters beyond strict police work and thus in matters with uncertain and possibly threatening repercussions. A senior Albany officer explained his objections in these words: "I don't believe in it [assigning juvenile officers] . . . Seems to me the policeman shouldn't try to be the parent. How can you be the parent? That's the parents' responsibility . . . You get into the homes and start telling people how to run their families and that causes bitterness against the police. I'm in favor of staying out of those situations."

Having a minimum number of specialized or special-duty squads has an important implication for organizational behavior: *there will be few places to which one can be transferred in the department and few incentives to seek transfer there.* Most men will spend most of their police lives on patrol; unless they make detective, they will be in uniform driving a car or walking a beat all their lives — even after making sergeant, in most cases. In Albany, a patrolman could get assigned to the traffic division, but that means riding a motorcycle or standing at a traffic intersection during long icy winters. *If there are few rewards to be sought outside the patrol force, there is little incentive to work hard to get out.* If there were a number of "cushy" jobs for patrolmen in the force — desk jobs, investigative jobs, staff jobs — patrolmen might become "producers" (writing tickets, making arrests) to attract attention and get those jobs. But there are not, and so they don't. Thus, an unspecialized department tends to be a watchman-like department that in turn tends to resist specialization.

Just as there is little incentive to specialize, so there is little pressure to seek promotion. In all three cities, a promotion was regarded by every patrolman interviewed as a "political" decision, though it was not always clear whether the politics was that of the city, the party, or the department. An examination must be taken to rise to the rank of sergeant or higher; though in most cities these exams are given by the state, for a number of reasons the final decision is left to the chief. There are comparatively few promotional vacancies, partly because in a watchman-style department relatively few men from the higher grades are lured away by more prestigious law enforcement agencies, such as the FBI and the state police, or by insurance companies seeking investigators. The stable rank structure, combined with the widespread belief (there is no reason to doubt its validity) that promotion is based on politics as much as achievement, leads patrolmen to judge situations involving contact with the public more in terms of protecting their present position than in terms of advancing to a higher or better position. And finally, pay differentials are very low. An Amsterdam patrolman gets $5,110; the chief gets only $6,400. Promotion from patrolman to sergeant in Albany is worth only $600 a year.

This preoccupation with conserving rather than enhancing their position gives them less incentive to initiate police-citizen contacts (to be a "rate-buster" with respect to traffic tickets), but it also gives them more leeway in handling those situations that are thrust upon them, provided they are not serious matters. Thus, in a watchman-like department a patrolman, who is recruited from the working class in the first place, has little incentive to "play up" to the citizens. By his class background — the focal concerns[8] of which include proving one's masculinity, not taking any "lip," maintaining your self-respect, and "giving as good as you get" — he is inclined to use rough language and a gruff manner when the situation seems to warrant them; a watchman-like department provides few incentives to change that manner. An officer directing traffic at a street corner is likely to yell at the motorist ("All right, come on, buddy, don't take all day!" "Move it! Move it!" "Where do you think you're going, lady?"), and a patrolman at the scene of a minor disturbance or fight is likely to assume a stance that immediately asserts his *personal* authority ("Shut up, wise guy, I'm asking the questions."

8. See Walter B. Miller, "Lower-Class Culture as a Generating Milieu of Gang Delinquency," *Journal of Social Issues,* 14 (1958), pp. 5–19, for a description of these "focal concerns."

"You want to start something, you start it with me!" "Beat it kid, this doesn't concern you.") A middle-class motorist thus addressed, or a middle-class on-looker at such a scene, is likely to assume that the officer is becoming "violent" or that he is in a "rage." This is not usually the case. The temper flashes suddenly, but it subsides just as quickly, unless the other person "escalates" the conflict by "talking back."

An officer under these circumstances is behaving no differently than a foreman supervising a street construction gang or a carpenter yelling at some kids who are annoying him while he works. What is different, of course, is that the police officer is in uniform and, by one view of the police function, supposedly exercising impersonal authority (applying the rule of law). But the watchman-style does not encourage playing an impersonal role — having, as the doctor is supposed to, a detached bedside manner. An officer is not taught to believe that what is done to him by a citizen is done to him as an officer and not as a man; there is, on the contrary, no distinction between being a cop and being a man. This is not to say that such officers indiscriminately insult or browbeat citizens. Like everyone else, they can distinguish among classes and personalities and they recognize that language appropriate to one class or personality type may not be appropriate to another. Indeed, the watchman style encourages officers to take personal differences into account both in enforcing the law and in addressing the citizen. Thus, citizens are viewed as "deserving"various forms of address.

Some Consequences

Because the watchman style emphasizes order maintenance, it makes distributive justice the standard for handling disorderly situations. Just as all patrolmen find themselves preoccupied with order maintenance to some degree, they also inevitably judge persons by what they "deserve." In a watchman-style department, however, use of the distributive standard is reinforced by administrative attitude and departmental ethos.

The consequences of relying on this standard might be important for any identifiable group in the community — the young, the poor, the rich, the female — but in this section attention will be paid only to its consequences for the Negro: partly because he is increasingly self-conscious about police treatment and partly because his arrest statistics are separately tabulated. Albany and Newburgh have sizable Negro populations, but there is almost no way to gather systematic evidence about routine police treatment of Negroes. Two questions can be asked, however: first, at what rate and for what offenses are Negroes in these two cities, as compared to Negroes elsewhere, likely to be arrested and, second, how does the city respond to such complaints as Negroes may make of their treatment?

In Albany and Newburgh, the police do not intervene frequently and formally in Negro neighborhoods — the total number of arrests is much less than in a city such as Oakland and little or no use is made of "field contact reports" or aggressive preventive patrol tactics. Just as there are few arrests in these two cities, as compared to Oakland, of whites for larceny, gambling, or driving while intoxicated, so also there are comparatively few arrests of Negroes for these offenses (Table 11). These, of course, are law enforcement situations that the police tend to ignore in watchman-style departments, unless they are very serious. But with respect to order maintenance situations, however, the record is very different — the police in Albany and Newburgh are significantly more likely to arrest Negroes for disorderly conduct than the police in Oakland, and those in Albany are much more likely than those in Oakland to arrest Negroes for drunkenness. (As one would have predicted from the discussion in Chapter 4, there is much less difference among the cities with respect to Negro arrests for assault. The handling of such matters, because they are private, is much harder to bring under the influence of departmental policy.)

In Albany and Newburgh the use of formal arrest to handle Negroes in disorderly but not in law enforcement situations is partly to be explained by the police tendency to use intoxication or disorderly conduct as "catch-all" charges, especially with respect to

Table 11. Arrest rates (per 100,000 population) for Negroes and whites in four communities, 1965.

Offense	Negro arrest rate				White arrest rate			
	Albany	Newburgh	Oakland	Syracuse	Albany	Newburgh	Oakland	Syracuse
Assault (aggravated and simple)	592.8	800.0[a]	1,099.0	960.6	97.1	226.6[a]	248.0	103.4
Larceny (all)	392.8	400.0	1,818.9	1,061.7	78.3	48.8	492.9	125.7
Driving while intoxicated	71.4	93.3	317.1	140.4	72.6	66.6	263.2	35.4
Gambling	7.1	26.6	337.8	202.2	7.5	8.8	25.3	40.5
Drunkenness	5,550.0	1,306.6	3,890.9	2,432.5	2,441.5	724.4	5,625.7	770.2
Disorderly conduct and vagrancy	1,157.1	1,226.6	381.9	735.9	607.5	262.2	197.2	99.3

Source: Report to FBI by local police departments, 1965. Negro and white population estimates for 1965 by local planning agencies.

[a] The assault arrest rate, Negro and white, was unusually high in Newburgh in 1965. In 1961, 1962, and 1963, it was more than 25 per cent lower.

offenses committed by Negroes. During an eight-week period in Albany, the police made 285 public intoxication arrests: of these, twelve (about 4 per cent) were in fact initiated because of behavior more serious than being drunk and, of these, eight involved assaults and cuttings, several serious enough to warrant a trip to the hospital. In every instance the person arrested for intoxication who had in fact committed an assault was a Negro. Of the other four, two were whites who had been arguing, one was a white Peeping Tom, and one was a Negro who had broken a window. The eight Negroes arrested because of an assault accounted for 10 per cent of all Negroes arrested during this period on intoxication charges. The four whites involved in a fight that led to intoxication arrests were only 2 per cent of all white drunk arrests made in this period.

But even if the Negro drunk arrest rate in Albany were reduced by 10 per cent to allow for arrests that in fact involved something quite serious, the police there would still pick up more Negroes on this charge, proportionally, than in any of the other cities. The reason may be that the watchman style, with its emphasis on public order and its general reluctance to handle minor offenses with an arrest, places heavy demands on the constraining influences of community and familial norms. If the police believe, rightly or wrongly, that those norms are weak — either because the person is in some sense "outside" the relevant (in this case, the white) community or because his family is, in general, weak and without sanctions — then an arrest, or the use of physical force, is the only way of maintaining order. In short, the Negro is assumed to be like the derelict drunk — he is "homeless." I have no evidence that would support this interpretation, and thus it must remain a conjecture. Three facts are at least consistent with it, however. First, the Negro arrest rate for intoxication in Albany is twice as high as that for whites. But, second, the Oakland police, who display a law enforcement rather than order maintenance police style, arrest *whites* for drunkenness at a rate much higher than that for Negroes (Table 11). If the police make an arrest whenever a law is broken, the pattern we observe in Oakland results, but if an arrest is made only when the law breaker is perceived to be "homeless," then the pattern of Albany may result. Third, the Syracuse police, who have been changing their police style in recent years from one similar to that in Albany and Newburgh to one more nearly resembling that of Oakland, have increased dramatically the rate at which they arrest Negroes for various crimes.[9] During the same period, however, the Negro arrest rate for intoxication *decreased* (from about 4,700 to about 2,400 per 100,000 Negroes). This means that the ratio of Negro to white arrest rates on this charge fell from about six to one to about three to one — a change that may be indicative of the gradual replacement of the standards of the watchman style with the standards of a different, more legalistic style.

In Albany and Newburgh, the complaints voiced by Negroes are of two kinds: that Negroes lack police protection (heard most often in Newburgh) and that the police are "brutal" (heard most often in Albany). Such complaints, to the extent they are well-founded, are precisely what one would expect wherever the watchman style operates: the police ignore minor matters but "get tough" when something important is at stake. The fact that Negroes in Albany emphasize one element of the style and those in Newburgh emphasize the other suggests that the concept of style may conceal certain differences in behavior.

In Newburgh every Negro interviewed — lawyers, ministers, night-club owners, prostitutes — agreed that the overriding characteristic of the Newburgh police was their tendency to under-enforce the law in Negro areas. One lawyer told an interviewer:

> We can't get police protection in this [Negro] community. They [the police] ignore the crowds. There's a bar right next to where my parents live . . . Every night there'll be a big crowd, especially in the summers, that will gather in the streets in front of this place. Sometimes we'll have to call the police four and five times before they even come. When they

9. The Negro arrest rate per hundred thousand Negroes in Syracuse increased between 1960 and 1965 from 108.3 to 398.9 for aggravated assault, from 383.3 to 634.5 for burglary, from 183.3 to 320.2 for auto theft, from 66.7 to 219.1 for robbery, and from 50.0 to 140.4 for driving while intoxicated.

do come, they often get out of their cars and just start joking with people standing there. The police are supposed to break up those crowds and move them along, but they don't do it.

Another Negro, well-known in the city, complained of a case in which the police did not respond to a matter more important than a crowd in front of a bar:

> Not long ago five men broke into my house. Five men! They came upstairs . . . If I didn't have a .22 rifle with me, I don't know what would have happened. I called the police three times and it took them a half hour to get there . . . When you complain to the police about their not giving you any kind of protection, you get answers like the one X gave me. He said, "I'll deny I ever said this if you repeat it, but you know how this police department is run. Our motto is, let the niggers kill each other off."

A minister complained that the police act slowly or not at all when there is a fight or a theft in the Negro community. He cited a case in which a dance was being held at a community center in the all-Negro low-income public housing project. When a fight broke out, a passing police car was hailed. It refused to stop. Another Negro who himself is engaged in some illicit enterprises in the city said contemptuously of the police: "The cops won't do anything if someone in the crowd motherfucks them. They're scared. A cop is afraid of a knife. If a kid pulls one, he'll never try to disarm him." A respectable Negro lawyer put it differently: when a police officer was called to check a disturbance at a bar, he did not enter. "He couldn't have scooted off faster if he had been on roller skates."

Though such anecdotes may be somewhat exaggerated, the testimony of certain police officers suggests that they cannot be dismissed entirely. One patrolman said to an interviewer, "What do they expect you to do if a few of them [Negroes] jump you? Don't kid yourself; I'd run like hell." When asked whether he would try to make an arrest if a hostile crowd gathered, he replied, "An arrest? What's that?"

It would be a mistake to assume that fear alone governs police behavior. The result would be the same if the police had a deliberate policy of leaving Negroes alone except in very serious matters, and the comments of some officers indicated that this is indeed the case. Although there may be, as we shall suggest in a later chapter, political reasons for such a policy, at least one widely affirmed reason is based on the police department's conception of the mores of the Negro community. Negroes have, in the eyes of almost all policemen interviewed, a different set of rules, a desire to be left alone, an unwillingness to cooperate with the police, and a preference for settling matters themselves. A Newburgh detective told an interviewer:

> When one of them [a Negro] gets cut, they don't come in here and tell us. He handles it on his own. He or his brother will cut the guy back. If we do get to question the victim, . . . he'll suddenly be unable to remember who did it. And if we can file a complaint, often he'll shake down the guy who cut him for fifty bucks, and withdraw the complaint.

The detective went on to say that this policy did not apply in a very serious matter: it was only for "small cases . . . no more than fifteen or twenty stitches." For these, "Off the record, we don't care." This indifference characteristically applies to family quarrels, personal disputes, and barroom disorders; it is, however, partially set aside when Negro behavior disturbs white residents. A Negro nightclub, once located in an all-Negro neighborhood, was forced to move by a land clearance project. It relocated in the middle of an old Italian neighborhood and the residents promptly began complaining to their city councilman and through him to the city manager and police chief. A few sporadic police "crackdowns" were launched, which left both the white neighbors and the nightclub owner dissatisfied — the former because the crowds and noise did not abate, the latter because she felt she was being harassed by police who had left her alone when the same things happened at her former all-Negro location.[10] Further, she felt that the police only responded to white complaints; when she had trouble with her cus-

10. On October 27, 1965, she paid in city court ten parking tickets at fines of from three to five dollars each.

tomers, they did nothing. The police and city officials were for their part angry at her for creating a situation they could not handle by their usual policy: "I don't believe in us serving as a bar owner's bouncer," one lieutenant told an interviewer. "I won't send a man in to serve this function when a bar owner calls and asks us to throw someone out." A city councilman told the newspaper that the bar would have to do its own policing.[11] Finally, some Negro leaders — some of whom were no doubt rather embarrassed by having to take up the case of a person they felt was "not respectable" — held a meeting in 1965 to protest inadequate police protection.

The police are disgusted by such representations. Though some will admit that fear may be a motive for ignoring Negro misbehavior, others see the problem as one Negroes themselves must solve. They must, in the eyes of the police, change their moral code so as to make misconduct a matter for collective repression rather than private vengeance and to make cooperation with the police the rule rather than the exception. Negro complaints are not to be taken seriously so long as Negroes commit such a disproportionate number of crimes, provide little or no information to the police, refuse to swear out complaints, and periodically assault police officers. Recently, a crowd of Negroes assaulted an officer and took away his gun. No arrests were made and the gun was not recovered. No one went to the assistance of the officer, according to a Negro witness.

The law enforcement system in Newburgh has institutionalized the view that certain offenses will be left to private recourse. As noted in Chapter 4, a person who alleges a misdemeanor and files a complaint against another party often must hire his own lawyer to prosecute the case. Because such complaints typically involve either an assault or a larceny and because Negroes comprise the majority of persons arrested on such charges (54 per cent of those arrested for assault and 73 per cent of those arrested for petty larceny), the burden of private prosecution falls primarily on Negro com-

11. Newburgh *Evening News,* September 4, 1965. Later, the bar owner offered to pay the cost of the assigned police protection. *Evening News,* September 13, 1965.

plainants (Negroes being the usual victims of Negroes) and thus it is they who are primarily discouraged from proceeding.

When the police do act vigorously against a Negro — or against anyone, for that matter — it is because a heinous crime has been committed or because the law has been flouted rather than ignored or broken. And it is flouted, in the eyes of the police, when the authority of a police officer is challenged, face-to-face. To them, authority rarely invoked should be given even greater deference than authority routinely invoked.

There is no way to know how many incidents of police abuse of authority occur, or even to know with certainty whether any occur; the abuses that have been alleged are neither as numerous nor as clear-cut as one would expect if the police were normally aggressive in their handling of Negro disorders. A Negro male was shot by a police officer in 1963. According to the police, he had assaulted an officer who had stopped him regarding a traffic infraction; according to Negro witnesses, there was no assault, but they concede the Negro did take the officer's nightstick away after the latter allegedly threatened him. In 1965 two officers shot and killed a Negro male who, they claim, tried to flee the scene of a burglary. Negro leaders claimed the shots were unjustified and filed suit; it was dismissed.[12] A Negro boy was allegedly beaten by the police after being taken from a theater where he had created a disturbance.

Such allegations are always difficult to interpret because the injured party is almost never wholly innocent and what constitutes necessary police force is a matter of judgment. An anecdote told by a Negro attorney in Newburgh illustrates the problem and suggests the way in which minor Negro misconduct and general police indifference can combine unpredictably to produce an "incident."

> Sometimes they [the police] over-enforce the law. I remember a case in which a boyfriend and girlfriend were having a fight. The girlfriend called the police. By the time they got there, they'd made up again and the girl told the police they were no longer needed. The man was told

12. Newburgh *Evening News,* June 28, 1965, and March 2, 1966.

by the police to leave the apartment anyway. When he got down to his car, a policeman hurled an insult at him and he hurled one right back. By this time there were several police officers there, maybe five or six, and they grabbed him and threw him up against the car and started beating on him . . . We sued the city on that, but . . . the case was thrown out . . . One of the problems in handling these cases is that a lot of the people who are the objects of police brutality have shady backgrounds, and often they don't want to get mixed up in any suit against the city. And even if they do, when their case comes up, they don't make a very good impression.

But at the time of this research there had been no major, large-scale police-citizen incidents in Newburgh and the city manager has taken some steps to reduce the chances that there will be. Additional Negro patrolmen have been hired (there were, in mid-1967, five on the force) and riot control training has been given to members of the department. In Newburgh, a high city official admitted, "We are walking a tightrope." The tightrope almost broke in July 1967 when a serious Negro disturbance occurred, apparently in protest against a rally of the National Renaissance (neo-Nazi) party in Newburgh; several Negroes were arrested.[13]

In Albany, the police arrest Negro drunks at four times the rate in Newburgh — partly because there are more drunks but partly because the police are more aggressive about maintaining public order. Indeed, there is not much evidence of Albany police timidity. A perceived challenge to police authority is met forcefully. During an eight-week period police records show nine persons arrested for disorderly conduct. In eight of the nine cases, the police report indicates that the person arrested used "abusive language" to the police or assaulted them; seven of the eight persons arrested for this reason were Negroes. The eighth person was a white man who had witnessed a police arrest of another person and said to the officer, "Why don't you let this man go?" He was ordered to move on; when

13. *New York Times,* July 30 and August 2, 1967. More than forty stores were looted, mostly in the Negro section, and over forty Negroes were arrested. The Newburgh police were equipped with "Chemical Mace" gas weapons, but did not use them.

he refused, he was arrested for disorderly conduct. On the other hand, in two of the cases Negro boys actually heaved bricks at patrolmen walking their beats. Whether from words or bricks, the Albany police do not passively accept challenges to their authority. Given these policies, the common Negro complaint against the Albany police is not so much lack of police protection as "police brutality." And because the newspapers are politically opposed to the local administration (in Newburgh the newspaper has been an ally of the administration), many incidents allegedly involving brutality receive considerable publicity.

Casual interviews with Negro men in the Arbor Hill section of Albany produced many heated complaints of excessive police force or verbal abuse; how common these are, or whether any particular incident occurred precisely as described to the interviewer, is impossible to say. One Negro spoke of being beaten on the legs at headquarters to extract from him an apology for an alleged insult; another told of being hit frequently by the police when he was a juvenile, because of being involved in gangs or the like, but of never being formally arrested. Though many Albany Negroes are as anxious as whites for more police protection, especially against Negro juveniles, several of the young Negro males interviewed were bitter about the way the police intervene in some situations. One expressed it this way to an interviewer:

> You can't stand up and be a man here. If you're walking down the street, they [the police] stop you, call you by your first name, call you "boy" or "nigger." If they see you out with a woman, they stop you. They insult you in front of your woman and you know you can't fight back. As a man you're not supposed to have to take that, but you have to take it from them or they'll hand you your head.

Between 1962 and 1967 police mistreatment of Negroes was publicly alleged in five cases. The facts in all the cases are in dispute and in one the local leader of the NAACP conceded that there was no evidence of police mistreatment. Of the remaining four, three became major issues. In 1962 a Negro postal clerk complained that he had been beaten by police officers at headquarters after having been arrested on disorderly conduct charges. The arrest, following his refusal to move a parked car blocking a street, occurred at 9:40 P.M.; he was released on $50 bail at midnight; shortly before 1:00 A.M. he was taken to a hospital and treated for bruises and swollen eyes.[14] The Negro claims the injuries were inflicted by the police; the police deny this on the grounds that the nature of the injuries — especially the scratches on the eyeballs — could not have been inflicted by blows. The police commissioner, after a hearing, dismissed the complaint. The Albany County grand jury then took up the case and subpoenaed reporters and editors from the newspaper that broke the story. After two years, a reporter was indicted for second-degree perjury (falsely swearing to a matter not material to the inquiry); he was later acquitted by the trial jury. An editor for the paper involved later told an interviewer that, in his opinion, the grand jury hearing was intended, not to uncover the facts, but to harass the paper for having printed the facts.

The second case involved a white man, of some stature in the community, who was arrested when he intervened to protest what he described as the beating of a Negro by the police.[15] The grand jury heard the case and refused to indict the accused officer, who in turn brought a multi-million-dollar damage suit against the newspaper that printed the story.

The third case arose when statements made to the local NAACP accused the police of beating a Negro male for resisting arrest after a relative of the man had called the police to complain that he was causing a disturbance. The president of the NAACP met with the police chief to discuss the matter and then, unsatisfied, asked for a meeting with the mayor. The mayor would not meet with him; instead, the grand jury was convened and the NAACP official summoned before it. When, by his own admission, he could not produce personal evidence of brutality, the police were officially exonerated. Only then did the mayor meet with the NAACP leader, but no program for improving police-community relations was offered.[16]

14. *Knickerbocker News*, June 6, 1962.
15. *Knickerbocker News*, April 11, 1963.
16. *Knickerbocker News*, April 22, May 4, May 10, 1966; *Times-Union*, May 17, 1966.

In the last case, the mothers of two Negro boys, with the help of a militant local civil rights organization, circulated a petition and presented it to the police chief accusing the police of having used unnecessary force and abusive language in arresting the two boys on disorderly conduct charges. The chief received the petition and, after a two-hour meeting with the mothers at police headquarters, announced he would meet with his commanders to reiterate that he would "not tolerate any unnecessary force," though he did not believe the facts in this case indicated that any brutality was proved.[17] (Subsequently, one of the two boys was rearrested on two felony counts charging him with knifing another boy and the other was arrested on charges of first degree arson and third degree assault.)[18] Then, to the surprise of almost everyone, the police chief agreed to meet with the civil rights organization (The Brothers) at their headquarters in a Negro neighborhood. After an unprecedented three-hour conference with no reporters present, the chief and the civil rights leaders announced the formation of an "Advisory Committee" to meet monthly with the chief and discuss police practices as they affected minority groups.[19] An NAACP leader was especially flabbergasted: "I have been trying for years to get the chief to discuss these things with us and to form some kind of organization," he told an interviewer, "but they wouldn't hear of it. Now all of a sudden they are meeting with The Brothers." Privately, some high officials of the city administration were critical of the chief for having gone to The Brothers but they were not certain this new initiative could now be reversed.

There is some evidence the Albany police may have decided to become slightly more circumspect in their handling of Negroes. The most widely advertised civil rights group in the city (The Brothers) is one that, unlike the NAACP, has explicit political aims — in 1967 it ran candidates in the primary election against the governing party in one of the Negro wards. (It lost badly.) A former Albany police officer, who in general believes the police are too easy on Negroes,

17. *Knickerbocker News*, March 28, March 29, and April 1, 1967.
18. *Knickerbocker News*, April 5 and May 16, 1967.
19. *Times-Union*, April 7, 1967.

told an interviewer that "In the old days, any Negro who talked back was hammered on the head, right, wrong, or indifferent, and nobody thought twice about it." If anyone complained, the grand jury was used to intimidate the critics rather than to ascertain the facts. He himself had observed two Albany patrolmen empty their revolvers into a Negro man fleeing the scene of a stabbing, even though after the first shot or two the man was no longer able to run. When on another occasion the officer was himself charged with assaulting a civilian, a white in this case, he said to the complainant, in his words: "You know how juries are picked in this county. You don't stand a chance. If you take this to court, I will be acquitted and then I'll slap a law suit on you." The complaint was withdrawn. In his view, the old ways of handling Negroes are slowly disappearing. "The Negroes were treated roughly; they got hammered around a lot; but the Negro community is slowly getting organized . . . At one time, the police had the backing of the community in dealing with Negroes. Now it's far from clear they do." [20]

Nor is it any longer clear Albany's Negroes are as passive as they once were. In July 1967 a rumor, later proved false, that a police car had struck a Negro girl caused a large crowd to gather in the all-Negro Albany Hill area. The Brothers went to the scene and dispersed the crowd. The next night, however, young Negroes would not be stopped; a large number of them congregated, some bottles and rocks were thrown, a few fires were started, and several store windows were smashed. The police arrested 54 persons, but no shots were fired. The police regarded the riot as proof of the need for toughness and determination and of the unfounded and perhaps incendiary nature of "brutality" charges — the riot, after all, was sparked by mere rumor. To the Negroes, the event was the culmination of grievances against the city and especially the police to which the authorities had shown no inclination to be receptive, much less

20. A white attorney with years of experience in handling Negro criminal cases told an interviewer: "A few nights ago there must have been four or five hundred people in front of that place [a well-known Negro night club]. They were watching a fight or something. The cops didn't even try to go near it. I can remember when they would have gone in there swinging. They used to beat Negroes over the head right on the street corner. They don't do that anymore. I think they figure they might lose the fight."

conciliatory. To an observer, the riot proved nothing one way or another: cities with every imaginable police style have had Negro riots. It is the daily and routine nature of police-citizen contacts, and not the occasional eruption of violence, wherein one finds the significance of a prevailing police style.

Six The Legalistic Style

In some departments, the police administrator uses such control as he has over the patrolmen's behavior to induce them to handle commonplace situations as if they were matters of law enforcement rather than order maintenance. He realizes, of course, that the officer cannot always act as if his duty were merely to compare observed behavior with a legal standard and make an arrest if that standard has been violated — the law itself, especially that governing misdemeanor arrests, does not always permit the application of its sanctions. But whenever he acts on his own initiative or to the extent he can influence the outcome of disorderly situations in which he acts on the initiative of the citizen, the patrolman is expected to take a law enforcement view of his role. Such a police style will be called "legalistic," and it can be found in varying degrees in Oakland and Highland Park and to a growing extent in Syracuse.

A legalistic department will issue traffic tickets at a high rate, detain and arrest a high proportion of juvenile offenders, act vigorously against illicit enterprises, and make a large number of misdemeanor arrests even when, as with petty larceny, the public order has not been breached. The police will act, on the whole, as if there were a single standard of community conduct — that which the law prescribes — rather than different standards for juveniles, Negroes, drunks, and the like. Indeed, because such persons are more likely than certain others to commit crimes, the law will fall heavily on them and be experienced as "harassment."

The Oakland and Highland Park police departments began functioning this way in about the mid-1950's; Oakland continues to do so, and Highland Park has modified its policies only slightly since the appointment of a new chief in 1965. Syracuse began moving in this direction in 1963, with the arrival of a "reform" police chief and deputy chief; it is too early to tell how far it will proceed. For now, it has only some of the earmarks of a legalistic department — and these primarily in the field of traffic enforcement.

The concept "legalistic" does not necessarily imply that the police regard all laws as equally important or that they love the law for its own sake. In all the cities here discussed, officers distinguish between major and minor crimes, feel that private disputes are usually less important than public disorders, and are willing to overlook some offenses and accept some excuses. Indeed, because the "normal" tendency of police officers, for reasons explained in Chapter 2, is to under-enforce the law, a legalistic police style is necessarily the result of rather strenuous administrative efforts to get patrolmen to do what they might not otherwise do; as such, it is never completely successful. Though there may be a few zealots in a watchman-like department, they will be few indeed and will probably concentrate their efforts more on making "good pinches," which in any department are rewarded, than on "pushing paper" (that is, writing tickets or citing juveniles). In a legalistic department, there is likely to be a sizable number of patrolmen with comparatively little zeal — typically older officers, or officers "left over" from a previous and different administration, or officers of any age who do not regard the benefits (in terms of promotions, official recognition, or good duty assignments) of zealousness as worth the costs in effort and possibly adverse citizen relations.

The legalistic style does mean that, on the whole, the department will produce many arrests and citations, especially with respect to those matters in which the police and not the public invoke the law; even when the police are called by the public to intervene, they are likely to intervene formally, by making an arrest or urging the signing of a complaint, rather than informally, as through conciliation or by delaying an arrest in hopes that the situation will take care of itself.

Though in many cases they are required by law to rely on citizen arrests, the police in following the legalistic style do not try to privatize the handling of disputes and minor offenses. Citizen arrests are facilitated, prosecution of shoplifters is encouraged, juveniles are handled formally, and drunks are arrested "for their own protection." Prostitutes are arrested (but drug-store pornography, because the law affords few grounds for an arrest, is pretty much left alone). Even in Highland Park, though a small town, drunks and juveniles have been handled more formally since the mid-1950's and bad-check passers are often prosecuted even when the merchant is willing to drop charges. As the chief told an interviewer, "Once we get that check, we'll sign a complaint and we'll prosecute. We've got the check with their name on it and the date, and it's marked 'insufficient funds,' so we've got all the evidence we need. A lot of the stores would just as soon not prosecute, I suppose, but . . . we're not a collection agency." At the same time, as Highland Park *is* a small and affluent town, the police are hardly eager to intervene in domestic disputes — to be precise, wife beatings — which, unlike the barroom brawls of the big city, are rich in opportunities for an officer to get himself in trouble. The police once handled such dilemmas occasionally by calling the local magistrate (until recently, an elected magistrate handled all local cases) and asking him to try informally to reach a settlement and, of course, to take responsibility. This is no longer the case; now, the victim would be asked to sign a complaint ticket.

Though the legalistic department will issue a large number of traffic tickets, not every department with a high ticketing rate can be called legalistic. Because he has an unambiguous performance measure, the police administrator can obtain almost any level of ticketing he wishes without necessarily altering the way the police conceive their function, as when ticketing is delegated to a specialized traffic enforcement unit. A legalistic department will typically go beyond this, however, and put *all* patrolmen, not just traffic specialists, under some pressure to "produce." To the extent this policy is followed, some change in the patrolman's conception of his function ensues. Sometimes, however, the opposite occurs. In Highland Park, the chief responsible for the heavy emphasis on traffic enforcement was replaced, in 1965, by a chief who shifted the department's strategy without greatly affecting its ticket productivity and without abandoning its general law enforcement orientation. He did this by substituting specialization for quotas — easing somewhat the pressure to produce on the force as a whole and giving the task to one or two officers who would do little else.[1]

A better test for the existence of the legalistic style can be found in those situations where the administrator's control of his subordinates' conduct is less certain and where therefore greater and more systematic efforts must be made to achieve the desired behavior. The handling of juvenile offenders is just such a case. In Oakland and Highland Park, and perhaps to a growing extent in Syracuse, the police take a law enforcement rather than familial view of their responsibilities in delinquency cases. Perhaps "institutional" view would be more correct, because the police in none of these cities feel their task is simply to make an arrest whenever possible. Indeed, the officers are keenly aware of the importance of the family and spend considerable time talking to parents, but the relationship between officer and juvenile or officer and parent is formal and institutional — the officer seeks to invoke specialized, professional services (probation officers, judges, child guidance clinics) rather than to apply his own form of discipline or to resort to appeals to clergymen or others presumed to wield "moral" influence. Of course, to take advantage of the professional services the community provides, the juvenile must be brought into these institutions — and that, typically, requires an arrest.

In Oakland, for example, the police do not arrest a large number of juveniles because they want to have the boys punished by the juvenile court (in 1965 only 11 per cent of the 6,772 boys referred by various police agencies to the juvenile division of the Alameda County [Oakland] probation department were sent on to court and of these only a fraction were placed in any correctional institution). Indeed, large numbers of juveniles are arrested *despite* the nine-to-one odds against the youth having to experience much more than a

1. When the specialized enforcement strategy replaced the quota system, the morale of the Highland Park patrolmen improved. But the new methods did not substantially reduce the chance that a motorist would be ticketed. In 1965, though the new chief was in office for about nine months, the number of moving violation tickets issued was about the same as the average for the preceding three years when the former chief, and thus the quota system, prevailed.

conversation with a probation officer. An arrest is made because, being official, it is thought to be the right way to do things and because experiencing an arrest, getting a record, and even talking to the probation officer may do some good. Nor do the police stop there. In recent years the Oakland police have operated a "Good Citizenship School" for children between the ages of eleven and fourteen, usually first offenders, who come with a parent to headquarters for a two-hour class every week for four weeks. During 1966 about a thousand juveniles attended and a version of the program has been incorporated into the curriculum of the public schools. The Oakland officers approve of such institutional programs; they are much less likely than officers from New York communities to approve of more informal methods of dealing with delinquency.[2]

The Oakland police also encourage citizens, such as store security guards, to handle by arrest persons caught perpetrating minor crimes, such as shoplifting. The police frown on stores that seek only restitution rather than prosecution. A sergeant assigned to the shoplifting detail regularly meets with security guards to discuss procedures for handling such cases. Partly as a result of this, of the 155 shoplifters processed by the police in December 1965, not one had the charges dismissed because the complainant failed to prosecute. (Not all were arrested, either. Some of the juveniles were reprimanded and released and some adults were given a "district attorney citation" which, perhaps extra-legally, requests the offender to appear before a prosecutor for what is in effect a lecture and warning.) As one Oakland officer told an interviewer: "We insist that the citizen come in and sign the complaint; most of them, of course, we

2. A survey of the attitudes of police officers of all ranks and specialties from 316 police departments across the country revealed that officers from the Middle Atlantic states, including New York, were significantly more likely than officers from the Pacific states, including California, to believe that the police should try to find jobs for older juveniles who come to their attention, that they should operate Boy's Clubs and Little League baseball teams, and that in minor cases the offending juvenile ought simply to report periodically to the police for informal probation. George W. O'Connor and Nelson A. Watson, *Juvenile Delinquency and Youth Crime: The Police Role* (Washington, D.C.: International Association of Chiefs of Police, 1964), pp. 115–126.

know, since they are store security guards. And if occasionally the citizen won't sign, we [that is, the police] will sign 'on information and belief' if we are sure of the facts."

The zealous police chief who served in Highland Park between 1956 and 1965 instilled a law enforcement orientation to juvenile offenses. "Laws," he told an interviewer as well as his own men, "are on the books to be enforced." The practice of dealing informally with juveniles "on the street" was to be discontinued. A sergeant explained the new philosophy:

> It's Chief X's philosophy that the case is either unfounded or you had better have charged them with the offense which they are suspected of having committed. When we come across a group of kids scuffling after a basketball game, there's no such thing as "messing around" in his eyes. Either there's no trouble and no reason to stop them or else you had better bring them in.

The results of these new directives were dramatic. Between 1958 and 1959 the number of juveniles brought into the station increased from 77 to 507.[3] That more kids were detained does not mean more were punished — there was no great increase in the number going to court, largely because the additional juveniles brought to the station had committed only minor offenses.[4] But the chief was determined to see that those sent to court were punished. The judge who handled juvenile cases in the county reported that when the new chief first came to town "He would come to court himself with every juvenile offender and would invariably complain that too many were being granted probation." But probation was granted

3. This figure includes all persons under the age of eighteen and thus is not comparable to the data for Brighton or Nassau County or for the data reported on Highland Park in Table 7. The latter figure is only for persons under the age of sixteen. Similar figures for earlier years were not available.

4. One anecdote makes the point. An officer patrolling a busy street in Highland Park saw a boy walking alone after the curfew hour. The officer recognized him and knew that he returned every evening at about this time on his way home from his girlfriend's house. The officer decided to give him a ride. He radioed the station to tell them what he was doing but the chief, who overheard the communication, cut in to tell him, "We're not running a taxi service," and ordered the boy brought to the station and his parents summoned to pick him up. (From an interview.)

anyway, and eventually the chief gave up. According to the judge, "He didn't come here anymore."

When the chief resigned in 1965, his successor, though a local man with a quite different personality, did not change fundamentally the policy on juveniles or, for that matter, on most other offenders. In 1963 the city had adopted a curfew ordinance that made it illegal for a person under the age of eighteen to be on the streets after 11 P.M. between Sunday and Thursday and after midnight on Friday and Saturday. The police enforced it, and from May 1964 to September 1966 they brought twenty-one cases charging curfew violation before the local court. When asked why, a sergeant explained: "The curfew law was passed so we would have a way of locking up kids who gather in gangs downtown looking for trouble. If you leave them there alone at night . . . they'll look for some way to prove what smart guys they are, such as by kicking in a plate glass window." The chief confirmed this:

> We used to be able to get a boy on a juvenile delinquency charge for almost anything. We never had trouble finding some grounds for bringing the boy in. The new [state] juvenile code makes it a lot tougher to arrest him, so we adopted the curfew law. It's in conformity with the state statute . . . We still have to bring him into the station, but at least we've got a charge on him that we can use to get him off the streets.

In Syracuse, also, the police have changed somewhat the manner of handling juveniles, though not as drastically as in Highland Park. Between 1961 and 1965, the number of juveniles disposed of by the police increased from 1,132 to 1,398, an increase that might reflect the growing number of young lower-income Negroes in the population. In the same period, the proportion who were referred to Family Court increased from 44 to 58 per cent; by contrast, the proportion referred to religious or church-connected welfare organizations for informal guidance decreased from 3.2 to 1.1 per cent. This greater reliance on formal, court-centered proceedings as opposed to informal, church-centered ones occurred simultaneously with the advent of the new police leadership and its emphasis on police professionalism. It is not clear that the "reform" caused a significant change in police treatment of juveniles — the available data are too skimpy and the officers involved deny it — but such data as exist are not inconsistent with that possibility.

The police in these cities, however, do not arrest because they like making arrests, or hate teenagers and Negroes, or love the penal code. Almost every officer interviewed in these departments said in one way or another, "We're not out to make arrests" or "We don't believe an arrest is always the answer." Such statements are quite sincere and not at all inconsistent with the fact that these men *do* make arrests and issue tickets at rates much higher than those found in other departments.

One reason the statement and the behavior can coexist is that the officers know that they see many offenses, usually minor, that they "let go" without an arrest or ticket; they are not especially aware — there is no way that they could be — that the police in other cities let many more go. Moreover, the average patrolman knows that most of his time is spent on things he does not regard as "real police work," much less on things that result in arrests. If anyone should suggest that he is "zealous" about making arrests, he would deny and perhaps resent it.

The fact that so many arrests are made, and that they are made as much as possible on the basis of a fixed, not a variable standard of behavior, is primarily the result of departmental policies. It is the administrators who devise these policies, manipulate the rewards and sanctions that get them carried out, and reflect on their justification. The patrolmen are primarily "doing their job" — making runs, stopping cars, filling out forms, and putting up with citizen behavior that is tedious, bizarre, or even dangerous. When he thinks of his role, it is usually with a mixture of irritation that the "brass" in the offices "don't know what it's like out here on the street," disgust that the so-called "good citizens" and the courts are not supporting the police, and anger that the people who misbehave show so little respect for the police and provide so little cooperation. These views are about the same whether one is in a legalistic or a watchman department. The police administrators effect the difference between these police styles in part intentionally and in part unintentionally.

To some degree they demand that their officers enforce the laws because they believe it is right that all laws be enforced. In November 1966 the Highland Park chief sent out a letter to local businessmen expressing concern that some were allowing persons under the age of eighteen to buy cigarettes and also "openly smoke them in their place of business." The chief reminded them that this was a violation of an Illinois law that the police intended to enforce. The Oakland Police Department announced in January 1967 that because of the number of stolen bicycles and the difficulty in tracing and recovering unlicensed bicycles, it would intensify the enforcement of bicycle licensing ordinances by issuing juvenile citations to owners of unlicensed bikes. Parents were warned that disregarding this citation could result in a juvenile court appearance. Such policies would be followed in a watchman department only if they were required by a public hue and cry, and that would be most unlikely. Moreover, the police in a legalistic city obey the law themselves. In Oakland, the police parking lot is across the street from headquarters. The direct route to take to and from the building is to cross in the middle of the block. Routinely, interviewers watching the shifts change saw officers leave the building, walk to the corner, wait for the light, cross, and walk back to their cars. "Once or twice, maybe, I'll dash across the street," a patrolman told an interviewer, "but you get used to not jaywalking, and that's the way it is all the time."

The administrators of these departments want high arrest and ticketing rates not only because it is right but also to reduce the prospect (or the suspicion) of corruption, to protect themselves against criticism that they are not doing their job or are deciding for themselves what laws are good or bad, and to achieve, by means of the law, certain larger social objectives. Almost invariably a legalistic department was once a corrupt or favor-doing department. In Oakland, the police had been accused of tolerating gambling, conniving with insurance companies, and rolling drunks in the city jail. In

Syracuse they had been accused of consorting with and accepting favors from gamblers and the political friends of gamblers. In Highland Park, they had been regarded as "sloppy," "ineffective," and interested in "looking out for themselves and their friends." Because police chiefs are broken by scandal, not crime, a new chief, hired to put an end to scandal, will seek to put an end to the officers' discretion concerning what laws will and will not be enforced. *All* laws will be enforced. Discretion, except under carefully defined circumstances, creates opportunities for officers to use that discretion out of improper or corrupt motives or, what is almost as bad, to *appear* to do so out of such motives. Police departments are judged by the public to a great extent in terms of appearances and rumors; the best way to stifle rumors of corruption or favoritism is to make sure that everybody gets a traffic ticket, every bookie is put out of business, and every glue-sniffing teenager is hauled in for questioning.

A police chief may also, for reasons to be developed in a later chapter, want to take the police "out of politics," at least formally. The most obvious way to achieve this is to assert that there is a clear difference between law-givers and law-enforcers or, more generally, between policy and administration. Every police officer likes to remark, "We don't make the laws"; in dealing with an angry housewife who has received a ticket or whose son has been arrested, it is a conventional observation intended, obviously, to reduce interpersonal conflict by representing the police officer as the impersonal, and slightly sympathetic, agent of a remote "Law." In a legalistic department, that view becomes the position of the chief as well as the patrolman, and partly for the same reason — to dissociate the department from the law-making process, which is essentially a political process, thereby making it clear that so long as the department "does its job" the responsibility is on others to decide what it shall do and thus no one can accuse the department of being "political" by making its own decisions as to what laws to enforce. It is harder to keep the department out of politics if it appears to be making political judgments, and it may appear in just that light if it does less than enforce all the laws all the time.

The chief also knows that the law is a device to achieve certain social objectives — order, peace, security, certainty, and liberty. He is aware that by enforcing certain laws he can achieve the purposes of other laws, and this gives him and his department a reason to enforce laws that otherwise might appear trivial and thus be ignored. Enforcing traffic laws is desirable not simply because it is their duty but because such enforcement is one way to prevent automobile accidents. (The police know it is not the only way, and agree that it is hard to prove conclusively that it is even one way, but it is, in their view, the only way open to them and they feel they must do something.) Furthermore, stopping cars for traffic infractions affords an opportunity to check the identity of the driver and the registration of the car; from time to time, the police discover fugitives, stolen merchandise, illegal weapons, and stolen cars this way. This, in turn, leads to even more arrests. This screening process is a kind of positive feedback system that helps explain why high-arrest departments are so *much* higher than low-arrest departments: the more traffic tickets you issue, the better the chance of catching a real criminal; if you catch a real criminal, you make yourself look good; thus rewarded, you have even greater incentive to make more car stops.

The same instrumental view of the law extends into other areas where the police act on their own initiative. A drunk becomes the victim of a strong-arm robber; arrest him and you prevent a robbery. Juvenile vandalism can, the police believe, lead to a career in crime; better to investigate now, and take it seriously now. Teenagers loitering on a street corner late at night might cause mischief later on; thus, in Oakland and Highland Park, the police enforce an anti-loitering or curfew law. Besides being illegal, vice also leads to muggings and the rolling of drunks; arrest prostitutes and you reduce the number of rollings.

In watchman-like departments account is also taken of the consequences of a law violation, but the consequences considered are limited, for the most part, to those which are immediate, personal, and direct. Will *this* drunk hurt *himself* or some nearby person *soon* if I let him go? Is *this* car driving so recklessly as to endanger others on *this road*? Are *these* kids getting into mischief *right now*? Legalistic departments, by contrast, additionally take into account consequences that are general, remote, and impersonal. For the patrolman from a working-class background, the pattern found in watchman-style departments may be in some sense "natural." In the management of violence generally, working-class persons are likely to take into account primarily the immediate consequences of actions, while middle-class persons are more inclined to take into account motives and long-term consequences. For example, working-class parents are apt to resort to physical punishment "when the direct and immediate consequences of their children's disobedient acts are most extreme, and to refrain from punishing when this might provoke an even greater disturbance." Middle-class parents, on the other hand, seem "to punish or refrain from punishing on the basis of their interpretation of the child's *intent* in acting as he does"; thus, a furious outburst will be punished if it represents a "loss of self-control" but not if it is merely an "emotional release." [5]

The Organizational Context

The legalistic style may result partly from administrative actions taken with other ends in view. A "reform" chief must get hold of his department. To break through the governing pattern of personal relations, loyalties, and feuds to which he, as an outsider, is alien, he seeks to centralize control, formalize authority, and require written accounts of everything that transpires. When the new chief arrived in Highland Park in the mid-1950's, each officer was required to keep a detailed daily account of his activities, to make complete reports of all investigations no matter how minor, and to submit all such documents to superior officers for review. When, at about the same time, a reform chief took over the Oakland Police Department, he promptly abolished the precinct stations and centralized the

5. Melvin L. Kohn, "Social Class and Parent-Child Relationships: An Interpretation," *American Journal of Sociology*, 67 (1963), p. 478 (italics added). See also Kohn, "Social Class and the Exercise of Parental Authority," *American Sociological Review*, 24 (1959), pp. 312–366.

entire department into one headquarters building, created the post of departmental inspector to investigate alleged police misbehavior and a planning and research section to gather and analyze data from the voluminous reports patrolmen were required to file, launched a nationwide recruiting program (after first having abolished the local residence requirement for patrolmen), established an elaborate and lengthy training program, and held inspections to check the appearance and equipment of the men.[6] A patrolman driving a beat in Oakland carries with him a fat briefcase filled with forms and notebooks on which he records every kind of investigation, complaint, report, and "field interrogation." Syracuse, beginning in 1963, underwent the same kind of changes: new records and reports procedures were adopted; an internal affairs and an inspection section were created to check performance and look into complaints; daily logs were to be filled out by all men; a planning section was to study beat boundaries and manpower allocations. In Oakland and Syracuse, the chiefs made major — and controversial — efforts to break up the informal organization of the department. Men who had been on the same beat for years were assigned new beats and made part of a general rotation system. An attempt — not wholly successful — was made to break down the long-standing separation between the patrol force and the detective force so that men could be assigned from one to the other.

It is easy to imagine the consequences of these changes. Formal, hierarchical authority was strengthened at the expense of informal, clique authority. The patrolmen were put on notice that they were continuously being evaluated, and evaluated principally by the only standard the department had available — vigor in imposing rules and efficiency in completing reports about incidents. Promotions were stressed and promotional opportunities increased — partly by creating new senior positions in order to staff the new specialized units (planning, community relations, internal affairs, and so on), partly by encouraging certain older officers to retire, and partly by recruiting college-educated recruits who, as they moved up through the ranks, would prove attractive to outside agencies and thus be

6. See *Oakland Tribune*, February 27, 1955.

lured away from the police department, thereby creating vacancies for more promotions.

Promotional opportunities, and the prospect of desirable working conditions in the new specialized units, made the patrol force a reservoir from which the "elite" units drew manpower. For example, the traffic enforcement section — especially the motorcycle unit — is for various reasons an attractive job for many men on the Oakland force. There has been a waiting list of patrolmen seeking to get in, from which the chief could pick the "best"; being the "best" means, among other things, having a proven traffic enforcement record — that is, having written tickets as a patrolman.

A legalistic department also values technical efficiency. Strictly speaking, of course, the concept "efficiency" has very little meaning in police work. Properly defined, it is a ratio between valued outputs and valued inputs — the higher the ratio (the more valued output per unit of valued input), the more efficient the system. But the police can neither evaluate their output nor measure that output which they can evaluate. *True* efficiency — accomplishing a given law enforcement objective at minimum cost, or accomplishing more of that objective at a given cost — is almost always very hard to attain. But legalistic departments do emphasize *technical* efficiency; that is, they try to produce as much output as possible, no matter how it is valued, for a given cost. In short, a legalistic department tries to get the men to work harder, confident in some areas (for example, vice suppression) and hopeful in others (for example, preventive patrol, field interrogation, juvenile citations, traffic summonses) that this will achieve a desired objective.

Such departments, if they are fairly large, will have a "planning and research" section, but they will rarely do much planning and not even much operational research. They will produce "studies" — largely fact-finding exercises about how many crimes are being committed, or the characteristics of certain offenders (for example, how many juveniles, when arrested, had been drinking), or the distribution of such offenses by beat, time of day, or season. Such facts are of some value. The number of calls answered by various beats can be equalized, so that no beat is being overworked; outside inquiries about the crime trend, or the "juvenile drinking problem," or the number of narcotics arrests can be answered factually; and some record can be kept of operating and maintenance costs. But little effort is made, except in unusual cases, to plan even for those police objectives that are amenable to research and measurement. For example, a police department may well want to minimize response time (the time between receiving a citizen call for assistance and the arrival of a police officer at the scene), or determine the patrol force's "down time" (the number of minutes during a day when no car is available to answer calls in a given beat), or calculate the "screening efficiency" (the proportion of fugitives caught by traffic enforcement car stops in various locales). Rarely is this done or, if done, done systematically and over time. As a result, planning and research sections often spend much of their time writing memos and draft orders or answering inquiries from citizens and visiting researchers. Administrative modernization, though apparently related to — and often justified in terms of — productive efficiency, is in fact designed to achieve control of the force, reduce such discretion that might be corrupted or abused, emulate accepted "professional doctrine," and recruit and train higher quality manpower.

Indeed, the manpower objective may be the ultimate rationale for many of the "modernizing" changes so eagerly pursued by a legalistic department. The reason there is not much systematic effort even to "suboptimize" — that is, to maximize the attainment of a limited and partial objective, such as minimum police response time — is that police departments, whether legalistic or not, are rarely judged or rewarded by the public on this basis. It is not response time in general that interests a citizen, but the response time to *his call.* And it is not even response time at all that produces the most serious citizen complaints, but rather allegations of discourtesy, brutality, indifference, or harassment. As we shall see in a later chapter, a legalistic department is often in a political environment that requires it to be exceptionally sensitive to (and about) such complaints. One way to cope with them is to take the complaints very seriously and, through departmental investigations, punish or correct misbehavior on the part of officers. The disadvantage of this approach is that it alienates the officers without satisfying the citizens — in Oakland almost every patrolman interviewed was bitter about the fact that the internal affairs section "harassed" them, investigated them, and disciplined them, often, they claimed, unfairly and over minor issues. But also in Oakland, the Negroes refused to believe that internal affairs was doing anything at all. That the truth probably lies somewhere between these extremes may be small comfort to the chief and his internal affairs investigators.

The chief hopes that the problem of citizen complaints will be eased if he can recruit "good men." A "good man" is one who finds it possible to play the police role impersonally — to distinguish between what a policeman must do and his feelings about doing it — and to play it both zealously and courteously. The administrators of legalistic police departments believe such men are more likely to be found in middle-class than in working-class neighborhoods and among the college-educated than the high-school-educated. The modernization of a police department — new buildings, shiny equipment, IBM punch cards, elaborate training programs, higher salaries, rewards for taking college courses in one's spare time, and the waived residence requirement freeing men to live in the suburbs — might all be viewed as an effort to attract middle-class men who both make and value a "good appearance" and who work hard. "Careers in law enforcement" and "professional police work" are emphasized, not only in recruiting posters, but in the appearance and procedures of the department itself. The image thereby created is probably well designed, whether by intention or not, to appeal to both the middle-class consumer of police services and the middle-class police recruit.[7]

In Syracuse, altering the appearance of the force was, next to the

7. Lest the reader assume that the college-educated Oakland patrolmen are humorless automata, it should be noted that not only are they very much subject to the attitudes described in Chapter 2, they also, as do all police, have a sense of humor about their job. In Oakland it can be a rather special one. One patrolman, trying to break up an argument between two Negro males on a street corner, stood glaring at them while they shouted the usual graphic colloquialisms at each other. Turning to the researcher, he remarked drily, "Here, sir, you see an example of an ethnically defined value system at work." Later the same night, he took a long switchblade knife from a Negro prisoner. He stood there, slowly flipping it open and shut and looking at it with a tough expression on his face. Finally he muttered, "I think it's a substitute oral fixation."

emphasis on traffic enforcement, the new regime's most important operational change. A captain told an interviewer:

> The big change as far as the citizen is concerned is in the appearance of the men. There's been a vast difference there. A lot of the men were allowing themselves to get a little ragged. They were messy . . . Now we have inspections at every roll call. If a man can't pass the inspection, he has to set the deficiency right. If he can't correct it, then he has to go home and he loses a day's pay.

A patrolman agreed, stressing the changes in attitudes that the concern for appearance was intended to achieve:

> The men really look nice now, but before, you saw men out of uniform, wearing the wrong uniform. They looked sloppy as hell. Now they look pretty well turned out. [And] a lot of the men, particularly the older men, had . . . a hard time getting used to the idea of being courteous to the public. The younger officers who are coming onto the force now are picking up the good habits much more easily than the older men who had been on for ten years or more.

Some Consequences

Because the legalistic police style encourages patrolmen to take a law enforcement view of the situations they encounter, it also encourages them to take as their standard of justice one which assumes that the function of the law is to punish, on the basis of individual culpability, those who depart from the behavior required by the law. Justice consists generally of equals being treated equally, but in the legalistic style equality does not depend on attributes of person but only on attributes of behavior. "All men are equal before the law" means that the only just distinctions that may be made among them are on the basis of their behavior in areas defined by the law. This criterion is, of course, rather different from the standard of distributive justice employed in the maintenance of order or the resolving of family disputes and thus rather different from the standard that the patrolman regards as somehow "natural."

Because what is expected of him is somewhat at odds with his inclination, the standard the patrolman actually employs will rarely be fully in accord with the standard required by the legalistic department. Just as no administrator can control perfectly the patrolman's behavior in order maintenance situations, so also it cannot determine perfectly the standard of justice he will employ in those situations. Nonetheless, such departments do have an effect on police behavior. In another study, I compared the way in which two big-city departments — one on the east coast, the other on the west — handled juvenile offenders. The western department displayed what I here call the legalistic style, the eastern department the watchman style. By examining juvenile records, it was possible to determine by race the proportion of juveniles coming in contact with the police who were arrested as opposed to being reprimanded and released. In the legalistic western city, the proportion arrested for eight major offenses was almost identical for the two races — whites were arrested in 46.5 per cent of the cases, Negroes in 50.9 per cent. Only for one common offense was there a significant difference — a higher proportion of Negroes than whites were arrested for loitering. In the watchman-like eastern city, however, Negroes were three times as likely as whites to be arrested — 42.9 per cent of the Negroes but only 15.7 per cent of the whites were taken to court.[8]

An explanation can only be speculative. Perhaps, as with the Albany drunk arrests, the watchman-like department regards the Negro as less constrained by community and familial norms; thus, an arrest will accomplish for the Negro what in the case of a white can be achieved by admonition or informal penalties. Indeed, given

8. James Q. Wilson, "The Police and the Delinquent in Two Cities," in Stanton Wheeler, ed., *Controlling Delinquents* (New York: John Wiley and Sons, 1968), pp. 13–14. Supporting evidence from another California police agency can be found in A. W. McEachern and Riva Bauzer, "Factors Related to Disposition in Juvenile Police Contacts," in Malcolm Klein, ed., *Juvenile Gangs in Context* (Englewood Cliffs: Prentice-Hall, 1967), pp. 148–160. But on court dispositions, compare Sidney Axelrad, "Negro and White Male Institutionalized Delinquents," *American Journal of Sociology*, 57 (1957), pp. 569–574.

the importance of family considerations for juvenile behavior,[9] the choice between arrest and warning may be especially important.

In Oakland at the time of my research, there was no significant difference in the arrest prospects of white and Negro juveniles once they had become involved with the police. (I could obtain no comparable data for watchman departments.) But the legalism that apparently produces equitable dispositions also produces frequent dispositions. Compared to a watchman-style department such as Albany, the Oakland police are over *four times* as likely to arrest a Negro (or a white, for that matter) for larceny and driving while intoxicated and almost *fifty* times as likely to arrest one for gambling (see Table 11). In 1965, over 15,000 Negroes were arrested by the Oakland police and perhaps another 27,000 were given tickets for moving traffic violations. If each arrest or ticket involved a different Oakland Negro (and, of course, they did not because some were picked up more than once and some were from out of town), then over 38 per cent of all Oakland Negroes had a formal involvement with the police that year. Syracuse, primarily because of its intensive traffic enforcement, produced a figure almost as high: 29 per cent. The comparable figures for Albany and Newburgh were much lower: 12 per cent and 9 per cent, respectively.[10]

This police style has two important consequences: first, any group that experiences such a high level of police activity and is self-conscious about these matters may feel that it is being "harassed" and, second, even though the proportion of improper police actions may be much smaller than in most other cities the absolute number of such incidents may be significant because of the high volume of police-citizen interactions. Exacerbating such feelings may be police

9. See, for example, Thomas P. Monahan, "Family Status and the Delinquent Child; A Reappraisal and Some New Findings," *Social Forces,* 35 (March 1957), pp. 251–258, and Ray A. Tennyson, "Family Structure and Delinquent Behavior," in Malcolm W. Klein, ed., *Juvenile Gangs in Context* (Englewood Cliffs: Prentice-Hall, 1967), pp. 57–69.

10. Arrests are tabulated by race, but traffic tickets are not. The figure for Negro ticketing was estimated by assuming that Negroes receive tickets in proportion to their percentage in the population. If in fact Negroes are ticketed excessively, the totals given above should be higher; if, because of lower automobile ownership rates, they are ticketed less than whites, the totals should be lower.

policies designed to prevent crime, such as aggressive preventive patrol and the preparation of field contact reports on "suspicious" street activities. Taken together, these elements of the legalistic style, even though wholly within the law, based on sound empirical generalizations as to the areas in which crime is most likely to occur, and as nondiscriminatory as organizational leadership can make them, may be experienced as "harassment." Every Negro interviewed for this study made this charge.

The police, in turn, are angered by these accusations. They know their department is honest, and that it enforces all laws strictly, tolerates no illegal enterprises, and employs the most modern police technology. Only such an organization, they believe, can give police protection to law-abiding Negroes and whites alike. To the police, the Negro leaders who charge harassment are competing for followings by creating issues where none in fact exist and complaining of police procedures essential to a proper enforcement of the law. By denouncing "harassment" they are promoting public resistance to police work; instead, they should be urging citizens to cooperate more fully with the police.

A Negro staff member of an important community agency that had become involved in the police issue described the problem in these terms:

> There's probably not really brutality — I mean no real physical abuse, or at least not much. It's harassment more than anything. What is harassment? Several things. Negroes are stopped by the police more than whites. Any group of Negro boys is stopped when any group of white boys might not be stopped. And of course they have this hang-up on [racially] mixed couples. You don't hear much police verbal abuse. There's not much of . . . officers saying, "Nigger, pull over" to a colored man driving a car . . . [But] you don't have enough Negro police officers.

A leading Negro officer of the NAACP agreed, and related his own experience:

> It's mostly demeaning treatment. I was stopped for speeding on [date]. I got out and gave him my driver's license. He looked at me and

said, "Joe [a pseudonym], where do you live?" "Well," I said, "it's right there on the license." And he says, "I didn't ask you that, Joe. Where do you live?" And he kept pressing me. I was getting mad and he was getting mad. And you could see what was happening. He was calling me by my first name. I was raised in the South where I know that a white man never calls a Negro anything except by his first name or "boy." You don't *do* that with a Negro [up here]. Now if he called you "Jim," you probably wouldn't think anything about it. But it's different for Negroes.

One of the reasons why the Syracuse police, under a reform administration, did not fully and immediately acquire a legalistic style may be that the modernization of the force began at about the same time as a marked increase in the tempo and militancy of civil rights agitation. The new chief and deputy chief found themselves facing incessant, vocal, and well-organized protest movements aimed at the police as well as at business firms and city agencies. The new chief and his successor devoted much of their time to handling these issues, partly by developing internal investigative procedures and partly by attending countless meetings with civil rights and community groups. By their manner — which is quiet and conciliatory — as much as by their policies, they won the grudging respect of many civil rights leaders without abandoning their view that the great majority of citizen complaints against the police are unfounded (see Chapter 7). Perhaps partly because of the need to come to grips with protest activities early in the modernization process, the department has not yet moved as far as Oakland's toward the legalistic style.

Reform came to the Oakland police department almost ten years before the civil rights movement came in force to the city. The style of the department was fixed by the first reform chief and his successor: to enforce all laws vigorously, recruit college-trained men into the force, maintain an appearance of modernity and efficiency, and answer calls promptly. By the time various leaders and organizations, both in Oakland and nearby Berkeley, had begun to mount intensive protest campaigns, zeal and courtesy had become operating rules on the force. But though these rules might appeal to the middle-class homeowner, white or Negro, the rank-and-file Negro, of working- or lower-class background, is likely to see only the zeal. More important, the leadership of the department was in no mood to be conciliatory — crime rates were rising, vacancies on the force were going unfilled, and the accomplishments of the department were not being recognized. And the men running the department were outspoken, often bluntly so.

To be sure, Oakland has had a few highly publicized cases of alleged brutality. The facts in all are in dispute, but taken together they do not suggest systematic or routine abuse. In one case, two vice squad officers in the wee hours of the morning saw two white boys acting suspiciously in a Negro neighborhood. When hailed the boys ran into the basement of a nearby house. The officers chased them into the basement and attempted to take them into custody. Here the stories diverge. The Negro man living in the home says his two sons heard their white friends call for help and, going to the basement, saw two white men struggling with the boys. Not knowing they were police officers (the men were in plain clothes), the sons freed the boys. The police say they identified themselves but that the sons and the father forced them from the house. In any case, the police returned with reinforcements and arrested all three Negroes (by this time the white boys had fled). The Negroes claimed they were hit without cause by the police; the police claim they were hit first, by a Negro boy wielding a pressure cooker; the arrest was on the charge of felonious assault and resisting arrest. Later, the Negro father picketed police headquarters and through a white lawyer brought suit.[11]

The second case involved a Negro itinerant who had built a fishing shack on private property near the estuary. When the owner of the property complained, two officers responded. On being approached, the Negro man reached for a piece of wood. The police said he swung it at them threateningly, and they shot him (not fatally); the man later denied having threatened the officers.

In the third, the police received a report of a boy trying to steal a

11. See *Flatlands* (a militant Negro newspaper), Vol. I, No. 4 (April 23–May 6, 1966) for an account of the incident from the point of view of the victim.

car. They went to the street and saw a white boy run into a house. Thinking he might be the culprit, they ran after him and knocked at the door of the house. The father who answered claimed the police pushed by him and dragged the boy from the house. The police claim — and say the boy's own statement supports their version — he was not dragged out but left peacefully.

There have been other cases. The police response is to point to their internal disciplinary procedures, which, they believe, are adequate to handle such complaints. The internal affairs section, consisting of two officers, reports directly to a deputy chief. In 1965 it received 160 complaints of all kinds against officers; it sustained the charge against the officer in 41.5 per cent of the cases. (Another 264 "miscellaneous incidents" were heard that were deemed not sufficiently important to warrant investigation.) Fifty of the complaints charged "unnecessary force"; four of these were sustained. The previous year 33 complaints of unnecessary force were heard, and four were sustained. A sustained complaint is sent to the chief and from him to the officer's immediate superior, who is asked to recommend punishment. The recommendation is returned to the chief for approval (he often increases the punishment because immediate superiors, in the opinion of the internal affairs section, tend to be "lenient"). He can only reprimand the officer; suspension or dismissal requires the approval of the city manager. The officer is usually not allowed to confront or question his accuser; by the same token, the accuser is not told of the disposition of his complaint unless he specifically requests it.

Civil rights leaders believe this procedure is inadequate. They distrust the objectivity of police officers investigating their own colleagues and have demanded an outside review board of some form. (The details are in Chapter 8.) The police officers, on the other hand, believe internal affairs is too strict and takes too many complaints too seriously. Every patrolman interviewed felt internal affairs was "unfair". One said:

> The majority of officers think . . . that 99 per cent of all complaints are unsubstantiated and they feel the internal affairs section sustains a

lot of them just to show outside groups that they're doing their job. This job, police work, isn't much. I wonder why I'm in it sometimes. But it's nothing—but nothing—if the department doesn't back you up.

The civil rights leaders argue that it is the attitudes of the department leadership more than its policies that must be changed. They believe the police have taken a "get tough" posture, that they refuse to admit errors, and that they rally political support among white conservatives in order to defeat critics and proposals for change. One attorney claimed that before the Oakland police were reformed in the mid-1950's, there were frequent cases of police brutality; indeed, a committee of the state legislature held a hearing in Oakland on the matter. One Negro won a damage suit against two officers charged with having beaten him. During the early reform years, however, cases of police brutality (according to the attorney, whose office has handled many) fell dramatically — "from an average of one a month to less than one a year." [12] Then a new chief, while still continuing the professionalization of the department, began to encourage, in the lawyer's words, a "get tough" policy that resulted in new complaints of "harassment."

Many police officers agreed that there had been these policy changes but argued that there were good reasons for them. Under the early reform administration, the crime level was fairly stable and there was little civil rights agitation. In 1960, when the new chief took office, "all hell broke loose," as one captain told an interviewer. "Crime began to shoot up, the civil rights movement became very militant, and student activists began to take over at Berkeley," the captain continued. The new chief "felt these things were morally wrong and would say so, publicly." Many, probably most, police officers agreed completely with the chief's public statements,[13] though a few felt it would have been better to say nothing in order to

12. See also the newspaper account of the hearings conducted by the California State Advisory Committee to the United States Civil Rights Commission: *Oakland Tribune*, May 26, 1966.

13. One police captain was quoted as having said in a speech to a business organization that cries of police brutality are part of a "conspiracy against law and order" and that "nearly all critics of police are from the radical left." *Oakland Tribune*, May 19, 1966.

avoid becoming an easy target for civil rights leaders who attacked the chief as the "tool of the white power structure." The chief's personality did not permit him to remain silent in the face of what he saw as a willful flouting of the law and an organized refusal to support the police despite their manifest accomplishments in ending corruption, modernizing the department, and recruiting college-trained officers. Besides, the chief had his own problems in the department. Many officers disliked him as "too strict" and "arbitrary"; in addition, he was then fighting a long, and ultimately inconclusive, internal political struggle over the assignment of men to the inspector's division. The rank-and-file support he had lost on administrative issues could be regained, in part, by firmly and publicly supporting his men on operational matters.

By 1966 this chief had retired and his place was taken by a former deputy chief. Though less given to public statements than his predecessor, he, like most senior officers, was dismayed by what appeared to be an absence of any community response to department initiatives designed to meet criticisms of police-community relations. A seven-man community relations section had been organized and its men regularly attended community meetings. The internal affairs section, in the opinion of the officers, dealt strictly with officers who had complaints brought against them. In the winter of 1965–66 and again in the spring of 1966 thousands of copies of a letter from the chief were distributed to individuals and organizations in the city, informing them how to make complaints — by phone, letter, or in person — regarding police misconduct. A form was provided on which complaints could be submitted. A community relations training program was maintained, including eleven hours devoted to the subject in the recruit school. A police baseball league was organized, a committee of police officers and clergymen was formed, and police officers were sent into the public schools to give talks. An effort was made to intensify recruitment of Negroes as officers (there were sixteen Negroes on the force of 661 men in January 1967 or 4 per cent of the total), but the police complained that very few Negroes could be found who both wanted to be officers and could pass the stiff entrance requirements. And in August 1965 a directive was sent to all officers ordering them to refrain from using language that "has a derogatory connotation" in dealing with minority group members; specifically, the men were instructed not to use these words: boy, spade, jig, nigger, blue, smoke, coon, spook, head hunter, jungle bunny, boogie, stud, burr head, cat, black boy, black, shine, ape, spick, Mau Mau.[14]

None of the programs seemed to impress the civil rights leaders. The members of the community relations section were regarded, in the words of one NAACP officer, as "just glorified messenger boys";[15] the internal affairs section was suspect because the "police were investigating the police"; the recruitment program did not succeed because "they didn't try hard enough" or Negroes "distrusted the police"; the human relations training was "inadequate." Above all, the police were "too defensive" and a "sacred cow." Most officers believed the Negroes were simply being unduly sensitive. One thoughtful sergeant, with long experience in certain community relations problems, explained it this way to an interviewer:

> [Negroes] simply live in a social situation that produces the most contact with the police. Furthermore, Negroes can't pass off harsh police behavior. If a police officer speaks roughly to you, you are sufficiently secure in your own social position to pass it off and simply say to yourself, "that dumb, fat-mouthed cop," and then forget it. The Negro can't pass it off. He's not so secure. He feels he has been "put down" by the police and he wants to get even. He assumes he's been put down because of his race. Sometimes that might be true, but just as often it's not.

The same policies and training that make some Negroes criticize police handling of routine patrol situations lead them to praise the police for their handling of some critical events. In October 1966 Oakland experienced a major disorder in a Negro area, in and around a high school that had been the object of a boycott organized by a

14. Oakland Police Department memorandum dated August 4, 1965.

15. There is some evidence that this charge was true. In the fiscal year 1965–66, community relations officers attended 357 meetings. Most of these were held by neighborhood groups, which did not discuss police matters. When police matters are raised they are typically requests for more protection or questions about police procedures. Some OPD officers believe the community relations unit should be more aggressive in seeking out potential trouble-spots.

militant civil rights group. Gangs of Negro youths on the street and in the school building began smashing windows and throwing rocks at cars. Five teachers and several students were assaulted; business places near the school were attacked; a convalescent home was hit with firebombs; passing cars were stoned.[16] Some Negro leaders claim the disorder started because of a rumor that a Negro girl was subjected to unnecessary force when arrested near the scene of the boycott (the girl was later convicted of having assaulted a police officer).

The police blamed the disorder on school officials who failed to call in the police when the disturbances began, thinking they could handle it themselves, and on television newsmen who set up cameras at the scene to film (and, in the opinion of the police, encourage) Negroes congregating and protesting. About 125 officers responded; over the three-day period, they arrested about eighty persons and confiscated a number of Molotov cocktails. The police strategy was to avoid mass arrests; the assembly was not declared unlawful; only individuals were arrested for specific and observed offenses. An assistant district attorney was on the scene with the police to advise on legal issues. A command post was set up on top of a building and the area cordoned off. A Negro leader who had played a key role in organizing the boycott said later to an interviewer that in the ensuing riot, which he denied was caused by the boycott, "the police behaved admirably." In the past, he said, he had seen the police react by simply trying to drive the people off the street; in this case, "They played it very cool." Both police and Negro leaders alike agreed that it was the tight administrative control and extended training of the police that in this instance enabled them to function in an effective, quasi-military manner.

In a later instance, however, this same military-like control led to police actions that were widely criticized in some circles. In October 1967 several thousand antiwar demonstrators attempted to block

16. *Oakland Tribune,* October 19 to October 21, 1966. Conditions in the area before the disturbance are described in William L. Nicholls II, *The Castlemont Survey* (Berkeley: University of California Survey Research Center, July 1966). The boycott was aimed at six high schools and eleven junior high schools; serious disorders occurred at only one high school.

access to an army induction center in Oakland. The police asked the mob to disperse; it refused, and the police formed a wedge and moved into the demonstrators, swinging billy clubs. Several persons required hospital treatment. Some praised the police action as being "swift and effective"; others criticized it as involving excessive force. The press reported as among the critics one or two police officers from neighboring cities, who argued that a wedge tactic is inappropriate because it does not allow the mob to disperse, that the clubbing caused needless injuries, and that in any event a club should be applied on the torso and not the head.[17] However one evaluates the police behavior in either the Negro disturbance or the antiwar demonstration, both cases reveal the strong command structure of the department. Sometimes the wrong order may be given, but there is little doubt of the ability of the commanders to give orders.

17. The incident occurred after the research for this book was complete, and thus I can offer no judgment on what happened or what should have happened. A useful account, critical of the police, is in the *Wall Street Journal,* October 20, 1967.

Seven The Service Style

In some communities, the police take seriously all requests for either law enforcement or order maintenance (unlike police with a watchman style) but are less likely to respond by making an arrest or otherwise imposing formal sanctions (unlike police with a legalistic style). The police intervene frequently but not formally. This style is often found in homogeneous, middle-class communities in which there is a high level of apparent agreement among citizens on the need for and definition of public order but in which there is no administrative demand for a legalistic style. In these places, the police see their chief responsibility as protecting a common definition of public order against the minor and occasional threats posed by unruly teenagers and "outsiders" (tramps, derelicts, visiting college boys). Though there will be family quarrels, they will be few in number, private in nature, and constrained by general understandings requiring seemly conduct. The middle-class character of such communities makes the suppression of illegal enterprises both easy (they are more visible) and necessary (public opinion will not tolerate them) and reduces the rate of serious crime committed by residents; thus, the police will be freer to concentrate on managing traffic, regulating juveniles, and providing services.

Such a police policy will be called the "service" style, and it can be found especially in Brighton and Nassau County. In such communities, which are not deeply divided along class or racial lines, the police can act as if their task were to estimate the "market" for police services and to produce a "product" that meets the demand. For patrolmen especially, the pace of police work is more leisurely

1. During the first week of June 1965, the Brighton police sent 124 nonadministrative radio messages to patrol cars and the Newburgh police sent 173; the towns are approximately equal in population, but the median income in Brighton is twice that in Newburgh. Furthermore, a substantially higher fraction of the Newburgh

(there are fewer radio messages per tour of duty than in a community with a substantial lower class)[1] and the community is normally peaceful, thus apparent threats to order are more easily detected. Furthermore, the citizenry expects its police officers to display the same qualities as its department store salesmen, local merchants, and public officials — courtesy, a neat appearance, and a deferential manner. Serious matters — burglaries, robberies, assaults — are of course taken seriously and thus "suspicious" persons are carefully watched or questioned. But with regard to minor infractions of the law, arrests are avoided when possible (the rates at which traffic tickets are issued and juveniles referred to Family Court will be much lower than in legalistic departments) but there will be frequent use of informal, nonarrest sanctions (warnings issued to motorists, juveniles taken to headquarters or visited in their homes for lectures).

Because the two departments which most clearly — and, to some extent, by their own admission — display the "service" style are Nassau and Brighton, one might suppose that they are merely watchman-style police departments with a different, less divided, or more demanding clientele: prosperous suburbanites want to be left alone with respect to their own minor indiscretions, to have "undesirables" kept away, and the peace maintained. To some extent this is true, but it is not the whole story. The Albany Police Department, if transplanted to Nassau, probably would not — and certainly without major internal changes, could not — begin to serve this new and different constituency in accordance with its demands. Those matters about which the Nassau police believe, no doubt rightly, that Nassau residents feel strongly — residential burglaries, teenage narcotics, juvenile misconduct, personal and courteous "service" — are best dealt with by specialized police units and a certain type of officer. Creating these units and recruiting and training these officers would alter fundamentally the character of the Albany force in ways described below.

---

calls (8.9 per cent) were for "crimes in progress" than of the Brighton calls (3.2 per cent).

The Organizational Context

It is more relevant to ask why or in what ways the Nassau and Brighton departments, which are composed of honest and well-trained men, do not behave like their counterparts in Oakland and Highland Park. With respect to some matters — maintaining good records, insisting on good police behavior — they do, but for them to have the same style as their western counterparts they would have to intensify traffic enforcement, use more formal and, from the point of view of the young person, more punitive means in handling juveniles, arrest drunks on sight, and neglect no laws on grounds that they are too trivial to be enforced. This would not require, as would the Albany to Nassau transplantation, a change in manpower — the Brighton officers could easily function in the Highland Park department and the Nassau officers in the Oakland department. It would require, however, a change in administrative policies. And, if the Nassau police had to face the Oakland problems — very high crime rates, a large lower-class population, conflict with organized Negroes — they might very likely adopt many, if not all, of the latter department's policies. The important point is that the Nassau department could adopt many of those policies now, especially with respect to traffic and juveniles, but it does not.

The fact that Nassau maintains a service style is all the more striking considering its size. With 3,200 members, one might expect that it would necessarily have many bureaucratic characteristics and that the administrative policies necessary to manage a large bureaucracy — a multiplication of reports, well-defined chains of command, the development of statistical measures of performance — would lead to emphasis at the patrol level on producing large numbers of whatever can be measured (arrests, tickets, and so on), "looking good on paper," handling situations uniformly "by the book," and keeping costs down. Though this sort of thing exists, it is less than one might expect.

The reason is that the Nassau department, especially in recent years, has deliberately adopted many practices that would institutionalize the service rather than the legalistic style. The ultimate motivation for this is political, not in the partisan sense, but in the sense of having regard for the opinion of the community. More immediately, however, these practices aim at keeping the department "small" and close to the people, emphasizing community and public relations, maintaining the best and the shiniest of buildings and equipment, and developing various control procedures that make service a major concern to officers at every rank. And community concerns over some specific law enforcement problem are met, and often anticipated, by the department by creating a specialized unit to deal with it.

Nassau's patrol force, and all its detectives except those in specialized squads, operate out of eight precinct stations scattered about the county. Specialized investigative units, plus all staff services, operate in the main headquarters building at the county seat. The eight precincts are not simply administrative conveniences, however; they are designed in part to keep the patrol force "local." When a citizen calls for police services, he calls his precinct; if a patrol car is required, the precinct calls the central radio dispatcher at headquarters. If the citizen calls headquarters directly by mistake, he is referred back to his precinct. Patrolmen work out of their precinct stations and, although the county is heavily residential, consisting mostly of low-density buildings, nearly 40 per cent of the precinct posts are manned by patrolmen walking foot beats. "Professional" police doctrine — and certainly the doctrine operative in Oakland — calls for motor patrols in all but the most congested areas, such as business centers and large apartment projects. When asked about the reliance on foot patrols, a senior officer explained that "the villages expect these foot posts . . . The villages would complain if we removed the foot men." [2]

Nearly every precinct station is of recent construction and all are immaculately maintained. A citizen entering is confronted by a desk where a lieutenant, sergeant, and patrolman are on duty (when a citizen enters the Oakland or Syracuse police headquarters, he faces a bank of automatic elevators). The room is air conditioned;

2. Some foot patrolmen are being shifted to scooters.

no other room, including that of the precinct commander, is similarly equipped. One precinct commander told an interviewer, "The air conditioning is to keep the citizen happy and the desk-officer cool-headed." The commander meets once a month with the local village leaders to discuss any local police problems. The needs of these groups are taken very much into account. One village, thinking of asking the NCPD to patrol its area and abandoning its own police force, told the NCPD, as reported by a senior officer who spoke to the local officials, that "They wanted to be sure they had as policemen, men who understood the special problems of a rich community." The NCPD, according to one official, assured them that it would "give them well-screened men who would understand their special needs."

Though understanding the "special needs" of a group may lead to leniency in such police-invoked actions as drunk arrests, it also leads, at least in principle, to strictness in handling citizen complaints such as those about the increase in residential burglaries. The problem is that burglary is one of the most difficult crimes to solve, no matter how efficient and determined the police department — there are usually no witnesses, few clues, and often not even a good estimate of when the crime occurred. The department does what it can — detectives follow up on every case, there is a specialized burglary detail which sometimes organizes stake-outs (that is, places a property or a suspect under surveillance), and in addition there is a "burglary patrol." During 1965 this patrol, operating in high-risk areas of the county, stopped and searched over twelve thousand vehicles and questioned over fourteen thousand "suspicious persons." Eighty-six arrests resulted, but only nine were for burglary.

On matters that are not serious crimes — that is, on most matters the patrolman deals with — the service orientation of the department is clear. At the time of this research, serious juvenile crimes (felonies, if committed by adults) were handled by the detectives; other matters were turned over to the Juvenile Aid Bureau for, in most cases, nonarrest treatment. In 1965 the JAB handled 2,711 such cases and less than 5 per cent were taken to Family Court. Most were handled through family interviews. Likewise with drunks —

though there are 2,869 liquor licenses in effect in the county, only 107 arrests on public intoxication charges were made in 1965 for a rate one sixth that of bone-dry Highland Park. And there is no traffic ticket quota. Though an "Enforcement Index" is used to plan the traffic enforcement strategy by selecting high-accident-rate areas for special attention, there is no general pressure to produce tickets like that found in Syracuse or Oakland. Perhaps more important, providing service to motorists is an important part of traffic work — of the three highway patrol vehicles regularly assigned to the busy Long Island Expressway, for example, two are specially equipped as "assistance vehicles" and in 1965 they provided services to 5,367 motorists who experienced engine trouble, ran out of gas, or the like.[3]

In Nassau, "public education" is an integral part of law enforcement. The NCPD increased the size of its narcotics squad from two in 1962 to forty-eight in 1966. Narcotics arrests increased correspondingly, from 70 in 1962 to 174 in 1965. Knowing that not every user can be detected or every pusher arrested, the commissioner assigned twenty-six of the forty-eight men to "public information" work — giving lectures, organizing displays, and the like. This serves two purposes: it alerts the public to the symptoms of narcotics use and thus produces some investigative leads, and it makes the community more aware of what the police are doing about a matter of deep community concern.

The "community relations orientation" is a central feature of the department's training, evaluation, and leadership. The commissioner put it frankly to an interviewer: "I believe very strongly that you have to sell modern police practices to the community. You have to have community support . . . I think it's important to have outside teachers and speakers come in . . . We want the civilian point of view . . . You have to sell police services to the public at large."

A public relations man is assistant to the commissioner; he and his staff, during 1965, escorted 139 groups through headquarters, pro-

3. There are in addition six patrol cars assigned to precincts, which work the expressway.

vided over one thousand lectures at public meetings, issued nearly 200 press releases, and distributed nearly three quarters of a million pieces of literature. A separate community relations bureau works especially with minority groups. A Police Boys' Club program operates under the full-time direction of a senior officer; it claims twenty thousand members organized into thirty clubs. At no charge to the community, twenty-four patrolmen are assigned full-time by the NCPD to provide supervision of these clubs. (That is enough men to handle all the foot beats in almost any precinct for one watch.)

More important than these organized programs are the efforts to get patrolmen to display the service attitude. As one precinct commander put it: "The wealthier people in Nassau County know we are servants and they demand service. The kind of service they expect is prompt appearance and frequent, high visibility of policemen on patrol in their areas."

An inspector agreed and indicated he was on the lookout for men who did not measure up: "Today, how you come across [to the public] is so significant . . . If I get five or more letters [of complaint] on a man, he's had it . . . How we look to the public, our image, is crucial."

This means, above all, being courteous. Another inspector said that "The men should accept abuse; this should have nothing to do with whether he [a citizen] gets a ticket or not." A traffic patrolman agreed that this, indeed, was the rule. "Maintaining self-control," he said, "is what we are supposed to do if the guy's obnoxious." In a watchman-like department, by contrast, one is expected to maintain self-respect first and self-control, if at all, second.

One way this service rule is enforced is by quarterly evaluation sheets filled out on each officer by his superior. Of the four items on the form in use when this study was made, three referred to relations with the public — cooperation, courtesy, appearance — and only one — dependability — referred explicitly to performance of duty.[4] These ratings are not the most important control device, however. Every officer interviewed in Nassau spoke, in one way or another,

4. According to the NCPD, the evaluation form now has nine rating areas and the categories have been somewhat revised.

of the NCPD being "tough on discipline." The man who created the modern NCPD, John M. Beckmann, was commissioner from 1945 until 1961. The "Old Dutchman," as he was often called, was a strict disciplinarian. "He had quite a temper," one lieutenant said, "and wasn't afraid to use it." Both Beckmann and the present commissioner were and are unpopular with many men on the force. The present commissioner defended the strictness of his rules on the grounds that it prevents corruption and laxity and makes for uniformity; a subordinate, chafing under the toughness, conceded that at least "You know where you stand."

To the commissioner, corruption begins with accepting a free ten-cent cup of coffee. "Dishonesty to even the smallest degree will eventually get you," he told an interviewer. The rules against solicitation and accepting gifts are strictly enforced. The commissioner himself neither drinks nor smokes, is a regular church-goer, and expects his men to lead exemplary private lives.

Discipline is formally exercised by a four-man board headed by the chief inspector (there is no civilian review board). The NCPD is not reluctant to demote or suspend officers for misconduct. One patrolman was accused of rape, but the grand jury felt it lacked evidence sufficient to indict him. It did request that he be "severely disciplined," and the commissioner dismissed him (to the disgust of many officers, who felt the commissioner had taken in their opinion, a "slut's word . . . over that of a cop"). A detective having, while on duty, an affair with a bookie's wife was broken, after departmental investigation, to the rank of patrolman. And in 1963 a burglary ring of seven officers was found operating within the department. The commissioner acted swiftly to dismiss the men; they were convicted and sent away for long prison terms. The supervisory personnel in the affected section of the department were reshuffled.

In 1965 the department dealt with 161 disciplinary cases; in 1964, 201. Most of these resulted in either a reprimand (125 in 1965) or a fine (in 1965 they totalled 218 days pay). In 1965 five men were discharged, three allowed to retire. Many patrolmen feel this discipline is both unfair and too severe. Several complained that the department accepts and acts on anonymous complaints by requiring the man to write a memo describing his actions on a given day and then, after further inquiries, deciding whether the complaint is justified and even whether the memo raises other issues for which the man might be taken to task. The system keeps the men alert to the sensibilities of the people they deal with, but at a price. One patrolman said, "We only want the same rights as the criminals get, that's all." Essentially the same system, and the same complaints, are to be found in Oakland; the difference is that in Oakland, the most common major allegation is "excessive force" brought by a Negro, while in Nassau it is more likely to be discourtesy or inattention to duty brought by a white.

The department tries to hire officers who will not produce citizen complaints. In 1967 the salary, including holiday compensation, for a first-year patrolman was $7,403; after five years, he will earn $9,138. Sergeants and third-year detectives received over $10,000; a captain, nearly $13,000; the commissioner, $26,189. Over 40 per cent of the men appointed patrolmen in April 1966 had some college training; 15 per cent had two or more years. College courses are offered during the evenings in the department's training center and the men are encouraged to attend. All this, plus the modern equipment of the department — a bomb disposal truck, a fleet of coastal patrol boats, closed-circuit television in the jail, a crime laboratory — cost money. Per capita police expenditures in Nassau are the second highest in the state, excluding New York City.

Competition for promotions is stressed. As the commissioner told an interviewer: "We fight hard against feelings of security and pension-motivated people. Everyone on this force should be aspiring to be commissioner."

A lieutenant felt this pressure. "I always take the exam," he told an interviewer, even though "I don't think I stand a chance of making captain . . . It doesn't look good if you don't."

Brighton, a much smaller community, displays to a great extent the same service style. Being small, Brighton, like Highland Park, makes many demands on its police for noncriminal services. In 1965 the Brighton police department received 7,677 citizen requests for service. Of these, 1,450 (19 per cent) were for "house checks" (checking the homes of people away on trips to make sure they had not been broken into), 978 (13 per cent) called for escort duties of various sorts (usually guarding money being sent to the bank by local businesses), another 623 (8 per cent) had to do with lost or injured animals, and 539 (7 per cent) required taking a report of a traffic accident. Thus, about half -- 47 per cent — of all requests on the Brighton police were for clearly noncriminal matters.[5]

The editor of the town paper — a weekly that features stories on antique sales and local architecture and is itself housed in an elegantly restored eighteenth-century building — told an interviewer what he felt the community expected of its police:

> The police in a town like Brighton are there mostly to handle emotional and psychological problems of the families and to handle traffic. We out here are more concerned that a family may tear itself apart from some problem than we are that some burglar takes $100 from a gas station. At this, I think the Brighton police are pretty tactful.

Though many officers can barely afford to, most somehow manage to live in the town. The consequences of these local ties and the service orientation of the men were explained by a senior officer:

> You have to know the local people. The State Police are not liked in this area. One of the reasons is that they cover eleven counties. They can come into town and set up a roadblock and start inspecting cars or, if they're running short on their traffic enforcement quota near the end of the month, they'll park down on Monroe Avenue near the stop

5. Brighton police reports contain unusually full accounts of what the responding officer did on these calls. One recorded a response to a "noisy dog" complaint. The patrolman located the dog and found where it belonged; the owners not being home, he left a message with the babysitter to tell them to keep it quiet and then called back later to make sure the babysitter had delivered the message. Calls to provide a service, rather than to take a report of a crime or deal with real or potential trouble, accounted for about half the radio dispatches sent out in a one-week period by the police in Brighton, Highland Park, and Nassau and for about a third of the calls sent out in Albany, Newburgh, and Syracuse. Oakland was in between these two groups. (Compiled from radio logs and complaint records of local police departments for the week June 3–9, 1965.)

light and just wait there until somebody drives through and then give them a ticket. These men don't care; they're here one day and the next they're in some other part of the state. They don't have any ties here.

The Brighton chief is concerned about traffic but, although he maintains a "norm" for ticket issuing, he has not induced his men to produce tickets at more than two thirds the rate of the legalistic department in Highland Park. Partly, the reason is politics — it is possible in Brighton but almost impossible in Highland Park to bring influence on the police regarding "overly zealous" traffic enforcement. But partly it is the attitude of the police themselves. As the chief wrote in a letter to the author, "It is a good idea to have a norm, but the norm should not be too high." And special circumstances should be taken into account. For minor infractions, such as faulty equipment on the car, a warning ticket is issued, which is forgotten if the defect is corrected. When police felt obliged to lower the speed limit on a straight, thinly populated road after a car hit a cow, they realized that the new limit (35 miles per hour) would be regarded as unreasonable by motorists accustomed to driving at the old limit (50 miles per hour). Accordingly, the officers were instructed to arrest only those driving over 50 and simply to warn those driving between 35 and 50.

In handling juveniles, a similar policy operates — unlike watchman-style departments, the police do not overlook violations of the law but, unlike legalistic departments, they are less likely to handle those infractions by taking the person to court. A Brighton detective explained the department's approach: "If we can possibly do it, we try to avoid an arrest. We don't want to send [them] into the courts. We try to handle it right here in the department. We bring the parents in here, and usually they're cooperative once we bring the situation to them."

Serious cases will be taken to court, but otherwise such action is seen as of little value — the court is "too busy" and anyway the juvenile will probably receive probation, which, in the eyes of many officers, is "nothing — you're supposed to come in, at first, maybe every two weeks and tell the probation officer what you've been doing, what your grades are like." A typical youthful offense in Brighton is larceny. In 1965 there were over 300 larcenies reported; sixty-three arrests resulted, twenty of which were of juveniles almost all of whom were released with no court action.

This informality and apparent leniency do not indicate that the police in a town like Brighton ignore such matters; on the contrary, owing to the greater visibility of misconduct in a "quiet" town and the lower tolerance for disorder among its residents, the police become involved in many situations — especially involving juveniles — that would be ignored in a larger or more heterogeneous community. For example, four boys who followed a girl into her driveway and "rocked her car" and made indecent gestures were picked up by the police on disorderly conduct charges. Though they signed confessions no charges were filed. Another group of teenagers were picked up because they had "stayed out all night" (a girl was with them); they were released to their parents. That same year four boys were arrested for annoying a resident by "ringing his doorbell"; they, too, were released without a court appearance. It is hard to imagine any of these matters leading to police involvement in larger cities. It should be noted that all of these incidents were counted as cases of "disorderly conduct" on the police records. They are obviously not comparable with similarly labelled big-city events in which, typically, an officer has been assaulted or a serious street fight has occurred. Of the 72 disorderly conduct bookings in Brighton during one year (May 1965–July 1966), only seven involved a fight; 58 involved primarily annoying others by language, manner, or action; the remainder involved miscellaneous offenses.

These considerations suggest that community size may be an important variable in police behavior. That it is not a controlling variable is evident from the great differences among Amsterdam, Brighton, Highland Park, and Newburgh. However, even though the Nassau County police display, and speak of themselves as having, a service orientation, they are nevertheless a large, bureaucratic organization serving over a million persons spread over a far-flung county. One might conjecture that such an organization would have to treat its clients more formally, more according to rule, whatever its animating spirit — that it could not give "personal service" to people it did not know and in violation of rules it must have for its own internal management.

Yet the arrest rates for disorderly conduct and drunkenness are significantly higher in Brighton than in Nassau. This, of course, might be the result of unknown differences between the two communities. A better test of whether a large, specialized police force is necessarily more likely to handle situations by arrest can be found in Nassau County itself where there are over twenty independent village police forces operating in those areas not patrolled by the NCPD. These villages are, if anything, of higher socioeconomic status than the county as a whole — they often are "estate"villages of very wealthy residents. Presumably, if intimacy or wealth or both lead to leniency, it should be evident in places such as Old Brookville, King's Point, or Cove Neck. Table 12 compares the arrest rate for two kinds of offenses — those involving breaches of the peace (drunkenness, disorderly conduct, assault, driving while intoxicated) and those involving theft (petty larceny and auto theft) — for areas served by the NCPD and areas served by small, independent village forces. To control roughly for the effects of population characteristics, the areas are grouped by median family income and per cent nonwhite, as of 1960. Because not all areas served by the NCPD could be matched with demographically comparable areas served by independent forces, and vice versa, not every village is included in the table.

For every community type, the NCPD arrest rate for breaches of the peace is significantly lower than for the corresponding independent village departments. For thefts, however, the NCPD rate is higher for three of the five community types. There are several possible explanations. Perhaps the NCPD, by providing more intensive patrol, prevents crimes from occurring and thus reduces the need for arrest. But it is not clear that the NCPD patrols an area, especially a higher-status "estate" area, more intensively than a local force; indeed, local communities often resist proposals to use NCPD patrol services on the grounds that the local force keeps a sharper watch on things — in several cases, it is claimed that every house

Table 12. Arrest rates for breaches of the peace and thefts, 1965, for Nassau County communities, by socioeconomic class and type of police organization.

Community type[a]	Arrests per 100,000 population for breaches of the peace[b]	Arrests per 100,000 population for thefts[c]
White, over $11,000		
NCPD: 5 places, pop. = 38,451	42	177
IND: 3 places, pop. = 29,644	68	67
White, $9,000–$10,900		
NCPD: 5 places, pop. = 98,074	60	43
IND: 3 places, pop. = 53,512	133	19
White, $7,500–$8,999		
NCPD: 14 places, pop. = 363,263	85	34
IND: 3 places, pop. = 76,975	422	136
White, under $7,500[d]		
NCPD: 4 places, pop. = 136,175	142	60
IND: 1 place, pop. = 29,000	2,217	234
Significantly nonwhite, $7,500 or less		
NCPD: 2 places, pop. = 33,996, 14.5 per cent nonwhite	182	194
IND: 2 places, pop. = 62,240, 16 per cent nonwhite	810	124

Sources: Arrest figures from local police authorities. Nassau County Police Department arrests are tabulated for each village where arrest made.

Population figures used for rates derived from 1965 special census, reported in *Population, 1960–1965*, Nassau County Planning Commission, July, 1966.

[a] "White" communities are those which, in 1960, had a white population that was 92 per cent or more of the total. Income figures are median family income as reported in the 1960 census. "Significantly nonwhite" communities are those which, in 1960, were 8 per cent or more nonwhite.

[b] "Breach of the peace" arrests are total arrests for drunkenness, disorderly conduct, assault, and driving while intoxicated.

[c] "Theft" arrests are total arrests for petty larceny and auto theft.

[d] The very high arrest rate for the independently policed white community under $7,500 exaggerates the actual amount of criminality there. A large, transient population is found in the city during the summers but is not, of course, reported in the census of residents. This rate should be deflated by a large but unknown factor to obtain a "true" arrest rate.

in town is inspected twice during each eight-hour shift.[6] In any case, disorderly conduct and assault are rarely premeditated offenses likely to be deterred by the knowledge that the police are around. And finally, if drunken driving is "prevented" by police patrol, why isn't auto theft prevented as well — presumably a sober thief is more likely than a drunken motorist to take into account the likelihood of apprehension.

Another explanation seems more satisfactory. Holding population characteristics constant, a police department is more likely to take seriously, by making arrests, problems of order maintenance when it is directly exposed to community concerns for public order than when, by its size or detachment, it is insulated from them. In earlier chapters we saw that though the highly political watchman-style departments generally made fewer arrests than the nonpolitical legalistic departments, they did make more arrests in situations of police-initiated order maintenance — partly because such charges are convenient "catch-alls" and partly because (except for felonies) public order is the primary concern of such departments.

A small, locally controlled department is more sensitive than a large one to whatever values are dominant in the community, and in middle-class suburbs these values presumably attach great importance to order. Although it may generally avoid arrests, such a department will make them if the peace is breached, especially if by someone who, being an "outsider," is regarded as unconstrained by community norms and, in addition, lacks a local family or friends to whom he can be taken for disposition. By contrast, the county-wide Nassau department, though close to the villages, is not governed by them. One precinct may include several villages. There is less pressure to keep the local peace or, to put it differently, the word "local" does not have the same meaning. Furthermore, a person who to a village is an "outsider" is to the county police simply a citizen — he is not necessarily presumed to be immune to communal norms because he lives in the neighboring village rather than in the one where his infraction occurred. Finally, the county police, if they are so inclined, can take a man (or see to it that he gets taken) home,

6. See *New York Times,* June 18, 1967.

at least within a given precinct, even though home is not in the village where the problem occurred. Thus a small, service-style department may arrest more persons in order maintenance situations because it regards order as more important and more precarious and because it has fewer nonarrest alternatives open to it. Being local, of course, the village department may show more favoritism than the county-wide department, but favoritism and leniency are not the same thing. This explanation, which, of course, is only a hypothesis, is strengthened somewhat by considering the special case of assault. Unlike drunkenness, assault produces a victim and unlike disorderly conduct an assault arrest usually requires the victim's cooperation in signing a complaint. For infractions resulting in a written complaint the differences between NCPD and village police arrests are fewer — if assault arrests are omitted from breaches of the peace tabulated in Table 12, the difference between the NCPD and the independent departments *increases* in four of the five categories.

Theft is a different matter. The community has not been outraged; rather, a particular individual has suffered a loss. That loss must be rectified, accounts squared, so to speak, and for that the reassertion of community controls is not enough. An arrest — which may result either in court action or, more likely, in charges being dismissed after restitution has been made, or the use of juvenile probation — is clearly more in order. Furthermore, a large specialized department is better able to detect thieves. Here, then, there is less difference between the NCPD and local forces. In three of the five categories, the NCPD arrests at a *higher* rate for thefts; in the two where it does not, the differences in rates are less for theft than for breaches of the peace.[7]

Some Consequences

It is often alleged that the police display unjust favoritism toward community notables by "letting them off" while cracking down on

7. A full test of the hypotheses suggested in this comparison of the NCPD and village forces would require a study of individual incidents and the nature of the police response in each. Such data were not available.

"nobodies." But although arrest statistics give the race of the offender, they do not give his income, status, or influence. Thus, evaluating the quality of law enforcement with respect to notables and nobodies is even harder, if that is possible, than evaluating it with respect to Negroes. But it is not simply the facts that are unclear; the meaning of justice or fairness is as ambiguous for notables as for Negroes. If having a black skin is an empirical clue to a class status that, though unjust in any particular case, in general indicates a higher probability that one has committed an offense, then having a rich and assured manner is an empirically useful indicator of a class status that increases the probability that one has *not* committed an offense.

Furthermore, because the patrolman is primarily concerned about maintaining order rather than simply enforcing the law, he must be especially alert for clues that will indicate the likely *future* course of action of the parties to a dispute or the perpetrator of a disorderly act. He must handle these matters in a way that, ideally, produces rough substantive justice; in addition, he will be concerned with other values — for one, deterrence; for another, peace. It is not unreasonable to suppose that a high-status person is deterred more easily than a low-status person from repeating an infraction and persuaded to cooperate in reestablishing the public peace. After all, a high-status person is less likely to commit an infraction or disturb the peace in the first place;[8] he belongs to a milieu in which peace and order (or if you wish, conformity) are highly valued; and he has a reputation for "respectability" to maintain. For all these reasons, a patrolman might be forgiven for concluding that, if deterrence and maintaining the peace are among his objectives, taking a high-status drunk home to his wife will prove as effective as giving a low-status drunk a night in jail. Of course, a high-status person who has committed a serious crime — a major theft, for example, or

8. It is sometimes alleged that traffic violations are disproportionally a middle-class offense. The only American study of which I am aware, done in Evanston, Illinois, concludes that "Traffic violators do not appear to possess significantly higher social status than the population at large" (nor, for that matter, a significantly lower social status). H. Laurence Ross, "Traffic Law Violation: A Folk Crime," *Social Problems,* 8 (Winter, 1960–61), pp. 231–241, esp. p. 240.

a felonious assault — must also be arrested: the cost to the community has been high, private vengeance must be averted, important laws must be upheld, and the risk of adverse publicity from giving such a person a break must be avoided.

It is difficult, of course, to distinguish between police behavior motivated by a careful consideration of what deterrence requires and behavior arising out of a self-seeking desire to cater to the powerful or to avoid their sanctions. It is a nice question whether, or to what extent, police motives — as opposed to police actions — are relevant. If under certain conditions a warning reduces the chance of recidivism, and if one empirically valid measure of the appropriate condition is the status of the suspect, then warning such persons and arresting others may, statistically, serve a generally valued social function, whatever the motives of the particular officer. Indeed, that a warning should sometimes be used is explicitly recognized by law: the juvenile code of many states permits police officers to warn certain juveniles who have committed an offense no different from that which, if committed by an adult, would theoretically require an arrest. If having the status of a juvenile is properly relevant, is there any reason in principle why having the status of a "decent citizen" should not be relevant?

One reason that such a status could not be, at least formally, recognized as proper grounds for police leniency is that the general awareness of such distinctions would encourage — indeed, license — persons having the relevant status to break the law. But the police rejoin by arguing that this is exactly what the juvenile law now does — it encourages kids to commit minor offenses knowing they will get off with a warning. And the police may be right. In fact, even if the juvenile law were not written as it is, the police would in most cities give first or second juvenile offenders a break anyway (if they are not "wise guys") because, as with notables, they think "it would be a shame" to give the casual offender a record and because they think that "decent people" who slip up in a way that hurts no one else can be "straightened out" by a warning. In short, the police instinct is to assert that deterrence and forgiveness are objectives equally valid as justice, strictly conceived, and that a reasonable person will know what status can properly be taken into account and what status cannot even though it is difficult, and perhaps undesirable, to put such knowledge in the form of rules.

It is another matter — and a candid officer admits it is another matter — when no reasonable person would find any relationship between one's status and the probability of being deterred. Being a member of the ruling political party, for example, carries with it no obvious grounds for supposing that one is more likely to obey the law than a member of the opposite party, or a member of no party. Here fear of reprisals or common political allegiance or both may lead an officer in a certain city not to ticket a rank-and-file politician. Albany and Newburgh, for example, are highly partisan cities (see Chapter 8) and in neither place was there much chance that a patrolman would knowingly pass out a ticket to a party leader. A former member of the Albany police said that when he stopped a motorist, his first concern was whether the ticket would "bounce." "I always checked to see where they lived and where they worked. This way I could tell whether or not he was a Democrat. You never know if the guy might be a big shot."

In Newburgh, one patrolman told an interviewer that, though he had "ticketed a lawyer once" he would never ticket a city councilman. "In a way, he's your boss, isn't he?" In most of the cities visited, the police were asked what they would do if they saw a car with a very low license plate number (such as "N Y 2," "N Y 3," or "N Y 4") speeding. In some communities, such as Nassau and Syracuse, the answer was equivocal — "It all depends," "Stop it and give it a warning," and the like. In Amsterdam and Newburgh, the answer was clear: "Mind your own business." Once an Amsterdam officer did give a parking ticket to a car with a comparably prestigious license plate and was later surprised, he told an interviewer, that his action was not reported, with unpleasant consequences, to the chief.

In a legalistic department such as that of Highland Park, on the other hand, a determined and largely successful effort will be made to end what some observers might call favoritism but what the police themselves, in most communities, regard as "common-sense" law enforcement. Before the arrival of the new chief in 1956, Highland Park had what everybody now looks back on as a "sloppy and undisciplined" police department. A former police magistrate, himself highly critical of the new chief's behavior, nonetheless admitted that "fifteen years ago there was virtually no law enforcement in Highland Park." Unlike the Highland Park police today, who, though not zealots, are hardly "sloppy," the police then were thought to countenance ticket-fixing, especially for the customers of the local businessmen who controlled the city government. Soon after the new chief arrived, he called his men into his office and asked them, "What would you do if you were patrolling the downtown area and you caught your wife making a U-turn?" Anyone who did not immediately say, "Give her a ticket," was sharply rebuked. Though it would be absurd to assume that he ever got his men to ticket their wives, he did make it very clear to everyone that, as far as he was concerned, "the law is the law."

The uniform application of the law did not stop with traffic. A high city official, himself a supporter of the new chief, reported later that the chief raided a bingo game in his own church and minor gambling at a carnival held by the Jewish women's society. There was behind-the-scenes criticism of these actions but, as the official told an interviewer, the chief "wouldn't bend."

Where the police department displays the service style, the extent to which personal factors are taken into account in maintaining order and enforcing the law probably lies somewhere between the extremes found in the watchman and legalistic departments. Because such departments serve communities in which the perceived level of tolerable disorder is quite low, the police feel obliged to "do something" about disorderly situations, and that can often lead, at least in small communities, to relatively high arrest rates for offenses involving public disorder. On the other hand, because the police serve a community where, in their opinion, there is general agreement as to the norms that ought to govern public conduct, the police feel that they can use their judgment in a particular case without having to choose, or without being thought to have chosen, between competing standards of order held by different persons or subcultures. And if the community is small in addition, the police are more likely to have information about the character of a large number of citizens and thus some grounds for making a valid judgment about their likely future conduct. Stated another way, the police in a small town may believe that they are treating equals equally even when they do not treat everybody the same (by, for example, an arrest). With their more intimate knowledge of the community, they can make more discriminating judgments about who is equal to whom.[9]

In Brighton, for example, there was a series of incidents involving a Peeping Tom. The police knew the culprit, a minor executive of an important local firm. When such an incident was reported the police would call the man's wife and tell her, "Your husband's at it again." An arrest, they told an interviewer, would be difficult to make because the victim would often be reluctant to sign a complaint, but a serious effort to secure an arrest, to say nothing of the arrest itself, would make public the behavior of the culprit and no doubt cost him his job. The embarrassment of being reported to his wife was punishment enough. On another occasion the police found the daughter of a prominent local citizen staggering drunk down the street at night with practically no clothes on. They brought her to the station and, although she was very abusive, made no arrest. Instead, the police photographed her in her disorderly condition and showed the picture to her parents to convince them of the seriousness of the problem and to induce them to "do something." The incident was kept out of the town newspaper, which ordinarily prints almost all local police news. At the same time, the officers involved were disgusted to encounter a family that "had everything" but could not handle its own children. "Most of these kids could be straightened out at home if the parents only took the time to give them a little discipline," said one officer, "but you don't find that much anymore." Nonetheless, they were sure they had done the

9. Because the inferences about "character" that the police must necessarily make are, in a small community, less dependent on easily discerned external attributes (race, age, and the like), the citizens in such communities should perceive such judgments as unfair less frequently than citizens in large cities where police judgments must be based more on empirical or quasi-statistical generalizations.

right thing, because they had no further trouble with the young lady.

Officers who stop motorists for traffic violations will take into account who is involved, and his attitude, in determining whether a ticket should be issued. One patrolman told an interviewer that if the driver is a doctor or a clergyman, "We just like to warn [them] to slow down for their own good; they may be tired and in a hurry to get home from the hospital."

A traffic ticket once issued in Brighton cannot be fixed — it is a numbered form, all of which must be accounted for to the state. But the police are aware that people who feel themselves unjustly ticketed will try to intervene with the judge or with other town leaders. A senior police officer explained what usually happens:

> I can't do anything about a traffic ticket. The judge, he can . . . do anything he wants with it . . . I'm glad. I'd just as soon not get involved in that. I will write a note to the judge asking for leniency in certain cases. I had one involving . . . a big political figure . . . When it came in I got a phone call saying that, "Do you know that one of your men just ticketed X's car?" I told him I couldn't do anything about it, but that I would write a letter to the judge explaining what had happened and ask him to go easy. I'm not sure what happened, but I imagine the judge probably dismissed or suspended [the sentence].

A small department may be more sensitive to circumstances of personality and politics, but by the same token this sensitivity need have nothing to do — indeed, it would create problems if it *did* have something to do — with vulgar bribery. A bribe induces an officer to act other than as his duty requires. Its value requires that an officer have something to sell — freedom from an arrest he is otherwise empowered to make — and that a citizen be willing to buy. Ideally, the transaction should be secret; even if higher police officials were willing to tolerate it, they could rarely do so publicly, and few important citizens concerned about their reputation want to be known in a small town as persons who buy special privileges. But keeping secrets in a small town is not easy. More important, it is not necessary — the officer rarely has anything to sell because his superiors expect him to treat "somebodies" differently from "nobodies." A prominent man who is drunk in a public place will, unless he behaves in an extraordinary manner, be taken home or turned over to friends. A shabbily dressed itinerant with no family or friends who commits the same offense will be arrested — there is no place to take him, it is unlikely that embarrassment or a hangover will prove an effective punishment, and he may, lacking a place to stay, hurt himself or endanger others.

Where a service-oriented police department operates in a large community, as in Nassau, the police have less detailed knowledge of personalities and therefore they must rely more on external characteristics. But because the administrator of a service department is particularly fearful of scandal or even controversy, he is strongly motivated to develop rules that insure that his men do not take the "wrong" characteristics into account. In a big department in a big community, anonymity and thus secrecy are possible. Thus, the police may take the wrong characteristics into account for the wrong reasons — as they *do* have something to sell, the possibility of bribery is a constant threat. The NCPD, accordingly, has a tight departmental policy against favoritism — by which is meant avoiding, at least in law enforcement situations where it *can* be avoided, consideration of personal characteristics. As a result many community notables get traffic tickets. The county executive, to whom the police commissioner reports, the district attorney, and the commissioner of welfare have each been stopped and some have been ticketed more than once. When he was interviewed, the commander of the NCPD highway patrol had just discovered his own son had been ticketed; he paid. And a powerful state legislator had his car stopped even though it is known to quite a few officers on the force.

The police do not ordinarily relish such encounters and they are often apprehensive after the event. An important local official who was stopped in Nassau called the nearest precinct station on his mobile telephone as soon as the officer departed in order to complain of being "harassed." The precinct commander backed up the patrolman, though afterwards he told him to "be careful" when dealing with politicians. A judge reports being approached by two officers who had ticketed a politician. They asked if the matter could be "taken care of" so they would not get into trouble. The judge refused and persuaded the officers that they had done the right thing and nothing would happen to them. Nothing did. The fact that the officers came to court indicates, in the judge's opinion, that, other than persuading a judge to give a suspended sentence, there is no way to fix a ticket in the county.

Sometimes drivers offer money to patrolmen. The officers, not surprisingly, denied they would take it but added that they would not arrest a person for attempted bribery unless he were quite explicit and insistent about it. Such charges are hard to prove, they said, and require "wasting a day" in court.[10] When asked what they would do with a proffered ten-dollar bill, most said they would simply give it back and forget about it ("I'd be scared to take a bill because it might be a checkup done by the department"); one bolder officer carries with him stamped envelopes addressed to charities into which he puts, and then mails, any money given to him.

A senior officer in the highway patrol summed up the prevailing view of equality in traffic law enforcement:

> No one can put pressure on me. I've never felt I had to worry about that at all . . . I'm active in my church and a lot of clubs in my neighborhood, and my friends know it and call me up about a ticket. I just tell them, pay it, pay it, it's only five dollars. It's simpler that way. I won't say that no important person has been let off by [a] patrolman. You know and I know that's going to happen from time to time. But I know that a lot of people who are important have got tickets and I know that no pressure is ever put on me . . . to do anything about the ticket. Once it's written, it's in and the only way you could handle it is to face the judge in court.

The service orientation of the department, combined with the efforts made, because of its size, to curtail patrol discretion, contributed to the good relations the NCPD enjoyed with the leaders

10. Cf. Peter M. Blau, *The Dynamics of Bureaucracy* (Chicago: University of Chicago Press, 1955), pp. 148–153, where employees in a federal investigative agency, though themselves above suspicion, were reluctant to bring bribery charges against people who offered them money in exchange for favors.

of the Nassau County Negro community at the time of this research. Of course, departmental policies were not the only reason — demography has made the task easier. The Negro population is only a small fraction of the total[11] and is, in general, so thinly spread (many Negroes are domestic servants living in or near expensive suburban homes) that there are very few concentrations of Negroes sufficiently sizable to produce a ghetto-like atmosphere or to support the bars and nightclubs that would be causes of frequent police intervention.

In 1960 the NCPD arrested 733 Negroes on all charges; five years later, the number was still about the same (804) despite a considerable growth in the Negro population. Some of these were picked up by NCPD detectives who serve almost the entire county, others were arrested by patrolmen who serve about 70 per cent of the area. If every Negro arrested for a misdemeanor or minor offense is included in a Negro arrest rate calculated on the basis of that portion of the Negro population patrolled by the NCPD, the rate (per hundred thousand Negroes) is very low indeed — about 57.8 for intoxication, 196.5 for disorderly conduct, and about 315.0 for third degree assault. These rates are much lower than those for any of the four high-crime cities — again, partly because of the Negro's low population density.

Perhaps because comparatively few Negroes come in contact with the Nassau police, perhaps because the NCPD has succeeded in handling Negroes in a manner that arouses a minimum of hostility, the local Negro leadership is, on the whole, pleased with the police. The chairman of the Long Island chapter of CORE and the president of the Long Island region of the NAACP both publicly praised the NCPD, referring to the "fine example" and the "good job" of the department. "I don't know of anywhere they've done a bad job," said the NAACP officials.[12] This congeniality was slightly ruffled in early 1967 when a CORE leader accused the NCPD of having

11. Of the approximately 40,000 Negroes living in Nassau County in 1960, about 25,000 resided in areas patrolled by the NCPD. This was 2.5 per cent of the NCPD-served population. By 1965 the Negro population for the county as a whole had grown to over 55,000.

12. *New York Times*, July 24, 1966.

beaten a Negro being arrested in Garden City Park.[13] The commissioner promptly issued a denial, saying his investigation showed that the arrested man complained of no injuries when arraigned in court the next day. In the course of his press release, the commissioner went out of his way to observe that "We have always enjoyed the finest relationship with all civil rights organizations, including CORE, and I look forward to the same fine relationship in the future." An official of the county human rights commission afterwards told an interviewer that the matter had been dropped and that relations with the police were, if anything, getting better.

The police have had to cope with incidents accompanying Negro efforts to move into white neighborhoods. In 1965 a gang of white youths broke windows with firecrackers and burned a cross on the lawn of a mixed couple (white wife, Negro husband) who moved into a white area; the police caught the offenders.[14] On another occasion, a civil rights protest march was held in the Roosevelt section of the county. The police precinct commander visited white bars in the area to warn bartenders that they would be held responsible if any trouble developed. There was none. There has been no agitation for a civilian police review board in Nassau; when a local patrolmen's association argued publicly against creating one, the NCPD leadership was dismayed, fearing such statements would create an issue where none yet existed.[15]

Opinions among the patrolmen — and perhaps, therefore, the behavior of the patrolmen — differ with respect to the existence of a double standard for Negroes. A patrolman working a Negro area said there was a tendency to under-report Negro crime: "I think it's wrong but it couldn't be avoided without a revolt in those neighborhoods. The people themselves don't think it is so bad. They would think you were crazy if you made a big deal out of everything."

Another officer disagreed and there is no way of telling who is

13. *Newsday*, January 5, 1967.

14. *Ebony*, October 1965 and *Newsday*, July 9, 1965.

15. In 1967 a proposal to create an "ombudsman" for Nassau County was supported by the police commissioner, the county executive, and both political parties; it was opposed by the Patrolmen's Benevolent Association and the district attorney.

right; both may be. What is clear is that Negroes as a group have not made organized complaints of either harassment or neglect. An active Community Relations Bureau, created in January 1966 works to maintain this situation. The six-man (one white, five Negro) unit meets with community groups, primarily Negro, and supervises the work of captains assigned to each precinct, who have as one of their duties "human relations work" — again, meeting with neighborhood and civil rights organizations. Whatever the value of such a bureau in dealing with leaders, it probably can do little to solve the kind of dilemma reported by one patrolman who is keenly aware of the department's emphasis on caution where Negroes are concerned:

> I had been warned that a robbery had just occurred and they gave me the description of this Negro man. A few minutes later . . . I saw a Negro fellow who fit the description waiting for a train . . . All of a sudden he bolted and took off. I just took out my gun, yelled "halt," and when he kept going I unloaded the whole barrel. I was really surprised I didn't get him. But it was lucky . . . We got him later and he confessed. If I'd have killed him, I would have lied and made up some story but they [the chiefs] probably would have branded me as "trigger happy" anyway . . . I was lucky, that's all there is to it . . . I thought twice about shooting him because he was colored. If he had been white, I would not have hesitated.

Ironically, one recent reported incident of "police brutality" in Nassau came from whites, not Negroes. In 1965 two young men were arrested after they had allegedly ignored repeated police warnings to move a car that was blocking traffic. The arrest was made forcibly and handcuffs used; onlookers in this predominantly Jewish section protested the arrests and accused the police of brutality. A number of women present beat on the officers with their handbags. "Who's brutal to who?" a police officer later commented, bitterly.

Eight Politics and the Police

To change a police style one must first understand the extent to which that style is subject to the decision-making processes of the community. Differences among police departments that are the result of explicit community choices can presumably be altered by making different choices. Because police practices have a considerable effect on the lives of many citizens and because, in addition, crime — especially "crime in the streets" — is an issue of great importance in many cities, one might suppose that politics (taken broadly as the conflict over the goals and personnel of government) would determine the prevailing police style much as it determines whether an urban renewal project will be undertaken, the water supply fluoridated, or taxes increased.

In fact, deliberate community choices rarely have more than a limited effect on police behavior, though they may often have a great effect on police personnel, budgets, pay levels, and organization. How the police, especially the patrolmen, handle the routine situations that bring them most frequently into contact with the public can be determined by explicit political decisions only to the extent that such behavior can be determined by the explicit decisions of the police administrator, and the administrator's ability to control the discretion of his subordinates is in many cases quite limited by the nature of the situation and the legal constraints that govern police behavior. The maintenance of order, unless it involves the control of large disorders (a riot, for example), is very hard to bring under administrative control and thus very hard to bring under political control — at least insofar as politics operates through the making of conscious decisions by formal institutions (mayors, city councils, and the like). And some law enforcement situations, especially those in which the police response is citizen-invoked, offer few opportunities to the administrator — and thus to his political superiors — for changing the nature or the outcome of police action.

Even in areas of police-initiated law enforcement, where the administrator does have the ability to make policy, that policy is often his and not the community's. He can determine how many traffic tickets will be issued and he can strongly influence, if he chooses, how many drunk arrests will be made, but in no city studied for this book were those decisions by the chief made at the direction of the governing bodies of the community. The reason for a city's failure to exercise influence potentially at its disposal is that in most cases, and certainly in all the cases reported in this study, such matters are not of general interest to the citizenry or to public officials. In these matters, citizen interest, and thus political interest, tends to be highly particularistic — it produces specific complaints regarding whether *my* ticket was fairly issued, whether there is a teenager racing his car in front of *my* house, whether *I* have been annoyed by a drunk on the sidewalk. The political institutions of the city may or may not amplify or pass on such complaints, but if they do it is in the form of issuing specific directives or asking specific questions of the chief; to such inquiries or orders, specific responses will be made, but such responses only rarely take the form of a change in over-all police strategy.

The community can determine police policy, within broad limits, when the public can observe some general condition for which the police can be held responsible (whether fairly or unfairly is another matter). The existence of widespread gambling or of organized prostitution is visible and the political authorities can decide how vigorously the police should crack down on these activities. Just such a decision was made in Oakland by the city manager when he ordered his new police chief to put an end to illegal businesses and, insofar as it was in his power, that is exactly what he did. The mayor of Syracuse expected similar action from his new police chief, and he got it. The officials in Albany and Newburgh, on the other hand, have been less interested in these problems, and the police have acted accordingly.

Other than vice, only two issues of general significance typically become matters of community discussion, but in neither is the discussion conclusive or the police response proportional to the intensity of the emotions aroused. The first is the issue of "crime in the streets"; the second, police handling of citizen complaints.

It is one thing to decide that something should be done about crime in the streets and quite another thing to decide exactly what it is that should be done. The politicians may ask the chief, or he may propose to them, that the police intensify their surveillance over public places in order to deter, or apprehend, persons who are about to commit, or have committed, street assaults, muggings, purse snatches, and the like. But most cities where such problems exist are also cities that are more and more deeply divided on the proper police response to these problems. What in Oakland is a sound police strategy to many whites and most police officers is "harassment" to a substantial part of the Negro community. Furthermore, because the law enforcement benefits of aggressive preventive patrol are rarely measured with any care and because there is almost no way even in principle to measure the costs in terms of good community relations, this police policy — and the political mandate that may underlie it — tends to become as much an ideological as a practical issue. The police quickly sense that their behavior in this area is being judged by conflicting standards and expectations and that one set of expectations (those opposed to "harassment") is being urged by persons who seek to "meddle" in the department or to "play politics"; thus the police often are led to insist that such decisions be made by the police themselves and not by the community.

Unlike a discussion of crime in the streets, controversy over police handling of grievances is at least over concrete alternatives, such as whether to create a civilian review board or an "ombudsman." In varying ways such an issue has arisen in Albany, Nassau, Newburgh, Oakland, and Syracuse; in Oakland it has been a major community controversy. But though the issue is passionately debated, it is not clear that, however it is resolved, it will have much effect on the *substantive* police policies that are in effect — partly because some are not "policies" at all but styles created by general organizational arrangements and departmental attitudes and partly because grievance procedures deal with specific complaints about unique circumstances, not with the general practices of the officers.

If an issue of substantive significance *is* raised, it is often raised by a member of the law enforcement system — a judge, prosecutor, probation officer, or a group of police officers. The controversy in Nassau County over how the vice squad should be organized and led was an issue between the (Republican) district attorney on the one hand and the (Democratic) county executive and his subordinate, the police commissioner, on the other. The controversy in Brighton and Highland Park over how many traffic tickets should be issued was in each case precipitated, not by the public, but by the patrolmen some of whom, of course, tried to involve politicians on their side. Complaints about whether judges are "too soft" on suspects or police "too zealous" in making arrests, though they rarely become full-scale public issues, are usually exchanged among members of the criminal justice system. And because the system lacks any central authority or decision-making process that supervises its component parts or that can set general policy for it, such complaints usually sputter out with no effect except to confirm in the eyes of all parties that the other fellow doesn't know what he is talking about.

In sum, the prevailing police style is not explicitly determined by community decisions, though a few of its elements may be shaped by these decisions. Put another way, the police are in all cases keenly sensitive to their political environment without in all cases being governed by it. By *sensitive* is meant that they are alert to, and concerned about, what is said about them publicly, who is in authority over them, how their material and career interests are satisfied, and how complaints about them are handled. In short, they are alert to their particular concerns as individual members of a bureaucracy. To be *governed* means that the policies, operating procedures, and objectives of the organization are determined deliberately and systematically by someone with authority to make these decisions. The policies described in this study — handling petty offenses and traffic violations, treating juveniles — are, with very few exceptions, determined by the police themselves without any deliberate or systematic intervention by political authorities. (These policies may be affected in *unintended* ways by various political actions, but that is another matter.)

Such intervention as occurs usually concerns the selection of a new chief or the career interests of the individual officers (wages, working conditions, promotions, charges of misconduct, and the like). Even the conflict over racial issues — obviously a matter of growing importance — is typically conflict over police behavior in the *particular* case and is framed in terms of whether an *individual* officer has or has not exceeded his authority and, if so, what procedures should be followed to punish him. The more general questions — how the police allocate their resources, which laws they choose to enforce vigorously and which they choose to slight, whether they employ warnings or arrest in cases where they have discretion — are rarely raised, even in racial issues. Thus, the police officer sees the struggle over police-minority relations primarily as political efforts to challenge the authority of individual police officers and constrain them by threatening their career interests — their salaries, promotion prospects, self-respect, and morale. He sees challenges by Negroes as no different from the challenges of politicians or any other outside group, all of which are equally resented even when they cannot be resisted.

In other words, the police view most issues — whether they arise from a city manager's efforts to "reform" a department, an alderman's efforts to name a new deputy chief, or a Negro organization's efforts to establish a civilian review board — as a struggle for control of the department by "outside" forces. Of course, the issues are in principle quite different in each case, but because they affect the individual officer in essentially the same way, by making him less certain of his position and prospects, these differences are not taken seriously. This is not to say that if public authorities made systematic and deliberate efforts to set law enforcement policies the way the Joint Chiefs of Staff and the Secretary of Defense presumably set military policy, the rank-and-file police officer would be content and compliant. Far from it; any organization resists change, and the police role, with its vulnerability to legal sanctions, its (perceived) low social esteem, and its absence of professional reference groups, produces a sufficient sense of insecurity to be especially resistant to change. But when public control over the police is exercised *primarily* in terms of complaints, grievances, struggles over salary and retirement benefits, and legal sanctions, then the normal resistance to change is greatly increased.

In general, then, understanding the political life of a community will not provide a sufficient explanation of the police policies in effect. They are left, in many areas, to the police themselves. There was no political involvement in the Syracuse police decision to intensify traffic and parking arrests or in the Oakland decision to arrest drunks in large numbers. There was public pressure to "do something" about juveniles in Nassau, but the means were left to the police, and, as we have seen, the Nassau police response was the opposite of that in neighboring Suffolk (the former created a bureau to emphasize prevention and counselling, the latter created one to increase arrests). The Highland Park chief in the mid-1950's introduced the legalistic police style without any particular directives from the city manager and when a new city manager privately decided that the chief should ease up a bit, he took no special steps to obtain a change in policy. Certain party leaders in Brighton tried to get the chief to abandon his traffic ticket "norm" (not so much because of public concern as police concern), but although the ticketing rate dropped for a while, it soon returned to its former level.

Organizational changes in all these departments (for example, hiring more men, buying major new pieces of equipment, and reorganizing important units) involve consultation with mayors and city managers; such changes have important legal and budgetary implications, and public approval is often mandatory and always prudent. And in almost all cases, public officials transmit to the police specific citizen complaints and demands.

But if the police are not, in the routine case, governed by the community, neither are they immune to community interests and expectations. As a source of pay and promotions, the city government naturally interests all police officers a great deal and in most cities they are well organized to express those interests. But in addition the community is a source of cues and signals — some tacit, some explicit — about how various police situations should be handled, what level of public order is deemed appropriate, and what distinctions among persons ought to be made. Finally, the police are keenly aware of the extent to which the city government does or does not intervene in the department on behalf of particular interests.

Thus, police work is carried out under the influence of a *political culture* though not necessarily under day-to-day political direction. By political culture is meant those widely shared expectations as to how issues will be raised, governmental objectives determined, and power for their attainment assembled; it is an understanding of what makes a government legitimate. Since community attitudes were not surveyed for this study, the political culture can only be inferred from the general behavior of political institutions. Nor does the word "culture" imply that everyone in the community supports and approves of the way things get done; it only suggests that most people would expect, for better or worse, things to be done that way. With respect to police work — or at least its patrol functions — the prevailing political culture creates a "zone of indifference" [1] within which the police are free to act as they see fit.[2]

The most important way in which political culture affects police behavior is through the choice of police administrator and the molding of the expectations that govern his role. Just as the most important decision a school board makes is its choice of superintendent, so the most important police decision a city council makes (or approves) is the selection of chief. In some communities, it is expected that he will be the "best man available"; in others it is that he will be the "deserving local fellow" or the man "closest to the party."

1. The term is taken from Chester A. Barnard, who applies it to the authority of an executive in an organization. See his *The Functions of the Executive* (Cambridge: Harvard University Press, 1938), pp. 168–169. Another study that has applied it to community tolerance of administrative discretion (this time in the case of public welfare agencies) is Alan Keith-Lucas, *Decisions About People in Need* (Chapel Hill: University of North Carolina Press, 1957), pp. 246–247.

2. The zone is probably greatest when people are deeply divided over law enforcement issues, as they were in nineteenth-century Boston over the question of liquor licensing. See Roger Lane, *Policing the City: Boston, 1822–1885* (Cambridge, Mass.: Harvard University Press, 1967) p. 131.

And once in office, the chief will confront a zone of community indifference to his policies of varying dimensions. In Albany, where political power is concentrated at the top in party hands, that zone may be very narrow for any matter that affects the party or its favored supporters but quite broad otherwise. Where the political system tends toward the nonpartisan, professionally administered, good-government ideal, the zone may be narrow only with respect to actions that could be construed as corrupt or self-serving but quite broad with respect to everything else (except, perhaps, for certain critical events). And the political culture acts as a filter, different for each community, that screens out certain complaints and demands, leaving the chief free to ignore them, and passes through (or even amplifies) others.

The character of the chief can have a great effect within the limits set by his ability to control his subordinates (as described in Chapter 4) and the zone of indifference of the community. The outsiders who came to Syracuse and Highland Park are the most striking examples, though there are others as well. The men who became chief in Oakland in the 1950's and chief in Nassau in the 1940's were both insiders, but both made sweeping departmental changes. In Highland Park and Oakland, police changes accompanied broader political changes (the arrival of a professional city manager) — that is to say, the zone of indifference changed. In Syracuse and Nassau, the police changed though the political system did not — the police moved within the existing zone of indifference.

Except in Albany, where the chief is part of the party organization, and in one or two other communities where political constraints on the police are numerous, the attitude of most city officials interviewed for this study suggested that their job was to select, within the latitude open to them, the "best man" for the chief's job and then let him run the department the way he wanted. Everyone conceded that who the chief was made a difference, and all mayors and managers spent a good deal of time on this decision. But rarely, with the exceptions noted, was there any strong desire to "get involved" in police matters. The police department is regarded as a city agency that provides a service, and the man in charge can be evaluated, so the theory goes, in terms of how well or how "efficiently" he provides it. As this study should have made clear, this view is not quite correct. The police are not a municipal service like trash collection, street sweeping, or road maintenance, and to govern them as if they were leads to difficulties. Trash collection or street sweeping is a *routine* service provided to the population *generally*. Everybody gets it (though perhaps some a bit more than others) and everybody can evaluate what he gets by reasonably evident standards. When citizens get too little, they complain, and the service level, if the city is alert to these matters, is adjusted accordingly or an explanation of why it cannot be adjusted is offered. Police protection is an *exceptional* service, which exists to prevent things from happening. It is largely invisible, and the average citizen comes into contact with it only in the exceptional case. He has no way of telling whether he is getting good service or not, except in the (rare) case when he experiences it — and perhaps not even then. He has no way of knowing if he is being treated, either as victim or suspect, differently from others. If his call for help is ignored or the response delayed, is it because the police are lazy or because all their cars are tied up on something more important? If the police fail to catch the burglar, is it because they are incompetent or because the burglar has left no clue? And if a mayor receives a complaint about the police, it is as likely to be a measure of how *well* they are doing their job as how poorly — what is "harassment" to one person is "good police protection" to his neighbor.

In short, if public authorities evaluate the police as they evaluate routine municipal services they cannot, except by happy accident, produce the kind of suboptimization that the "service-adjusted-to-complaints" system of managing street sweeping produces. Just as the absence of reliable performance criteria makes the police administrator's task so difficult and gives rise to many of the tensions within the police department, so the mayor's, or manager's, lack of reliable performance criteria gives rise to the same kinds of tensions between the mayor and the police chief. The difference, of course, is that the mayor can, more easily than the chief, wash his hands of the whole affair or confine his concern with the police to particularistic matters

— promotions, budgets, assignments, favors, citizen complaints — rather than law enforcement, which is just what he is likely to do.

The ways in which the political culture affects the police can be suggested by examining briefly the politics of the eight communities studied and the police issues that have arisen in those communities; in the final section of this chapter, some data will be provided from a nationwide sample of cities to indicate the extent to which political culture, crudely defined, shapes at least one aspect of police behavior — the arrest rate.

Politics and the Watchman Style

The three cities that display the watchman police style have political systems with certain important similarities. Each is led by politicians who appeal to a predominantly working-class and lower-middle-class constituency on the basis of party loyalty, ethnic identification, the exchange of favors, personal acquaintanceship, and the maintenance of a low tax rate. None of the three has a high level of public services and, given the absence of industrial growth and the determination to keep taxes down, none is likely to change in this regard. In Newburgh, outside experts — professional city managers — have been employed from time to time, but aside from this important exception, government is in the hands of "locals" — professional politicians, Main Street merchants, local attorneys — who operate essentially caretaker governments.[3]

The caretaker political style seems to be so naturally associated with the watchman police style that one might suppose that the former is a sufficient explanation for the latter. And to a considerable degree it is. Providing the voters with a minimum of public services at the lowest possible cost seems, logically and politically, to be a corollary to leaving them alone with respect to law enforcement, except on important matters. Winning and holding office by main-

3. For the concept of "caretaker" government, see Oliver P. Williams and Charles R. Adrian, *Four Cities* (Philadelphia: University of Pennsylvania Press, 1963), pp. 27–28.

taining a network of personal relationships and attracting the support of the party leadership seems, again, logically and politically equivalent to judging the misdeeds of citizens on the basis of who they are as well as what they did and on the basis of the immediate consequences of those acts as well as their legal significance. The motto for both the politicians and the police might well be "Don't rock the boat" — and if the boat is rocked, make sure before doing something that you know who is doing the rocking and who is likely to get hurt.

Such an explanation can be carried too far, however. Despite their similar political systems and police styles, there are important differences among the three cities in the methods by which political power is acquired, the community context in which it is used, and the substantive issues facing both the politicians and the police. Without abandoning the general point — that the political system and the police style are congruent — it is important to introduce some qualifications and distinctions. A caretaker political system is not everywhere the same; it varies depending on the formal and informal political institutions and on the kinds of community cleavages. Albany has a highly centralized political machine with almost unchallenged control of the city and much of the county; Newburgh has a somewhat more faction-ridden (though still powerful) machine, which has recently lost a few elections to the opposition; Amsterdam has little stable political organization and is governed by men who, though avowedly partisan, win power mainly through personal followings and ad hoc alliances. In Albany and Newburgh, but not in Amsterdam, the politicians and the police have had to confront a large and growing Negro population. A sizable racial minority not only divides the community between black and white, it also divides the white majority among itself over how best to cope with the racial issue. The result can be a bitter conflict, as it was in Newburgh when its welfare program became a major political controversy.[4]

The Albany Democratic machine dominates the police department

4. On the Newburgh welfare controversy, see Joseph P. Ritz, *The Despised Poor: Newburgh's War on Welfare* (Boston: Beacon Press, 1966).

as it dominates everything else in the city. Under the leadership of Daniel P. O'Connell it has controlled the city and most of the county continuously since 1923. In the ensuing forty-five years, only one Republican, and no dissident Democrat, was ever elected to office in the city, and he lasted but a single term. Although O'Connell himself has held no office since a term as assessor in the early 1920's, his organization, at the time of this study, controlled the mayor, all nineteen members of the common council, the city controller, the city treasurer, the police court judge, and important county offices, including the district attorney and the county judges. Needless to say, the police chief is a part of the organization, picked by it and loyal to it.

Although a political machine this powerful might in some communities tolerate large-scale police corruption and organized crime, there is little evidence that this is the case in Albany. On the contrary, even the strongest critics of O'Connell concede that he has kept "organized" crime out of Albany and that the department is "tough" on important criminals. This policy apparently results from a love, not of purity, but of monopoly. No organization, legitimate or illegitimate, is to have influence in Albany except the O'Connell organization. Beer, during and after Prohibition, was provided by the organization, not the syndicate. O'Connell owned Hedrick's Brewery (recently sold to a national firm) and its product was supplied — often to the exclusion of others — in Albany tap rooms.[5] An important law enforcement official, a member of the party, told an interviewer how the party looks at police corruption: "The political organization is well established. It doesn't want people to rock the boat, and it doesn't need to engage in the sorts of things that go on in other cities."

A number of persons interviewed claimed they had seen police officers being paid off by prostitutes and madams; it is, of course, im-

5. The famous gangster, Jack "Legs" Diamond was arrested and chased out of Albany during Prohibition. One personal reason for the anti-syndicate attitude of the party may result from the kidnapping of Dan O'Connell's nephew by some racketeers during the 1930's. They were caught and convicted but feeling ran so high in Albany the trial had to be held in Binghamton.

possible to confirm or deny such reports.[6] To the extent brothels and gambling are tolerated, they are tolerated by the party and thus it is likely, though not certain, that any money exchanged goes largely to the party in the form of "campaign contributions." A few individual police officers may, as several ex-pimps alleged, have served as collectors, or they may have tried to pick up a few dollars on the side for themselves, or both. What is clear is that such illegal enterprises as have been allowed to flourish have been locally owned

6. One Negro man who once ran a brothel in the Gut before it was torn down described to an interviewer how he had operated before he went out of business: "When I had a trick house I was running two or three girls . . . I paid off two or three times to a cop named Sergeant X . . . We got busted once or twice and the girls had to pop for $500. [That's] what it cost to get a whore off in Albany. You give the money to a lawyer . . . I don't know exactly where he spends it, but I know I've had girls pay off to him and never have to spend a day in jail."

According to such information as is available, the machine has relied for the income of at least some of its members more on the manipulation of property assessments, contracts, and purchasing arrangements than on illegal businesses. In 1961 the State Board of Equalization and Assessment found very large differences in the property assessment ratios in Albany. One motel, owned by the executive secretary of the Albany County Democratic Committee, was assessed at 18 per cent of true value, compared to a citywide average of 56 per cent for all properties and nearly 100 per cent for commercial properties. An official of the State Board told a reporter that there is in Albany "the biggest spread between high and low percentages of assessment that can be found anywhere in the state." (*Knickerbocker News*, November 18, 1964.) A 1961 report by the State Commission of Investigation found that Albany County had accumulated almost eight million dollars in tax delinquencies, equal to a full year's worth of county taxes. The advantage to the party of allowing taxes to fall delinquent are several: friends of the party can have their taxes forgiven or compromised, the cost of running the city can be shifted to residents of the county (by law, the county must credit the city for all delinquent taxes and make up the difference out of its own resources), and the government can retain the good will of voters whose taxes are delinquent and not collected.

The New York State Commission of Investigation in a 1964 report found shortages in commercial deliveries to Albany County government agencies (such as the jail), a lack of competitive bidding among suppliers, and ties between favored commercial suppliers and a "sales corporation" owned by the nephews of the county purchasing agent and represented by the county district attorney as part of his private law practice. Suppliers using this sales corporation as an intermediary increased their sales to the county substantially in return for a very large fee—between one half and two thirds of profits, in some cases. (See SIC, *Report*, 1964, pp. 101–112.) Following these disclosures, some merchants but no politicians were indicted by the Albany grand jury. The grand jury is, of course, led by the district attorney who represented the sales corporation. See also Jonathan Kapstein, "Uncle Dan's Feud With the Albany Newspapers," *Reporter*, March 9, 1967, and a story by Joseph Lelyveld in the *New York Times*, March 27, 1964.

and operated; on this, machine members and their critics are agreed.

However the party may or may not have profited from illegal businesses, it rarely felt any compulsion to close down the famous "Gut." A high city official was asked whether the once-gaudy, now rather modest night life in the area ever produced any citizen complaints.

No, I don't think we ever got any complaints about Green Street. There used to be several Negro whore houses down there. They've mostly been closed down now . . . We never really got any complaints from people here in Albany. We used to get complaints from people out of town. I used to get an annual report from the American Social Hygiene Association which would do a survey of B-girls and the like . . . I would always tease the lady who brought in this survey . . . I'd tell her the report was interesting, but it was really terribly incomplete. She had left out the three biggest action spots in town: the Jones Hotel, the Smith Hotel [pseudonyms], and the State Office Building! When they were tearing down the Mall area, one of the last buildings to go . . . was the Hotel Franklin [pseudonym]. The reason was because it was the place patronized by legislators who went there for, well, I needn't tell you . . . Everybody knew why [that hotel] was being saved till last.

The city administration has changed its policy on vice slowly but in accordance with what it thinks public opinion expects. The Gut was once defended by officials who felt that it kept the "riff-raff" in one place; no decent citizen would be offended unless he went there looking for action, in which case he could hardly complain. Toward the end, however, it was receiving too much unfavorable publicity. Most of the honky-tonks and brothels torn down by the governor did not reopen; in any case, it was no longer clear the market was still large enough to support them. Albany was once a working-class city with factory workers, railroad and river boat men, and lumber jacks from the north looking for a good time. Now it is a city of civil servants, and elderly, and Negroes.

Law enforcement officials have used their power to suppress immorality that might offend the "decent people." The district attorney periodically wages war on "obscene" literature; at the time of one visit by an interviewer to the city, it was harder to find *Playboy* than a prostitute.[7] (The magazine, but scarcely anything more erotic, has since found its way back onto the newsstands.) And lurid, or at least luridly advertised, films do not appear in Albany theaters, though they appear outside the city limits. A high city official explained how this was done:

> [A] bishop called me to say that there was an improper movie being shown in town. We called up the head of the theater and told him to close down immediately and not to reopen the next day, and he didn't. The police chief in a nearby town called to ask what law we had been able to use to close it down. Of course, there was no law at all. We just did it. Theaters, what with licensing requirements and all, are pretty vulnerable. If you really want to get them, you can get them. It's not strictly legitimate, of course, but it's effective. Now the word is out, and the movie people don't try to put that kind of film in Albany any more.

Entry to and promotion within the police department are controlled by the party. A former police officer explained that being appointed or promoted "first has to be cleared with party headquarters; as a first step, this involves getting the endorsement of your ward leader." Albany is one of the few cities in the state that uses a local rather than state civil service examination.[8] Within the force, no challenges to party loyalty are permitted. In 1961 a group of patrolmen tried to organize a Patrolmen's Benevolent Association in Albany (it is the only large city without one). The effort was de-

7. At one time the district attorney had the novelist John O'Hara under indictment for having written *Ten North Frederick.*

8. In April 1960 the State Civil Service Commission ordered seven patrolmen and one sergeant on the Albany Police Department to show cause why they should not be dismissed because of irregularities, including erasures and changed answers, in their civil service test papers. The Albany Municipal Civil Service Commission denied there had been any tampering and the city obtained an injunction to block the removal of the men. Finally, a state Supreme Court justice (elected to that post by the O'Connell organization) ruled the action of the State Commission invalid. In 1965 the state was still complaining of the "woefully inadequate" local civil service procedures. It alleged that 142 city and county employees were improperly holding jobs on "provisional" appointments. (See *Knickerbocker News,* December 11, 1965.) In New York, about 86 per cent of all cities use state-administered civil service examinations; Albany is one of the few (Buffalo and New York are two others) that do not.

feated by the police chief, and the organizers resigned from the force.[9] The chief later told an interviewer, "They wanted to break up the political organization and get [me] out of office, but I'm still here and the organization is still here. But they're not." (The officers involved deny that was their intention.) The chief has also opposed the creation of a Police Athletic League, arguing that funds for it would have to be raised by officers selling tickets or getting contributions.

The strong and unchallenged party control of the police influences law enforcement in a number of ways. On most matters, of course, the party has nothing at stake and the police are free to set their own course. But even here the expectations of the leadership are understood. The citizens are not to be "over-policed." People should be allowed to double-park outside the stores. Motorists, unless they are rowdy youngsters about whom the police have received complaints, are to be left alone. The police are not to try to substitute for the parents in handling juveniles; unless it is a serious matter, let them go. But if the citizens are being annoyed — as by vagrants and alcoholics panhandling or otherwise creating a nuisance — they are to be protected. An assistant district attorney told an interviewer: "We're pretty tough on vagrants here. We give them summary justice and send them to jail. There, the police rough 'em up a bit and then send them out of town. These people could work if they wanted to. There's plenty of jobs here . . . The only reason these men don't work is that they don't want to work."

The police can also be used to create obligations to the party. Several informants, including former members of the police department, claimed that many parking tickets are handled in this way. One former officer with several years experience said: "Parking tickets are a way by which the organization creates little favors . . . that it can do for other people. You get a parking ticket for one dollar or two dollars or five dollars, and you take it to your ward leader. He sends them in to [party] headquarters and they're fixed."

Finally, the police are used to protect the party when that becomes necessary. Out-of-town businessmen wishing to do business

9. *Times-Union,* November 21, 1961.

in Albany have been, on occasion, checked out by the Albany police so that the party would have a better idea of whom it was dealing with. When a party leader breaks the law, the entire system, including the police, mobilizes to protect him. (Later, after any public discussion has subsided, the offender may be discreetly dropped from public office; the party does not like to have tainted personalities on the ticket.)

In contrast to the stable, orderly machine politics of Albany there is the unstable and faction-ridden machine politics of Newburgh. The Orange County Republican Committee has been the dominant force in Newburgh politics for many years. Headed by a local funeral director, the organization usually held a majority of seats on the five-man Newburgh city council. Its strength has rested on shrewd appeals to conservative opinion, the jobs and favors at its disposal, and the absence of a large upper-middle class in the city (most of which has moved out to the rapidly growing suburbs).

In recent years there have been two successful challenges to it, one by "reform" Republicans, the other by Democrats, but neither challenge endured nor while in office were the challengers able to take full control of the government. Each time their majority on the council was slim (three-to-two), badly organized, and politically inexperienced. Owing in part to the factionalism within the Republican party and to the frequent instability of the council majority, Newburgh has seen a rapid turnover in its city managers. Between 1916, when the plan was adopted, and 1967, Newburgh had twenty-one managers — seven of them since 1952 — each serving an average of about two years. The manager, usually a local, has been the instrument of the council majority but because there has not been, especially in recent years, a stable majority, the city has either been run on a caretaker basis or by an occasional aggressive manager who has precipitated, but been unable to resolve, a major issue.

Rapid growth in the Negro population has combined with the presence of many very conservative elements (both the John Birch Society and the neo-Nazi party are active in the area) to create a situation in which crime is often a political issue, each party or faction charging the other with not doing enough. In 1960 there was a series of muggings, allegedly done by Negro youths in white neighborhoods. The council instructed the city manager to report on how to handle the matter. He recommended giving the police power to break up crowds on the streets and to search cars at night for weapons; the courts, in turn, were to regard possession of a weapon by one member of a gang as presumptive evidence against others. A demand for hiring police dogs was deferred for more study. The following year the city judge ran for reelection, and a newspaper editorial supporting him stressed that "He has not been a 'soft' judge"; he gives out "jail sentences and heavy fines." [10] In 1965 more muggings and the murder of an elderly white man led to more charges of a "crime wave" and a Republican demand (by now the Democrats were in power) that police "secrecy" about the "true" crime picture be ended.[11] A council candidate ran on an "anti-crime" platform and was elected. In early 1967 a wave of burglaries and the murder of a businessman led to another city council meeting on crime and a "call for action" from the Chamber of Commerce. At the special council meeting a Negro minister charged the city was "wide open" with gambling and prostitution — an unexpected and somewhat embarrassing charge to city fathers who do not think of those things as "crime."

The cleavages between and within the political parties have also made it possible for the organized police officers, and the firemen, to play an important role. Appointment to and promotion within the force have always been strongly influenced by political considerations; in practice, this has meant that the Republicans, most often in power, have made most appointments. A recent city manager told an interviewer that "This police department has more loyalty to the Republican party than it does to its own administration." Nonetheless, the police are quick to see and to take advantage of opportunities to advance their interests no matter who is in power. In 1963, for example, they and the firemen backed the Democrats because that party had supported a referendum to raise police and fire salaries (the Republicans did not). The pay raise went through

10. Newburgh *Evening News,* November 4, 1961.
11. *Ibid.,* August 31, 1965.

and the Democrats got in and hired a "reform" city manager. His actions so thoroughly antagonized the police — he changed their shifts and tried to change their ways — that they picketed city hall and in 1965 vociferously supported the Republicans.

Though crime in the streets and police pay raises are important issues that concern many politicians, prostitution and gambling are not. Many party leaders see nothing wrong with them, and several public officials think there are more important things to worry about. A top Republican leader defended the bookies and whore houses:

> I'm not a do-gooder. I go to the track and I like to bet at the track. I'm in favor of legalized gambling and the fact that there's gambling around doesn't get me very concerned. I see prostitution the same way. I think there should be licensed houses of prostitution. I think if we did that there'd be a lot less raping going on.

A Democratic leader agreed with his Republican counterpart:

> There was gambling in the Stone Age, there's gambling today, there will be gambling when your grandchildren are as old as I am. I can't see enforcing a law against nature. Anyway, there's never been any gang murders or stuff like goes on in New York as a result of gambling and prostitution. The gamblers up here are nice people, otherwise; they're businessmen.

A former city manager with a strong sense of professionalism tried to change other things but felt, in view of the political and administrative realities, that it would be foolish to try to change this. He told an interviewer:

> If a city manager goes after this like a crusader, and he doesn't have his people in key positions, they can make him look like an ass. If prostitution and gambling got out of hand, I couldn't do anything about it with our police department. The older men were involved in payoffs in the past. Unless the situation becomes unbearable I won't try to do anything about it.

A high city official told an interviewer that "Nobody wants to eliminate all of the gambling and prostitution, especially among the

Negroes. We feel that some of it has to go on, but it should be kept down and under control." After the charges made by the Negro minister at the February 1967 council meeting, the city announced that gambling and prostitution had been shut down.[12] Some arrests were made, in fact, but privately a high city official told an interviewer afterwards that the city was not "closed tight"; he explained that "We couldn't close the place down totally with the minority group that we have here — we have to allow some safety valve."

Recent city managers have instead tried to get control of the police department, to modernize its equipment and procedures, and to improve the use of its manpower. A former manager bought radar units and ordered the men to start writing speeding tickets, changed the shift hours to put more men on the streets at night, bought more patrol cars, and tried to standardize procedures. Many of these changes were bitterly resisted, in part because they imposed some inconvenience (few patrolmen wanted additional night duty, for example), but in part because it appeared to the men to be an effort to "take over" the department and to make rules, hierarchy, and formal procedures determine what once had been guided by custom, cliques, and personality. And on the whole the resistance was successful. The city manager had the formal authority but not the real power to make his wishes stick.

In Newburgh, unlike Albany, the dominant party is not so strong as to be able to use the police as an instrument of party control nor can it specify a precise level of law enforcement for the community. The watchman police style that results is more the product of police inclination than party directive. Because the Negro and crime have become political issues in Newburgh, there are sporadic "crackdowns" to deal with community fear. Albany politics is not preoccupied with the Negro or with crime: there is no opposition to raise such issues, the party does not need such issues in order to win elections, and organizations that might agitate such issues are discouraged from forming. Indeed, the police seem to act somewhat more vigorously against Negro crime in Albany, where it is *not* an issue, than in Newburgh, where it *is*. The answer seems to lie in

12. *Ibid.*, February 23, 1967.

the presence or absence of central authority. The Albany police style is centrally determined: leave citizens alone in their minor indiscretions, arrest, or otherwise dispose of, persons who disturb the voters, and protect the party. In Newburgh, the police style emerges out of a number of conflicting stimuli (protect the Republicans, get benefits from the Democrats, cope with a reform-minded city manager, ignore vice that no one cares about, leave ordinary Negroes alone, crack down on trouble-making Negroes, and stay out of trouble) and seems to be shaped by default rather than intent. The Newburgh police are more likely to take the attitude that it's every man for himself, whereas the Albany police are likely to assume that the party is watching. It is interesting that Newburgh officers complain bitterly and publicly about many of their superiors, but the Albany police either praise their superiors or keep their views very much to themselves. The latter receive clear and consistent cues as to proper behavior, the former unclear and inconsistent ones.

Amsterdam lacks the political machine of Albany and the Negroes (and crime) to be found in Newburgh. With no major law enforcement problems, the politics of the city is concerned with other matters (chiefly, the shrinking tax base and the resultant lack of municipal revenues). The local businessmen, salesmen, and factory workers who win office on the eight-man common council do so on the basis of personal contacts with friends and neighbors in their wards; political parties are weak, and their membership on the council varies frequently, with neither side having a large margin. In 1966, for example, there were four Democrats and four Republicans, but Amsterdam politicians attached little significance to these labels. The mayor has little formal power (he is limited to one term and can only vote in the council in case of a tie); there is no professional manager.

The result of a situation characterized by few resources and little political power is that not much money is spent on public administration, including law enforcement. Of the three hundred or so city employees in 1966, only thirteen civilians were paid more than the base salary of a patrolman. And that base, as the police never tire of pointing out, is low indeed ($4,510 in 1966, $5,110 in 1967).

Once the policemen threatened to resign *en masse* if they did not get a pay raise. The city administration told them to go ahead, Pinkerton men would be hired to replace them. There was no mass resignation. The police have also participated in a lobbying effort to persuade the legislature to enact a statewide mandated police minimum wage law, which the mayor of Amsterdam opposed. Police salaries in 1966 were nearly one thousand dollars below Amsterdam's median family income in 1960. As a result, most patrolmen hold two jobs and many have working wives.

Equipment and facilities are in a similar state. Police headquarters, built in 1896 for the fire department, is badly run down and needs paint and repairs. There is no jail; to be confined, prisoners must be driven twelve miles to the county seat, a trip that ties up one fourth of the department's cars. A person who is being detained only briefly can be put in a detention cell, but it has no toilet facilities. There are only three marked patrol cars (there is one unmarked detective car) but one is kept as a reserve; thus, two simultaneous calls for police service will tie up the entire mobile patrol force. And the force has many vacancies. With 1.21 officers per thousand population, it has fewer men than the vast majority of American cities its size.

Because the city has so little serious crime, there is no political pressure to do more for the police department — or more accurately, the concern for low taxes outweighs whatever political pressure the police and their families can bring for higher salaries. The police believe the citizens want to be left alone — they think of "us as glorified night watchmen," one told an interviewer — and they act accordingly. Their indifference does not mean the police have been left outside the political system. Officers and politicians alike admitted that promotions and command assignments have been made on political grounds, often by the common council acting in accordance with the current distribution of party strength and ethnic representation among the aldermen. Though a civil service examination is nominally required for promotion, the council is free to pick among the top three or to postpone the appointment until the "right" man comes along. The chief, accordingly, is sensitive to the desires of the council and, perhaps because of this, tries to return to the city each year an unexpended portion of his meager budget. He attends the weekly council meetings but, because it would cost money and because no one is interested anyway, publishes no annual report. The politicians feel little pressure to deal with the small-scale local gambling. A high city official explained why to an interviewer:

People don't care about gambling. The only call you get is when the wife of a man who has lost his weekly paycheck at Angelo's or Nick's [pseudonyms] calls you and wants you to do something . . . Usually they won't sign a complaint; they don't want to get involved. Even when she does, the word gets out and so Angelo or Nick returns the guy's money and then the wife, she wants to forget all about it . . . When I came in [to office] I heard rumors about people in City Hall getting payoffs. I wanted to do something to allay suspicion. We could close down gambling if we had the money to hire out-of-town investigators to set up a raid. But we don't. So we asked the sheriff. He tried for awhile . . . but his men were known, too . . . Then the DA said the only thing to do is to call in the State Police. We said, OK, and so he did. They made that raid last year . . . I never found any evidence that the gamblers were paying off. I don't think [gambling] is a moral issue, or if it is, it has been pretty well fuzzed up. You can buy a lottery ticket now *in a bank* [the official New York state lottery].

In Amsterdam, in short, the caretaker spirit is natural (that is, not the conscious decision of a party organization) and not disturbed by the challenge of either crime or racial conflict. Indeed, the only conceivable threat to the present style would occur if the officers became so discontent with their salaries that they quit to take better paying law enforcement jobs with the railway police (the New York Central runs through town), the state police, or the capital police in nearby Albany.

Politics and the Service Style

The political leaders of Brighton and Nassau County believe that their citizens want something more from law enforcement than they would get in Amsterdam and something different from what they would get in Albany and Newburgh. Politics in general is regarded, at least by the politicians, as providing services and amenities to persons clearly able to afford them. Though taxes are an issue, the politicians believe that people are willing to pay for programs that improve the quality of community life beyond what is minimally necessary. Government, besides keeping the streets clean and putting fires out, is also expected to sustain a prosperous business life, provide excellent public schools, hire courteous and obliging public officials, and maintain the "character of the community." The political consumer — the voter — is thought to have high standards and thus would be impatient with a caretaker government and outraged by a corrupt one. If the politicians are to make money out of their public life, it had better not be obvious or clearly at the public's expense.

Size, of course, makes a difference. In Brighton, everyone interviewed agreed, there has not been any controversy over law enforcement, with one exception — a brief and very discreet argument over whether the police chief should use a "norm" for traffic tickets. Nassau, many times larger, has had several law enforcement issues — in part because the county is sufficiently diverse so that there is bound to be some disagreement as to how the police operate and in part because it is sufficiently large to sustain organized groups that, in and out of politics, take an interest in law enforcement, as well as everything else, and make proposals for improving it. Though large, the county has deliberately avoided creating a highly centralized government: careful attention is paid to the wishes and prerogatives of the many local villages by the county government and, accordingly, by the county police.

Though both communities are service-oriented, neither is in any sense nonpartisan. Elections in both places (in Nassau, only at the county level) are on a partisan ballot and the local parties, both Democratic and Republican, take local issues seriously and participate in statewide party politics. Brighton is strongly Republican — no Democrat has been elected to local office, as far as anyone can remember, in the 150-year history of the town. Nassau has been strongly Republican in the past, but of late enough Democrats have moved in from adjoining New York City to have made possible the election of a Democrat as county executive and to place Democrats in three of the twenty district judgeships. Both places have a strong chief executive — a town supervisor in Brighton (elected for two-year terms and paid $11,500) and a county executive in Nassau (elected for three-year terms and paid $30,000).

Politics does not, of course, determine the police style in Brighton or Nassau; indeed, there is much less political intervention (in the narrow sense of partisan political intervention) in police affairs in these two communities than in even the least organized of the cities with a watchman police style. "Playing politics" with the police would be almost as unpopular as playing politics with the schools and, though politics is evident, especially and inevitably in the selection of the chief, it is more circumspect, less obvious, and less constraining on the day-to-day behavior of the officers. Size again makes a difference. The service orientation of the Brighton police is maintained by the attitude, widely shared among the officers, that this is what the community expects of them; no one has to give orders to see that the style is followed. But if the community is small enough to communicate its expectations directly, it is also small enough to be satisfied with nice, courteous officers who give prompt and personal service. Nassau, being much larger, must institutionalize its style by careful training, by organized public relations, and by an internal investigative unit that handles complaints. And when organized groups or politicians struggling for office demand that "something be done" about a number of "issues," it must respond within a political system that is both more competitive and more dependent on newspaper publicity for the discussion of issues. Thus, it creates and heavily publicizes specialized units to deal with burglary, narcotics, juveniles, community relations, highway accidents, and almost anything else one can imagine. Inevitably, therefore, the Nassau police department must be both more bureaucratic, that is, more reliant on formal rules and standard procedures and more specialized than the Brighton force; and these organizational differences, though inspired by the same concern (to serve the community), acquire a logic of their own which leads to significant differences in the handling of law enforcement matters.

The effect of politics on the police in both communities is largely indirect. In Brighton, for example, most of the officers interviewed were Republicans and locals (by law all men on the force must take up residence in the town within six months after their appointment; most usually live there to begin with). They go to the Republican town picnics and believe that political activity is not irrelevant to their role as policemen. On the other hand, they speak very critically of the sheriff's office, which, because he is directly elected, they feel is "too political." The Brighton chief told an interviewer that the local Republican leader (at the time of this study, he was a prominent attorney and bank president) had never tried to interfere in matters that normally prove attractive to politicians:

> He's left me alone, I'll say that for him. When he took over [as town leader] he asked me how I took care of my purchasing for the police department. I told him I put it out to bid and took the lowest bidder who produced something that would meet community standards. He said, "Okay, go on that way, and don't let anybody pressure you." You've got to respect him for that.

The only law enforcement issue that has arisen concerned traffic law enforcement. The local newspaper got wind of the ticket "norm" the chief enforced on his men and printed a story. About the same time, a local justice of the peace, an elected official, began to feel that the increased ticketing was unnecessary. He later told an interviewer that the extra tickets were not for speeding but for things like faulty equipment which used to bring only a warning. "It used to be handled informally out on the street, now we handle it informally in court . . . We just suspend sentence. I don't think this crackdown on traffic violations affects traffic safety at all." One of the justices of the peace was a law partner of the Republican town leader; not surprisingly, the latter heard of the issue. Some police officers also complained to him of the pressure on them. The leader spoke to the chief and asked him to ease off. "I don't think the police officers should be questioned about the number of tickets [they write]," he later told an interviewer. The town supervisor supported the chief. When the issue first came up, there was a temporary drop in the number of tickets written,[13] but thereafter the number began to climb again.

At no point did the *public* seem to be involved. The justices of the peace were concerned, the officers complained, a newspaper story appeared, but the average citizen was not aroused. "I don't think we've ever had any [public] complaints about enforcement," the town leader said. "Usually we get complaints from the officers." Like many issues in law enforcement, it arose because of disagreements among members of the law enforcement system.

The Nassau department, being a much larger, more complex, and thus harder to control organization, cannot afford to be casual about political contacts if it is to preserve its reputation for "professionalism" and honesty. Happily, the political system of Nassau County is well designed to maintain a balance between the strong central administration necessary for organizational control and management and the close attention to village interests necessary to the service orientation.[14] Towns and villages with strong traditions of home rule coexist with a county government that pursues a vigorous program of providing certain services, including police protection for most of the county, on a centralized basis.

Even at the county level, careful checks and balances are imbedded in the formal structure. The executive is elected by the entire county; he chairs the board of supervisors, appoints, with the board's consent, department heads, and prepares the annual budget. Like most elected chief executives, he takes a county-wide view and tends to be a source of innovation, and he has in recent years been a Democrat with ambitions for statewide office. The board of super-

13. In the first quarter of 1963, the Brighton police wrote 478 tickets; in the first quarter of 1964, after the intervention, they only wrote 196.

14. On the history and political development of Nassau County, see Edward J. Smits, *The Creation of Nassau County* (Nassau County Department of Public Works, 1963) and Michael S. Wald, "Nassau County: A Case Study in Suburban Political Institutions" (unpublished honor's thesis, Cornell University Department of Government, May 1963). When the NCPD was founded in 1925, there were 38 independent police forces. Fifteen of them were dissolved and the villages used NCPD patrol services instead.

visors consists of six men, four elected by the three towns and one each from the two cities. The board is dominated by Republicans who are oriented to local interests (most of the town representatives are also the chief executive officers of their towns) and who legislate with a view toward the preservation of home rule and an eye on the tax rate.

The key power held by the towns and villages, and safeguarded by the board of supervisors, is control over the use of land; the key power held by the county executive is control over a large, highly expert administrative apparatus with a capacity to produce attention getting proposals. (The present county executive has supplemented his staff with an elaborate array of citizen's advisory committees on everything from welfare to "county goals.") The village and town officials, in turn, can extend the range of their influence through the many voluntary fire departments, which not only control local fire protection services but also constitute an influential set of social clubs.

The Nassau County Police Department partakes of elements of both political systems. The commissioner is appointed by the county executive and serves at his pleasure; central police headquarters is located near the county executive building; the commissioner works closely with the county executive in acquiring modern equipment, planning new programs, and improving the quality and image of the force. At headquarters, investigative and staff services are provided to all local police agencies in the county. At the same time, the NCPD operates eight precinct stations, which provide uniformed patrol services for all unincorporated areas plus those incorporated villages that voluntarily elect to take advantage of this service in exchange for a fixed charge, applied to their tax rates. These district forces, and the commissioner in his capacity as head of these forces, stay in close touch with village leaders, pay careful attention to village demands, and try to woo more villages to use NCPD services (there are still twenty-three independent police forces in the county).

Centralized management, especially in the hands of strong commissioners, has kept the NCPD free of party politics in the narrow sense — merit examinations govern recruitment and promotions and purchasing appears to be carefully nonpartisan. Partly because of the skill of the commissioner and the county executive, most police matters — other than problems of salary and other benefits for officers — have been defined as a debate over "community needs" rather than as a conflict among particular interests.

Sometimes, of course, an issue involving police policy arises. One involved the handling of juveniles. Democrats demanded that something be done about juvenile delinquency; the police countered with the argument that there was no need for a specialized bureau and that compartmentalizing juvenile matters would reduce the interest of patrolmen in the problem. A woman who later became a Nassau district judge was especially outspoken in favor of a juvenile bureau, and the head of the Family Services Association also supported the idea. The county executive took up the issue in his campaign in 1961. When he was elected, he replaced the commissioner (the disciplinarian who had built the department had died and another man was in office), and his new appointee created the bureau in 1963. In part to soften its impact on a somewhat resistant department, the bureau was given authority only over minor juvenile offenses; arrests for serious matters would still be handled largely by the detectives.

Other than the controversy over the juvenile bureau, the striking thing about the political environment of the Nassau police is how rarely law enforcement policy is set as a result of organized community demands or overt political pressure by the county executive. To some extent this has been because of the department's skill in anticipating possible issues and adapting to meet them before they arise. The narcotics squad was one instance; others were the creation of a community relations bureau to deal with minority groups and a specialized burglary patrol to demonstrate a concern for the large number of housebreaks. These and other innovations were proposed by the department itself; the county executive approved of them and helped get community backing for them. The service style in police work is accompanied by exceptional sensitivity to community interests: do something before it occurs to anybody to demand that something be done. As the commissioner told an interviewer, half in jest, "We try to get the community involved so that if anything goes wrong we can blame the community." Beyond this, the county executive deals primarily with problems of resources — budgets, pay scales, equipment purchases, and the like.

The other police issues have been organizational rather than substantive, and they have arisen, not out of demands placed on the system by community groups, but out of conflicts among members of the law enforcement system: principally, conflicts between the district attorney and the police commissioner or between the organized police officers and the commissioner or the county executive.

The district attorney is a Republican, the county executive a Democrat. Conflict is inevitable, and it is frequently intense. One issue arose when the district attorney, believing that there was gambling and prostitution going on in the county jail (under the control of a Democratic sheriff), tried secretly to plant two out-of-town detectives in the jail as "prisoners." When he learned of it, the county executive objected. Eventually, the governor ordered a special inquiry. Not long afterwards, the acting commissioner decided to rotate the NCPD detectives assigned to the district attorney as members of his vice squad (the squad had been under the district attorney's control since the 1946 gambling scandal) and to replace the commander of that squad. The district attorney objected strongly, charging that the acting police commissioner had "covered up" corruption and wrong doing in the NCPD.[15] The acting commissioner, supported by the county executive, denied the charges.[16]

15. The main charges given to the newspapers were that the acting commissioner had attempted to conceal the involvement of a police officer in a prostitution ring and had failed to take criminal action against four New York City detectives accused of shaking down a Nassau bookie (they were instead turned over to the New York City Police for disciplinary action). The DA also accused the police of not cooperating in raids on teenage drinking spots and in failing to release the names of persons in whose homes stolen loot had been hidden by a police burglary ring. *Newsday,* January 30, 1965.

16. According to the acting police commissioner: the officer involved in the prostitution case had resigned before departmental charges could be brought, the DA's office was notified, and in time the man was indicted and tried but allowed by the DA himself to plead guilty to a lesser charge; the New York City detectives were

Finally, the vice squad was transferred to the NCPD.[17] Throughout the bitter feud, neither side accused the other of covering up vice cases — under the district attorney, the squad made many vice arrests and under the NCPD it has made even more.

The other major source of controversy among law enforcement officials is the Patrolmen's Benevolent Association. The PBA has fought to get status as the official bargaining agent of the police officers, to obtain higher wages and more benefits, and to have the prior police commissioner removed. (It also lobbies the state legislature; the head of the Nassau PBA spends up to three days a week in Albany.) On one occasion PBA members demonstrated before the county executive building in Mineola, carrying a mock coffin and an effigy of a patrolman with a knife in his back. The picketing, carried on over several weeks, was an effort to pressure the board of supervisors and the executive into voting a pay raise. Finally, the head of the PBA has publicly supported candidates for political office (technically, it is illegal for a civil servant to "endorse" a politician, but no action has been taken). Though most candidates with (unofficial) police backing are Republicans — one was the district attorney — the Democrats are not reluctant to seek their support.[18]

Politics and the Legalistic Style

The most obvious difference between the two cities with a legalistic police style and other communities is the presence, in both Oakland and Highland Park, of a strong, professionally oriented city manager. Highland Park, for example, is demographically very much

turned over to the New York police because they had jurisdiction and in any case, the DA's office was notified; the loot from the burglary ring was recovered using search warrants naming the persons and these are matters of public record; finally, it is the job of the police and not the DA to enforce drinking laws. *Newsday*, February 1, 1965.

17. *Newsday*, March 3, 1965.

18. At one point in a wage dispute with the county executive, some NCPD officers threatened to resign and, to give credence to the threat, they took the entrance examination for the Suffolk County police. In the end they did not resign.

like Brighton; the difference is primarily political — two vigorous city managers recruited from outside the city have, in recent years, been in complete charge of local administration and have alone and unaided selected the police chiefs. In terms of its population, Oakland is not so very different from Albany or Syracuse; it is utterly different, however, in its political system — since the mid-1950's administration has been in the hands of a professional manager hired from another city. In both Oakland and Highland Park the appointment of the police chiefs responsible for developing the legalistic style (and for other professional innovations) were made by city managers who had come to the city with a mandate for change. The Oakland manager was hired to take the place of a caretaker local manager who proved unable to handle fiscal problems or prevent a police scandal; the Highland Park manager was the first ever, the city having only recently abandoned the commission form of government.

Behind each city manager there is a mayor and city council elected on a nonpartisan ballot from the city at large. The councilmen have not always shared the manager's desire for change or his determination to be the sole head of the city bureaucracy; though nonpartisan, many have the more particularistic and conservative views of the middle-class voters and on occasion have tried to check the policy leadership of the manager or intervene in the city administration. But despite the great changes brought in city government by the managers (and nowhere were these changes more dramatic than in police work) the councils did not fire — or even seriously try to fire — either manager. Police behavior became a political issue in both cities — in Highland Park because the police resented certain of the chief's policies, in Oakland because of that and also because Negroes criticized police behavior — but in neither case did the controversy materially alter that behavior. The manager, with few exceptions, stood as a buffer between political pressure and police administration (though not necessarily between *police* pressure and local politics — it was a bit easier for the police to influence politics than for politics to influence the police). This does not mean that a manager could always count on a council majority; in many cases, they have had to work hard to get and keep one. What they *could* count on — and this helped them get the council majorities — was the backing of the city's upper-status business executives. The men who ran Oakland's largest enterprises (the *Oakland Tribune*, Kaiser Industries, the larger banks) or who in Highland Park were important businessmen or lawyers in nearby Chicago were usually behind the manager. The city councilmen, on the other hand, were more likely to represent, in the case of Oakland, the white middle-class homeowners or, in the case of Highland Park, the local businessmen and noncommuting voters and to object to some of the manager's plans.

Syracuse is a mixed case. Its police force is in transition and displays some aspects of the service style (in handling drunks or juveniles, for example) and some elements of the legalistic style (in handling traffic enforcement). Its political system is similarly mixed: power is concentrated at the top, not in the hands of a manager, but in the hands of a strong mayor and his colleagues in the Republican party organization. Though intensely partisan, politicians have not seriously intervened in police affairs since 1963. The scandal then made it desirable to take politics out of the police; the newly elected mayor was shrewd enough to see this and powerful enough to do something about it. He hired outside administrators to "reform" the department and left them alone while they did it. How far the department will change remains to be seen; thus far, it has stressed improving its service aspects (in the appearance and manner of the officers, and in its sensitivity to civil rights complaints) as well as changing some aspects of its law enforcement functions (in traffic primarily).

In short, the principal effect of the political culture on police behavior in these three cities has been to make possible the appointment of chiefs strongly committed to the doctrines of "police professionalism," to permit them to acquire control over the department free of the lateral interventions of politicians or special-interest groups, and to insulate the department from community pressures seeking changes in police policies. The principal sources of controversy have thus been internal — conflict between the administrator and certain groups of police officers over their respective powers and prerogatives.

The first city manager of Highland Park, installed after the government was changed from the commission form, dominated by local businessmen, to the council-manager form, dominated in its formative years by high-status executives who commuted to work in nearby Chicago, was hired from out of town and given a free hand and the strong backing of the mayor, a wealthy Chicago tax attorney. The manager, in turn, brought to the city a police chief from out of town and gave him an equally free hand. There were no local political parties to intervene in these matters; indeed, the largest and in some ways most influential organizations in town were the League of Women Voters and the Parent-Teacher's Association.

When the new chief installed a legalistic police style, the citizenry did not rebel but the police officers did. Some citizens complained about the great increase in the number of traffic tickets or grumbled when the chief raided a church bingo game, but on the whole there were few pressures from voters to which the city council felt it had to respond. At least while the wealthy Chicago commuters dominated it, the manager and his chief were supported. When the chief became involved in a dispute with a popular, old-time sergeant over promotions, the issue was raised in a councilmanic election (the sergeant had many friends in the community), but the incumbent councilmen supported the chief. Whatever the new chief's faults might be, a majority of the councilmen felt that he was a great improvement over the days when the police were run in a haphazard fashion by one of the elected city commissioners.

A member of the League of Women Voters expressed this view when she told an interviewer: "The old [police] department was very friendly; every officer seemed to know you. If you were going too fast they would give you a warning instead of a ticket. But I suppose the way the department operates today is the only right way to go about it. The laws should be enforced to the letter."

A high city official who himself thought the chief was too rigid nonetheless denied that citizen complaints had much effect: "I don't think that the complaints against [him] had too much to do with law enforcement. The average citizen might complain if he got a ticket, but most citizens didn't get tickets and they were proud of their police department. Nobody criticized the department for being too good."

The grumbling that went on among the voters was quiet, did not affect elections, often took the form of jokes about zeal, and was easily countered by the city manager. The grumbling among the patrolmen was another matter. To them, the legalistic police style had been purchased at the price of excessive discipline, arbitrary rules, and unfair personnel policies. In the past, discipline, such as it was, had been handled casually by the chief within the department. The new chief brought formal charges against some officers before the local civil service commission. Promotions, salary increases, and assignments had in the past been determined largely on the basis of seniority; now elaborate personnel evaluation procedures were put into effect to decide such matters on the basis of what the chief thought was "objective merit." When an officer resigned from the force, allegedly because he had been caught pilfering, he made public a letter accusing the chief of "intolerance" and "harassment."

A popular officer was not allowed to take the examination for lieutenant on the grounds that he was not a sergeant and therefore not qualified, but he felt that since he was serving in a capacity (juvenile specialist) with the pay and prerogatives of a sergeant, he was qualified. He appealed the ruling to the courts. Finally, the patrolmen organized a protective association to demand changes in the promotional system and to complain of the discipline and lowered morale in the department. The chief asked the city council to appoint a committee to investigate his administration; reluctantly, they agreed and after private hearings issued a report upholding him. The patrolmen attacked the report and argued again for seniority-based pay increases. "To merit, in our opinion, is to earn or deserve," they wrote. "We feel that anyone who is doing average work on the . . . department deserves and earns automatic periodic raises in pay. Anyone doing below average, or inferior work, could and should have charges preferred against him." They also criticized the city for appealing a court ruling upholding the officer who was denied permission to take the lieutenant's examination (ultimately, a higher court upheld the city). Some officers supported the chief and this made matters even worse.

A senior officer later described to an interviewer the state into which the department had fallen during those bitter months:

> It was really terrible. I can't begin to describe to you what the situation was like. The men weren't even speaking to each other. When a police officer clams up, he really clams up . . . You'd walk into a room and nobody would say anything to you, and nobody'd talk to anybody else. Everything was falling apart. The men were just going through the motions. You can't run a department unless the men'll cooperate. A department depends on the exchange of information and if people aren't talking to each other, there's not a damn thing you can do.

Finally, the city manager left to accept a job elsewhere. A new city manager was hired — also a professional, also from another city — and he was faced with the police problem. From the outset he took the position that it was his concern and that he would tolerate no political influence on his decisions. He kept the controversial chief in office, though privately he advised him to adopt a more "flexible" attitude. By this time certain officers had mounted a steady campaign against the chief consisting of letters and phone calls to the council and leaks to a local newspaper (two newspapers serve the city and as a result of the competition one of them is aggressive in a way not typical of most suburban papers). Finally the chief took a job in another community, apparently believing he had outlived his usefulness. The city manager appointed a new chief, this one from inside the department, but only after a general canvass throughout several states and many interviews. The new chief was more tactful and popular but retained many of the old chief's law enforcement policies and introduced further "professional" changes.

The new chief, like the old one, was aware that some citizens did not like to get traffic or parking tickets or wanted special considerations. But he felt protected by the city manager and free to pursue his own policies:

The biggest source of these complaints is discourtesy. Often it's not real. It's just the style of the officer . . . without meaning to he can sound discourteous. But whatever the reason, this is the thing you can get hit with. Fortunately, the city manager is my boss . . . As long as I've got a city manager like [the present one] I can ignore it. Of course, I'm a realist, I listen to them. I'm polite, I don't turn my back on them but I don't do anything about these complaints unless the city manager and I feel it is a serious matter.

He is buffered against particular complaints about specific actions; with respect to general law enforcement strategy, he gets almost no pressure at all. When a child is killed at an intersection, there will be, as there have been, demands for a new stop sign at the corner or closer police patrols. In one such case the chief thought such measures were not justified, but when several people went to a city council meeting to demand a stop sign, the council overruled the police and ordered it installed. Such demands are, again, highly particular in nature. There is no organized concern about how many traffic tickets are issued or how many juveniles arrested or the relative advantages of a specialized detective force over a beefed-up patrol force in coping with burglaries.

Because Oakland is a racially divided city, it has not been possible for the city manager to treat the police function as if it were a purely technical one with no large policy implications. Students from the University of California at nearby Berkeley have organized antiwar demonstrations and marches in Oakland; local Negroes have demanded changes in the handling of complaints against the police. When the police department was reformed and reorganized in the mid-1950's, the city manager and the new chief had to devote a great deal of effort to coping with the complaints of organized police officers. None of these issues, however, has caused any modification of the over-all police strategy and only one (the Negro demands) has even been concerned about that strategy.

At first, the manager's principal problem was to protect the reform chief against efforts to replace him or to reverse his policies. The chief and the manager were offered, and refused, large bribes to permit gambling to continue; one councilman fought the manager bitterly, but unsuccessfully, over the location of the new police headquarters building; other officials have tried to influence the choice of a replacement for the reform chiefs who died or retired. Organized officers resisted a plan to abolish the rank of inspector and another to give the city manager, on the recommendation of the chief, the power to appoint deputy chiefs (formerly, such promotions, like all others, were made on the basis of civil service examinations). They were successful on the first issue and unsuccessful on the second.[19]

In recent years, however, the major political issues involving the police have concerned the handling of certain groups in the community. The city manager has taken an important part in most of these controversies; only when there was no manager (for a few months after the first reform manager resigned to take a job elsewhere, there was only an acting city manager) did the political leaders of the city — the mayor and city councilmen — play an important role. When a civil rights march occurred in 1965, the manager assumed personal charge and, with the chief, saw to it that the marchers were given the freedom to parade and assemble under clearly defined rules and with ample police protection. There were no incidents. Later that same year, an antiwar demonstration was announced. The manager having resigned, the mayor and others took charge and tried for a while to forbid it, thereby precipitating a long political and legal fight over the right to parade, which resulted in the defeat of the city and the growth in the number of marchers from the few hundred who originally sought to display their antiwar sentiments to the several thousand who sought in addition to defy the Oakland authorities.[20]

19. See *Oakland Tribune*, February 22, 1965, and November 17, 1954. City law required that there be the rank of inspector, in addition to patrolman, sergeant, and so forth, and that men holding that rank perform only investigative duties. The chief believed this arrangement was too inflexible and prevented him from assigning men to various duties as he saw fit. Because the chief cannot be required to *appoint* anybody to the rank of inspector, in time this rank will probably die out through attrition and the criminal information division will assume all investigative duties.

20. On their first attempt to march, the antiwar group was met at the city line and turned back by about two hundred Oakland police officers. The second attempt,

The other major political issue involved the proposed creation of a civilian review board or some extra-departmental arrangement for handling citizen complaints about police behavior.[21] The Oakland Negro community has an especially large number of civil rights organizations and spokesmen, ranging from the moderate to the radical, from integrationist to "black power." Such a situation leads inevitably to a good deal of competition for leadership, resources, and attention; when, in addition, elements of the city government show little inclination to be conciliatory with respect to at least some of the demands made on them, it is not surprising that Negro protest should tend to become steadily more militant, more strident, and less compromising.

In September 1965, at the climax of a period of repeated demonstrations, one civil rights group began demanding the creation of a civilian review board, charging "police brutality" and a failure to hire sufficient Negro officers.[22] The city council rejected the plan. The following spring, critics of the police testified before the State Advisory Committee of the U.S. Civil Rights Commission; the chief denied their charges. When it became evident that the city would not create a review board, a plan was devised by certain white and Negro activists to create a private or "shadow" review board, called the "Police Affairs Committee." The plan was taken up and, after some modifications, endorsed by the Oakland Economic Development Council (OEDC), an organization created the previous year by the city as the community action agency for local poverty programs.

After a long period of public controversy and private negotiation, the mayor proposed creating a "Citizens' Grievance Representative" to be appointed by the manager, who would hear complaints about

---

the following day, was similarly repulsed. This time the peace marchers were attacked by members of the "Hell's Angels" motorcycle club; one Angel was arrested. See *Oakland Tribune,* October 14, 16, and 17 and November 18, 19, 20, 1965.

21. The background of and arguments for and against civilian review boards are discussed in "The Administration of Complaints by Civilians Against the Police," *Harvard Law Review,* 77 (January 1964), pp. 499–519. One of the cities in which interviews were conducted for that article was Oakland.

22. See *Oakland Tribune,* December 12, 1964; February 19 and 20 and September 27, 1965.

the workings of any municipal department or appeals from the decisions of departmental grievance procedures. When the mayor submitted the idea to the city council, it was rejected.

Here, as on the question of the civil rights marches, the so-called "power structure" that supposedly "runs" Oakland from behind the scenes was deeply divided, if indeed it exists at all. A majority of the city councilmen favored a "get tough" policy with marchers and Negroes. One mayor agreed with them; his successor disagreed. The *Oakland Tribune* supported resistance to the antiwar march, and lost; it favored the mayor's plan for a grievance officer, and lost again. The police department opposed the grievance officer plan, and won, but the mayor, who had favored it, was nonetheless reelected to office by an overwhelming majority. One city manager allowed the civil rights marches over the private objections of many influential persons but suffered no costs as a result; his successor, the acting city manager, opposed the peace march but was passed over when it came time to pick a regular manager. One city councilman who led the struggle against the grievance officer proposal had been opposed for election by the *Tribune*; he won anyway. Each of the last three police chiefs was picked by the city manager with, apparently, a free hand, and each chief has been able to run the department in his own way except when a mass demonstration occurred; then they have collaborated with either the manager or, in his absence, the mayor — with, as we have seen, very different results.

In Syracuse, a strong mayor has acted more or less like the strong city managers in Oakland, with the important difference that, because he is an elected official, he has paid more public attention to the popular concern over "crime in the streets." Together with his solid Republican majority on the common council,[23] he dominates

23. Syracuse, though demographically similar to Albany, has been solidly Republican for as long as the latter has been solidly Democratic. One reason was the strong Unionist sentiment in Onondaga County, of which Syracuse is part, during the Civil War; another has been the strong antipathy displayed by Syracuse voters toward New York City and "Tammany Hall," which, in their minds, is coequal to the Democratic Party; a third has been the skill and success with which the Republican Party in Syracuse has been led. See Roscoe C. Martin, et al., *Decisions in Syracuse* (Bloomington: University of Indiana Press, 1961), pp. 35, 46, and 318–319; Ralph

the city's politics though in recent years agitation among Negroes over the poverty program and certain police and civil rights issues have made those politics more turbulent than usual. But the Republican party remains strong and united, whereas the Democrats are weak and divided.

Until 1963 political involvement in police affairs was commonplace. A high police official told an interviewer, "Mayor *X* was terrible. Nobody could get promoted or assigned to anything within the police department without clearing it with him. And the salaries were terrible. The mayor never did anything for the department; he only did things to it." Nonetheless, many officers were reluctant to see the old order change, less from any attachment to it than from fear of what might replace it. They were concerned about ranks, duties, salaries, and promotions, and they were as skeptical of entrusting such affairs to a strong chief as they had been of entrusting them to a strong mayor. They preferred these matters to be governed by rules that *nobody* could change. The new city administration, while searching for a new chief, encountered this resistance and an accompanying lack of central authority in the department. A high city official later remarked to a researcher: "[The department was] incredibly faction-ridden . . . There was an Irish faction, an Italian faction, a sergeants' faction, a detectives' faction, a PBA faction, and so on. Each had their own rival candidates for leadership positions and each was jealous and suspicious of the other."

The fact that an outside chief was recruited and then backed up by the mayor must be explained by the mayor's temperament and personality as well as by his political needs. He was newly elected, one of the first under a charter amendment that permitted him to succeed himself at the end of his four-year term. He had a master's degree in social work from Syracuse University and a strong desire to make a name for himself. He consulted with many people in professional law enforcement at the state and federal level and

---

A. Straetz and Frank J. Munger, *New York Politics* (New York: New York University Press, 1960), pp. 39–67; and John H. Lindquist, "An Occupational Analysis of Local Politics: Syracuse, New York, 1880–1959," *Sociology and Social Research*, 49 (April 1965), pp. 343–354.

in New York City before making up his mind. By picking the man everybody recommended, he deprived the Democrats of a police issue. He also insisted that subordinate officers in the department be promoted strictly in accordance with civil service examinations. As he later explained to an interviewer, "If you always appoint the person who scores highest on the civil service list, then you can protect yourself from pressure. It's the perfect out when dealing with people who want you to do favors for them." His strategy worked: after the furor created by the report of the state investigating commission, prominent Syracuse citizens began to praise the police department and its "new look."[24] When the next election came around, the only law enforcement issue the Democrats could raise was that the city needed more policemen. The mayor, naturally, could agree but point out that this would cost money, which the city did not have.

The new chief, as a result, had a relatively free hand on personnel and organizational matters. Though there have been one or two efforts by certain officials, as well as by one important religious leader, to help someone on the force they liked, a high police official said to an interviewer, "We told [them] no and fortunately we had our heavy artillery lined up with lots of good reasons why it couldn't be done."

City hall has been more concerned with certain law enforcement issues than with internal departmental affairs — especially with civil rights demonstrations, demands for civilian review boards, and public concern over rising crime rates. Various public officials tried to tell the police how to handle the demonstrations, generally by urging them to take a tougher line. One high police official told an interviewer that this had been a mistake: "[The mayor] could be a

24. The "Citizens for an Informed Public," a Syracuse civic group, mailed to the voters a brochure entitled, "How Good is the Syracuse Police Department?" in which they concluded that it was now very good indeed. The newspapers, once critical of the department for incompetence, now occasionally criticize it for excessive zeal. A former key official of the SIC later told an interviewer that "Syracuse has been our big success story," unlike other cities he felt "had probably slid back to just about where they were before the investigation."

great mayor . . . if he was a little calmer in these crises." Some Republican politicians agree and apparently the party is divided between those who fear "over-reacting" and those who fear being "too soft." The mayor has stated his unequivocal opposition to the proposed civilian review board but, perhaps because of changes in the police department and the work of the human relations commission, the issue had, in late 1966, died down. To cope with complaints about rising crime (because of improved police statistics in Syracuse, it appears to be rising faster than it is), the mayor appointed a "Commission on Law Enforcement and Criminal Procedure" and provided it with a small staff. It reviewed all agencies of criminal justice in the area, but seemed concerned mostly with certain city judges whom the mayor felt were too lenient and were thus letting too many criminals, especially chronic young offenders, stay on the streets.[25] However, its report, submitted in December 1966, was, in the opinion, and to the relief, of most law enforcement persons, innocuous; other than reaffirming the city's opposition to a civilian review board and recommending the hiring of more police, prosecutors, and judges, it suggested little of consequence and created no public stir.

Issues such as "crime in the streets" and "police brutality" are highly dramatic and freighted with real and symbolic importance for both Negroes and whites. But they have relatively little to do with the day-to-day operational policies of the police department, despite the fact that those policies have changed sharply since 1963. One might suppose that the 58 per cent increase in traffic tickets during the first full year under the "reform" chief and the somewhat tougher policy toward juvenile offenders, to say nothing of clamping down on gambling, were changes of sufficient significance to justify the involvement of the mayor in making them or to provoke some kind of public reaction to which the mayor would have to respond.

In fact, except for some isolated and ineffectual complaints there has been no political issue generated by these changes. A county official accused the Syracuse police of being "over-zealous" in check-

25. Syracuse *Post-Standard,* May 27 and December 1 and 7, 1965.

ing bars for liquor law violations,[26] a judge criticized the police for arresting some people for engaging in "friendly" drinking in a tavern before official opening time,[27] a newspaper accused the police of emphasizing parking tickets more than serious crime and of using the tickets "principally for revenue." [28] None of these complaints was taken seriously by the police, partly because they were trivial and partly because they came from third parties, not injured parties. Far more common have been demands for "more police protection," many of them inspired by the 1965 mayoralty election campaign. Newspaper stories and editorials called for more policemen downtown, more at an athletic field, and more near gas stations; in addition, the district attorney was urged to show "no quarter" in dealing with people who attack police officers.[29] The mayor responded by announcing that he would add twenty men to the force and by instructing the police to be "tough but fair." [30]

The police tend to view such public maneuvers somewhat skeptically. To them, these periodic outbursts of concern are politically motivated and, what is worse, ephemeral. Though they are happy to have more men on the force, or better yet, higher pay for those already on, they know from experience that putting a cop on a particular street corner or by a certain gas station will not stop crime, it will only displace it. In any case, the demands never last long and, because everybody would like a cop on his corner, they tend to cancel each other out. In the end, the police know, things will return to normal.

What does concern them, here as in all cities in this study, is job security and departmental control. As in Oakland, Syracuse officers fought some of the early reform moves, they opposed in court the selection of deputy chiefs by the chief himself rather than through civil service procedures, and they opposed transferring men be-

26. *Post-Standard,* August 2, 1963.
27. *Post-Standard,* September 16, 1964.
28. *Post-Standard,* February 10 and April 25, 1965.
29. *Post-Standard,* October 8 and 10 and November 26, 1964; January 13, 1965.
30. *Post-Standard,* September 9 and 13, 1965.

tween the patrol and investigative divisions.[31] In addition, the officers wanted, over the chief's objections, to keep certain organizational perquisites — the right to sell tickets and advertisements for the policemen's ball and to issue windshield stickers and wallet cards to "honorary" members of the PBA. On all of these issues except the ticket sales for the dance, they lost.

Some Findings from National Data

Ideally, one would like to measure the extent to which a police style is constrained by a city's political culture with data from a large number of cities. The relationships described in the preceding part of this chapter may, after all, be peculiar to these eight communities or the causal connections may be more apparent than real. But if this study has made nothing else clear, it should have explained why this would be exceptionally difficult if not impossible. Measuring a political culture — assuming we could agree on what is to be measured — would require fairly elaborate and expensive surveys conducted in fifty or a hundred communities. And measuring police policies would be even harder. As indicated in Chapter 4, many of the most relevant elements of such policies are not made explicit by the department; indeed, the department may not be aware of such "policies" themselves (in which case they cannot, strictly speaking, be called policies but only "styles"). And even if the measurement problems could be solved, we would not expect anything like a perfect fit between policy and culture, for as we have said, the latter constrains the former but does not uniquely determine it.

Nonetheless, some effort of this sort might be useful. As a substitute measure of political culture, we here use form of government modified, in the case of the city manager form, by the degree of apparent "professionalism" of the manager. Four kinds of cities

31. *Post-Standard,* July 17, 1963.

are used — those with a mayor and council chosen by districts on a partisan ballot, those with a mayor and council chosen on a nonpartisan ballot, those with a council-manager government and a manager ranking low on a scale of "professionalism," and those with a council-manager government in which the manager scores high on such a scale. The theory underlying these categories is this: the more partisan the political system, the more politicians represent small geographic constituencies, and the more nonprofessional the executive head of the government, the more likely the city will have a political culture favorable to the watchman police style. By contrast, cities electing nonpartisan officials at large and vesting executive authority in a highly professional city manager will more likely have a political culture favoring the legalistic police style.

As a substitute measure of law enforcement policy or style, we use the arrest rate for certain offenses where we know police discretion is great and thus where police style is likely to be most evident: larceny, simple assaults, drunkenness, disorderly conduct, and driving while intoxicated. It must be emphasized, however, that police style is not always best measured by arrest rates, even for high-discretion offenses. Albany and Oakland both arrest a lot of drunks, as we have seen, but for quite different reasons, and those reasons are relevant to the likelihood that any given drunk will be arrested.

A list was made of all cities that in 1960 had a population of between 25,000 and 100,000, a median family income of between $5,000 and $7,500 a year, and a nonwhite population that did not equal or exceed 5 per cent of the total. Eliminated, therefore, were cities that were either very large or very small, very rich or very poor, or more than slightly Negro. Controlling for such factors should eliminate any large differences in the true, but necessarily unknown, crime rate because crime varies significantly with city size, social class, and racial composition. The form of government of these 188 cities was ascertained; for those with the council-manager form, data gathered from the files of the International City Managers' Association were used to assess the degree of apparent "professionalism" of the manager holding office in 1960. Two extreme types of council-manager cities were used — those with a manager having none of the "professional" attributes and those with a manager having all or most of these attributes.[32] The "high professional" manager cities are in general those where the manager has a postgraduate degree, has had previous experience in city management or other public capacity, and was brought to the city where he was serving in 1960 from another community. The "low professional" cities are those where the manager has no more than a bachelor's degree, has had no previous experience in city management, and was recruited from the same city where he was serving in 1960.[33] It was possible to sort 161 of the 188 cities into one of the four political types — partisan mayor-council, nonpartisan mayor-council, "low professional" city manager, and "high professional" city manager. The Federal Bureau of Investigation supplied arrest statistics, as of 1960, for the 146 cities on which they had data; many of those missing did not have independent police forces.[34]

32. The incumbent managers were scored as follows:

Education

2 points = graduate degree
1 point = bachelor's degree or other undergraduate degree
0 points = no college degree

Experience

3 points = previous experience in city management in another city
2 points = previous experience in another city but not as a manager
0 points = a local hired as manager from same city in which he is now serving or with no previous experience in another city

Managers scoring 4 or 5 points were classified as "high professional"; those scoring 1 or 0 points were scored "low professional." Intermediate score positions were omitted.

These data were abstracted from the files of the International City Managers' Association by research assistants under the supervision of Robert L. Crain of the National Opinion Research Center.

33. In another study it was found that the more professional managers were more likely than less professional managers to serve in cities where the decision to fluoridate the water supply was made by administrative action. See Donald B. Rosenthal and Robert L. Crain, "City Government and Fluoridation" in James Q. Wilson, ed., *City Politics and Public Policy* (New York: John Wiley & Sons, 1968).

34. Arrest data for individual cities are not published by the FBI but are kept on file. I am indebted to the Uniform Crime Reporting Section of the FBI for making

The specific hypotheses were that cities with professionalized, "good government" regimes would be likely to have legalistic police forces that made more arrests than other cities in law enforcement situations (that is, for larceny and driving while intoxicated); that cities with partisan, mayor-council regimes would be more likely to have watchman-style police forces that would make more arrests in order maintenance situations where the action is typically police-initiated (that is, for disorderly conduct); that in order maintenance situations where the police response is citizen-invoked (that is, assault), there would be relatively little difference between police departments, and thus between cities, because arrests in these cases require citizen cooperation and therefore depend more on the characteristics of the citizens than on the characteristics of the police; and finally that drunkenness arrests might or might not differ, depending on whether the police saw such matters as problems of law enforcement or order maintenance, but that professionalized cities would probably show a higher arrest rate because they were more likely to take the law enforcement point of view.

Somewhat surprisingly, given the crudity of the measures, Table 13 tends to confirm these hypotheses. The arrest rate per 100,000 population for larceny and drunkenness is nearly twice as high in the professional as in the partisan cities, whereas the rate for driving while intoxicated is about 50 per cent higher. The arrest rate for disorderly conduct, on the other hand, is 42 per cent higher in the partisan than in the professional cities. The assault arrest rate, however, is about the same in the two extreme city types.

The intermediate cities — low-professional manager and nonpartisan mayor-council cities — show no consistent pattern, as one might expect. On larceny and drunkenness, they are quite similar to the high-professional manager cities — suggesting that if any one of the elements of municipal reform is present (nonpartisanship or the council-manager form), the political culture becomes more

these figures available to me. It would be interesting to see if differences in arrest rates for major crimes exist that are comparable to the differences found for these minor offenses and also how much of the difference in the latter rates results from police policies toward juveniles.

Table 13. Arrest rates for certain common offenses, by community political system, 1960.[a]

Offense	High-professional council-manager cities ($n = 43$)	Low-professional council-manager cities ($n = 19$)	Nonpartisan mayor-council cities ($n = 50$)	Partisan mayor-council cities ($n = 34$)
Larceny	251.1	204.6	230.1	121.9
Drunkenness	1,185.8	1,113.6	918.0	656.5
Driving while intoxicated	194.6	159.2	136.8	132.2
Disorderly conduct	224.9	259.1	211.9	318.2
Simple assault	108.2	101.2	66.3	94.0

Source: 1960 reports of arrests by local police departments to the FBI.

[a] Arrest rates are the total for all cities of that type; that is, the total number of arrests for all cities in each column is divided by the total population for the cities in that column.

conducive to the legalistic police style. With respect to driving while intoxicated, however, only the manager cities arrest at high rates; rates for both partisan and nonpartisan mayor-council types are lower. One somewhat anomalous finding is the very high arrest rate for disorderly conduct in the nonprofessional manager cities. This high rate may be due in part to the fact that the nineteen cities in this category include, quite by chance, two resort cities where the summer population is abnormally large (and of course, not counted in the census) and unusually boisterous. Removing these cities from that category reduces the disorderly conduct arrest rate by 7.0.

It may be objected that there is a regional effect at work on these data. A large number of the council-manager cities (thirteen of the sixty-two, to be exact) are in California where city government, one may conjecture, operates in a statewide political culture that has for so long stressed nonpartisan, professional administration and that has given such strong encouragement to police professionalism that one would expect, almost regardless of who is in power in a particular city, a legalistic police style. The thirty-four partisan, mayor-council cities, on the other hand, are largely (twenty-six of the total) from the northeastern region where, presumably, the tradition of the "Irish cop" and the fact of strong party organization may contribute to a watchman police style almost regardless of who is in power.

To check this possibility, all California cities were deleted from Table 13 and the rates recalculated. With respect to larceny, drunkenness, and driving while intoxicated, there is very little change — the high-professional manager cities still arrest at a rate much higher (88 and 66 per cent higher, respectively) than the partisan, mayor-council cities for the first two offenses and at a rate somewhat (27 per cent) higher for the third offense.[35] With respect to disorderly conduct, the partisan cities continue to arrest at a higher rate than the professionalized cities (33 per cent higher, to be exact).[36]

In sum, the theory that the political culture of a community constrains law enforcement styles survives the crude and inadequate statistical tests that available data permit. This exercise has also

35. The rates for the sample, excluding the California cities, were:

Offense	High Professional ($n = 34$)	Low Professional ($n = 15$)	Nonpartisan ($n = 48$)	Partisan ($n = 34$)
Larceny	229.0	162.3	228.8	121.9
Drunkenness	1,061.2	1,084.6	914.2	656.5
Driving while intoxicated	168.3	129.1	128.5	132.2
Disorderly conduct	239.2	267.3	215.7	318.2
Simple assault	112.2	103.4	65.6	94.0

36. One would also want to know the effect of political culture on local traffic enforcement but traffic ticket figures are not reported to the FBI and few departments keep such records locally for as far back as 1960; thus, ticket rates cannot be used in an analysis based on 1960 population characteristics. Gardiner ("Police Enforcement of Traffic Laws") finds that, using 1964 data on tickets, the rate at which they were issued increases in cities with high rates of population mobility and that mobility, in turn, increased the likelihood that a city would have the city manager form of government.

confirmed the judgment offered in the beginning of this study—that a full explanation of a police style requires first-hand observation of the behavior of the police in order to discover what that style is and first-hand knowledge of the community in order to discover what the political culture is. Nevertheless, there is good reason to believe that police professionalism and municipal reform apparently have real consequences for the substance of law enforcement, not just in the eight cities studied intensively but perhaps in cities generally, even though the effects may be less dramatic in the typical case than in the "pure" types selected for this study. And thus there is also good reason to believe that politics, in the broadest sense, influences law enforcement but that the influence is more indirect than deliberate.[37]

37. This emphasis is quite different from that of the Wickersham Commission, which, in its 1931 report on the "principal causes of the defects in police administration which too generally leave the citizen helpless in the hands of the criminal class," found the "chief evil" to be "the insecure, short term of service of the chief . . . and in his being subject while in office to the control of politicians in the discharge of his duties." National Commission on Law Observance and Enforcement, *The Police* (Washington, D.C.: Government Printing Office, 1931), No. 14, p. 1. And, indeed, the office of chief did seem then to be a political football: Detroit had four police chiefs in one year, Chicago fourteen in thirty years. This has apparently changed: the chiefs in most of my eight communities had been in office for over eight years. The police have clearly been taken "out of politics" in the narrow sense, except in Albany and Newburgh, but it is far from clear that this change has made the citizen any less helpless in the hands of the criminal class.

Nine Conclusions and Policy Implications

The patrolman, in the discharge of his most important duties, exercises discretion necessarily, owing in part to his role in the management of conflict and in part to his role in the suppression of crime. In managing conflict, his task is to maintain order under circumstances such that the participants and the observer are likely to disagree as to what constitutes a reasonable and fair settlement and he is likely to be aware of hostility, alert to the possibility of violence, and uncertain that the authority symbolized by his badge and uniform will be sufficient for him to take control of the situation. In suppressing crime, his task is to judge the likely future behavior of persons on the basis of their appearance and attitude and to deal with those he deems "suspicious" under the color of laws that either say nothing about his authority to question and search short of making an arrest or give him ambiguous or controversial powers.

In any particular case, the patrolman may act improperly by abusing or exceeding his authority, making arrests or street stops on the basis of personal prejudice or ill-temper, or handling a situation differently from the way the administrator or mayor might handle it. But to say that in a given case the observer or the community could have prescribed a better course of action is not to say that a better course of action, applicable to all or most situations, could be prescribed generally and in advance. Put another way, the possibility of deciding in a particular instance that the police behaved wrongly does not mean that one can formulate a meaningful policy for how the police should behave in all cases.

The problems created by the exercise of necessary discretion are least in communities that have widely shared values as to what constitutes an appropriate level of order and what kind of person or form of behavior is an empirically sound predictor of criminal intentions; the problems are greatest in cities deeply divided along lines of class and race.

Though the police administrator, and thus the city government, cannot prescribe in advance the correct course of action for handling order maintenance or crime suppression situations, this does not mean that their actions and policies have no effect on the patrolman's behavior. They have, but that effect is gross, imprecise, and hard to predict — they shape the over-all style or strategy of the police but they cannot direct or guide police behavior in the concrete case. Or, more accurately, such guidance as the policies provide is more a list of things *not* to do rather than a statement of what the officer *should* do. Negative policies, of course, have their effect. Historically, police departments have changed partly because patrolmen have been increasingly constrained by departmental rules to avoid certain actions they once regarded as natural. These rules and understandings are the product of the changing views of administrators, the rapid spread of that form of government (nonpartisan, "professional" city management) that is supportive of the legalistic police style, and the particular interventions of specific political groups seeking to change police conduct toward them. The differences between certain southern and northern police departments have been due, in the past at least, to the exclusion of Negroes from political participation in the southern communities and thus to the inability of Negroes to compel the police to avoid certain anti-Negro actions.

But there are at least two limits to the value of negative policies. First, they leave untouched a large area of necessary discretion and, second, they are perceived by the officers as irrelevant and unhelpful restrictions — as rules that "tell us what we shouldn't do" and thus "give the brass plenty of rope with which to hang us," but that "don't tell us what we *should* do." Precise, positive guidance is, as we have seen, made impossible by the nature of the situation, even though the patrolman's desire for positive policies probably increases with the number of restrictions placed on him. And such policies as exist are hard to implement. For example, an ideal policy for patrolling the streets of a low-income Negro area would be to leave alone persons "known" to be law-abiding and to question or investigate persons who are acting suspiciously. It is difficult for a well-intentioned and conscientious observer to make such distinctions; it is almost impossible for an organization to get hundreds or thousands of members to make them and make them consistently and in the same way. Thus, patrolmen will alternate between periods when they believe "The brass wants us to leave them alone" (leading to complaints of neglect and underenforcement) and periods when they believe "The brass wants us to crack down" (leading to complaints of "harassment").

Because the control the organization has over the behavior of its members is imprecise, efforts by a social scientist to explain that behavior are likely to be imperfect. The sources of discretion can be described, the key elements of the situation, from the patrolman's point of view, can be identified, the outer limits to discretion that are set by police policy or style can be suggested, but how officers routinely handle their discretion in the least visible situations can only be stated and explained in approximate terms. Furthermore, many possible explanations have not been considered here. Middle-class officers may systematically behave differently from working-class ones; older officers differently from younger ones; west coast officers differently from east coast ones. About these and other matters, this study could provide little information.

And from the point of view of the police administrator or the city official, it is by no means clear that such other explanatory variables would have much interest. The mayor cannot move his city from the west coast to the east coast, replace younger officers with older ones, or even (in the short run) do much about the class background of his recruits. He may, of course, make a determined effort to attract "better men" to his force by raising salaries, engaging in nationwide recruiting campaigns, and sending his men to, or getting them from, college. To a limited degree and in some cities, these efforts have substantially changed the class and educational attributes of the force (Oakland is a good example). But it would be a mistake to rely very heavily on such methods. For one thing, it is not yet clear exactly in what ways, if at all, middle-class, college-educated men make better police officers. For another, it is most unlikely that many such persons are ever going to find a police career very attractive — especially in the big cities, where police work is much of the time a boring, monotonous, messy routine occasionally interrupted by intense hostility, physical danger, and social conflict. Finally, even if getting such men were a good idea and some were interested, we could not expect enough of them to be available to fill even a fraction of the more than 400,000 police positions in the country or even a large fraction of the 100,000 positions in cities of over 250,000 population. According to the President's Commission, most departments are under-strength today even though the vast majority require nothing more of their recruits than a high school diploma.

In short, police administrators and mayors are going to have to work with the human material they now have, or something very like it. And this means that the available ways of getting the police officer to "do his duty," when what that duty requires is far from clear, will be mostly confined to organizational and legal factors. Here, there are two competing values — bureaucracy and professionalism. For some purposes or to some people, the problem with the police is that they don't follow the rules. They question when they shouldn't, search when they mustn't, arrest when they have no grounds. The remedy, therefore, is to bureaucratize, or "judicialize," [1] the police: make them subject to more and more explicit rules, have these rules reviewed by the courts or by other nonpolice agencies, and reduce their discretion wherever possible. Lawyers, for whom "clear standards" is always a favorite remedy for administrative discretion, are especially inclined to take this approach.

Police administrators have taken it also, though for very different reasons. The general drift in police management has been to convert, wherever possible, matters of order maintenance into matters of law enforcement, to substitute the legalistic for the watchman style, and to multiply the rules under which the patrolman operates.

1. Cf. Herbert L. Packer, "Two Models of the Criminal Process," *University of Pennsylvania Law Review,* 113 (November 1964), pp. 1–68.

Partly this drift has been a consequence of political reform: reduce corruption by reducing the amount of discretion the officer has to sell. Partly it has been to give the appearance of efficiency and vigor — make as many arrests as possible with as few officers as possible and evaluate the individual officer by his arrest record. And partly it has been in order to achieve law enforcement objectives — vigorous police activity, a high arrest rate, and intensive surveillance over suspicious street activity will, in this view, deter criminals, apprehend fugitives, locate stolen goods and other contraband, and even reduce auto accidents.

Other persons, and in different circumstances, some of the same lawyers and administrators mentioned above, want the police officer to perform as a "professional" who has a service function. He should be freed from "objective" evaluation on the basis of arrest records and should emphasize creating and maintaining "good community relations." Training and supervision, this argument goes, should encourage the patrolman to take a broad view of his role, exercise initiative and independence, appreciate the discretion he necessarily possesses, and learn his beat and work with the people on it. Traditionally, this is exactly what the patrolman did — he tried to keep a "quiet beat" and to "handle" such situations as they arose. His traditional role was changed for various reasons — riots and civil disorders led him to be mobilized and armed more as a combat than a beat patrol force. Crime waves at the end of the nineteenth century and again in the period from the First World War through the depression led to a public demand that law enforcement be emphasized, and Prohibition and other restrictions on the sale of liquor brought him into an adversary relationship with his beat[2] (for the first time, he was supposed to do things many citizens did not want done) and created the opportunity for large-scale corruption. Public disagreement as to the legitimate uses of discretion and public concern over the officer's capacity to use it honestly and without favoritism led to its progressive curtailment.

2. See, for example, Roger Lane, *Policing the City: Boston, 1822–1885* (Cambridge, Mass.: Harvard University Press, 1967), Chap. 12.

The patrolman is neither a bureaucrat nor a professional, but a member of a *craft*. As with most crafts, his has no body of generalized, written knowledge nor a set of detailed prescriptions as to how to behave — it has, in short, neither theory nor rules. Learning in the craft is by apprenticeship, but on the job and not in the academy. The principal group from which the apprentice wins (or fails to win) respect are his colleagues on the job, not fellow members of a discipline or attentive supervisors. And the members of the craft, conscious of having a special skill or task, think of themselves as set apart from society, possessors of an art that can be learned only by experience, and in need of restrictions on entry into their occupation. But unlike other members of a craft — carpenters, for example, or newspapermen — the police work in an apprehensive or hostile environment producing a service the value of which is not easily judged.

An attempt to change a craft into a bureaucracy will be perceived by the members as a failure of confidence and a withdrawal of support and thus strongly resisted; efforts to change it into a profession will be seen as irrelevant and thus largely ignored.

Faced with these difficulties, it is tempting to devise ways whereby the police can be bureaucratized for some purposes, professionalized for others, and left alone for still others. Perhaps the leniency and neighborhood orientation of old-style departments can be combined with the honesty and equity of the new, in order to have the best of both worlds and the worst of neither. If this means simply putting the "old-time Irish cop" into a department where careful attention is paid to warning suspects of their rights and assigning patrolmen by computer, it does not seem very plausible. If it means that a department should be honest but not zealous, fair but not "harassing," there is something to be said for it but a note of caution is required. This study has suggested, but obviously not proved, that *there may be a trade-off between leniency and equity*. While a legalistic department, by being more "bureaucratic" (that is rule-bound) treats persons more evenly it also tends to reward officers for following rules, including legal rules, which stipulate that it is the officer's duty to make an arrest wherever he can.[3] A watchman style department will overlook "minor" offenses and events that do not unduly disturb the public peace, but it will treat harshly and sometimes extralegally serious matters, disturbances of the peace, or challenges to police authority, and this treatment is often experienced as brutality or discrimination.

The "friendly cop" who ignores minor misdeeds is often thought to be benevolent, but because he must choose which and whose misdeeds to ignore, he is in some sense discriminatory. The requirements of justice are quite different from those of benevolence: the former enjoin us to treat equals equally, which is to say by rule, and the latter encourage us to be considerate even though a rule must be broken and thus one person given (unfair) consideration over another. Justice can be a duty under all circumstances, but benevolence cannot — if it were, everyone would be impoverished by constant alms giving and the equal protection of the laws would be supplanted by the injustice of compassion. Though benevolence may not logically imply unfairness — one could overlook a certain offense under all circumstances — there is at least an empirical tendency for discrimination to accompany benevolence, so that what is benevolence to the beneficiary becomes malevolence to the neglected.[4]

What some proponents of a return to the service-oriented patrolman have in mind, however, is not hiring benevolent officers, but redistributing authority in the police department so that the patrolmen are to a substantial degree commanded by those whose disorder

3. In Oakland, a person might feel himself the victim of the legalistic style if he should be arrested, but once arrested he will become its beneficiary. From personal observation, there is little doubt, in my mind at least, that a suspect is more likely in Oakland than in most of the other eight communities to be charged, booked, and jailed in an orderly manner, without violence, and with due regard for his rights. This was not always the case — reforming the administration of the jail was one of the major objectives of the police chief who came to power in the 1950's.

4. The meaning of benevolence and its relationship to justice has been considered in Adam Smith, *Theory of Moral Sentiments,* 11th ed. (Edinburgh, 1808), Vol. I, Part 2, Section 2; John Stuart Mill, *Utilitarianism* (New York: E. P. Dutton & Co., Everyman's Library, 1951), Chap. V; David Hume, *Enquiries Concerning the Human Understanding and the Principles of Morals* (L. A. Selby-Bigge, editor; Oxford: The Clarendon Press, 1927), pp. 176–182, 304–305.

they must regulate and whose misdeeds they must correct. If it is so difficult to insure police fairness by rule — if, in short, so much must necessarily be left to police judgment — then let us, some say, reduce the scope of police authority or make it more subject to the control of those neighborhoods or groups most likely to experience a sense of injustice. Politics, in the broad sense of community involvement in policy making, will be used to achieve what administrative rationalization cannot. Adherents of this view propose giving a policy role to neighborhood organizations, developing citizen police patrols partly or wholly independent of the regular department, and utilizing more foot patrolmen under the control of local precinct stations and fewer radio car patrolmen under the direction of central headquarters. Such arguments are directed most often at departments with the legalistic style — the Oakland and Los Angeles police have heard them — perhaps because the rate of Negro involvement with such departments is so high.[5]

The issue involves two competing models of how best to maintain order. One, held by professional police officers, might be called the *institutional.* In this view, the law must be vigorously enforced because to do otherwise would call into question the law itself. Though community and familial norms are the ultimate foundation of public order, the fact of high and rising crime rates shows that such norms are less and less able to serve the function they once performed in a more stable and traditional social system. Indeed, the law must be enforced with special vigor in those areas where

5. See Paul Jacobs, "The Los Angeles Police: A Critique," *Atlantic,* 218 (December 1966), pp. 95–101; Byron E. Calame, "Community Patrol," *Wall Street Journal,* August 2, 1967; and President's Commission on Law Enforcement and Administration of Justice, *Task Force Report: The Police* (Washington: Government Printing Office, 1967), pp. 157–158. The idea of "neighborhood patrols" is not new. For many years the Soviet Union has had a system of "People's Patrols" that operates, with millions of volunteers and under Communist party leadership, to perform primarily what I call the order maintenance function. They are locally controlled and charged with maintaining order, combatting petty crime (including drunkenness), enforcing traffic regulations, and similar matters. As Harold J. Berman describes them, "They roam the city in pairs, taking issue with conduct of which they do not approve, such as boisterous parties, wearing of 'Western' clothes, or dancing of 'Western' dance steps . . . They are apt to be rough and discourteous and to exceed their powers." *Justice in the U.S.S.R.: An Interpretation of Soviet Law* (rev. ed.; Cambridge, Mass.: Harvard University Press, 1963), pp. 285–288.

community norms appear weakest; failure to do so would penalize law-abiding persons in those areas and inhibit the development of a regard for community norms among the law breakers. Furthermore, high-crime or high-disorder areas offer too many temptations for police officers. Gambling, prostitution, loan sharking, narcotics traffic, and moonshining create possibilities of corruption so great that only the strictest, most centrally directed police work can survive untainted. Finally, whatever frictions may be created on the street by vigorous law enforcement, the crucial threat to personal liberty is a denial of due process in the handling of persons after they have been arrested. A street stop inflicts no penalty and should bother only those with something to hide; an arrest, with subsequent detention and the creation of a record, can inflict a penalty and inconvenience the innocent. But insuring due process of law requires administrative regularity, strongly enforced departmental rules, and central authority. These are weakened, and thus regard for the rule of law is weakened, by decentralization. The old precinct station house may be a romantic memory to some, but one should not forget that it was typically there — rather than downtown, where lawyers, reporters, and senior officers were present — that bribery, third-degree interrogations, and prisoner shake-downs were once practiced. Indeed, in an era now past in most cities, the precinct station was a key organizational unit in ward and machine politics, and though such political systems may have acted benevolently toward friends and the party faithful, they were inclined to use the police to harass political enemies, protect the racketeer, and conceal corruption. It is hard enough to run a good police department when it is subject to second-rate politicians in city hall; it would be much harder if it were subject to fourth-rate politicians in the wards and neighborhoods.

Opposed to this is the *communal* model. Because most police work is concerned, not with serious crime, but with regulating public conduct, whatever may be the virtues of centralization and expertise when it comes to catching the murderer or rapist, maintaining order on the streets and handling domestic quarrels require different virtues and accordingly a different organizational pattern. Various neighborhoods and subcultures have their own levels of tolerable disorder; what may appear to be weaker norms are only different norms. Nor are the members of such subcultures a threat to persons in other neighborhoods — police statistics show that almost all disorder, tolerable or intolerable, occurs among persons who are likely to share common norms because they are acquainted or related. Justice is not an absolute; it can be rationed, providing more or less of one kind rather than another to different neighborhoods.[6] In any case, law enforcement — like any system of compliance — cannot operate effectively without the support and cooperation of those subject to it. In this regard, community norms need not be changed so much as understood, and they are best understood by police officers who are not isolated from them. This requires hiring officers who are Negroes, or Puerto Ricans, or whatever, even if they do not measure up fully to the standards of professional police departments, and assigning them to Negro or Puerto Rican neighborhoods. But most important, it requires the officers to be controlled by the neighborhood. Though there may be some risk of corruption, this is not the greatest problem we face; or if it is, the real corruption is that practiced by big-league, downtown interests — racketeers, politicians, businessmen — and not by the corner saloon. Machine politics is dead; recreating the neighborhood precinct police will not restore the boss to power. New bases of power are being forged in the neighborhoods to perform, out of community-regarding rather than selfish motives, the functions once performed by the political party. Humanizing the police will be one of these.

In principle, any police style is compatible with the distribution of authority specified by either model. Though the institutional model often displays the legalistic style, it need not — the example of Nassau County suggests how the service style may predominate even in a department where the command function is highly centralized and rules and "professional" training methods abound. And the Albany department is certainly centralized but its leadership does

6. For an argument that justice can be "rationed" in ways comparable to that by which society rations welfare, service, or education, see Geoffrey C. Hazard, Jr., "Rationing Justice," *Journal of Law and Economics,* 13 (October 1965), pp. 1–10.

not see fit to adopt the legalistic style. What the proponents of the communal model are, in effect, recommending is that we "suburbanize" the central city — let each neighborhood (usually defined along lines of class and race) determine its own style of law enforcement. This view of the police is in keeping with the recently acquired opinions of certain liberals and radicals that decentralization and "participatory democracy" are among the chief remedies for social problems.

The matter, unfortunately, is not so simple. Though there is a great deal to be said for involving the police more deeply in neighborhood affairs, for choosing more explicitly what police style we prefer, and for providing the patrolman with more guidance in keeping order, it is not clear that redistributing authority over the police is the proper means. For one thing, a central city cannot be fully suburbanized however much we may want to — it is, by definition, *central,* which means that many people from all over the metropolitan area use it for work, governing, and recreation and that, as a result, competing life styles and competing sets of community norms come into frequent and important contact. Necessarily, this generates political pressures to maintain order at the highest level expected by groups who use the city — central locations create demands for the "highest and best" level of order just as they create demands for the highest and best use of land. Some residents may not like having the police try, for that is about all they can do, to maintain order at a level demanded by the businessmen, shoppers, theater-goers, students, and public officials who use the central city, but to say they should not try is to take a deliberate decision not to have the area serve the function of a central city, except for those persons who come to the city in search of disorder — prostitution, dirty-book stores, cheap bars, and the like.

Furthermore, many of the deepest social cleavages are within the central city, not between the city and its suburbs. The working-class and lower-middle-class members of certain white ethnic groups who still live in central neighborhoods are the persons who most bitterly resist school and residential integration; by comparison, the upper-middle-class suburbs are usually the areas most willing to accept, admittedly often on a token basis, Negro school children (even to helping pay the cost of bussing them out) and Negro families who might wish to live there. And when such integration is attempted, suburban police forces are rarely used, at least deliberately, to block it. Giving central city neighborhoods, many bitterly apprehensive of and hostile toward adjoining neighborhoods, control over their own neighborhood police would be to risk making the police power an instrument for inter-neighborhood conflict. Proposals for communal police often are based on the tacit assumption that, somehow, only Negroes, and poor Negroes at that, would get control of the police.[7] In fact, legislation that would give the police to Negroes would, out of political necessity, give it to others as well. The exclusion of Negro residents, school children, and even passers-by that is now accomplished, to a degree, by informal controls and threats of violence could then be accomplished by police harassment, the subtle withdrawal of police protection, or both.

Besides deep racial divisions, there are issues of order maintenance and law enforcement in the central city that are of such emotional and political significance that the police are already under intense political pressure from competing forces seeking to exploit these issues. Allowing them to be governed by neighborhoods could only intensify that pressure, putting the police at the mercy of the rawest emotions, the most demagogic spokesmen, and the most provincial concerns. If the study of urban politics has taught us anything, it is that, except on referenda, and perhaps not even then, "the people" do not govern — organizations, parties, factions, politicians, and groups govern. The people choose among competing leaders and thereby constrain them. Such constraints are hard to maintain even in citywide elections where the interest in local politics is greatest. Even socially heterogeneous big cities often have one-party government, or something very like it. But if the unit of government becomes the neighborhood, interest will become even less (witness

7. It is not clear how far the President's Commission meant to go in this regard. It argues for the creation of "neighborhood committees" that would act as a "real participant in policy formation." It seems to have in mind, judging from the context, mainly Negro and Puerto Rican neighborhoods. President's Commission, *The Police*, p. 158.

the miniscule proportions of persons voting in "poverty neighborhood" elections) and the opportunities for a small, self-serving minority to seize control of the police or the schools will become very great indeed.

When a community is deeply divided and emotionally aroused, the proper governmental policy is not to arm the disputants and let them settle matters among themselves; it is, rather, to raise the level at which decisions will be made to a point sufficiently high so that neither side can prevail by *force majeure* but low enough so that responsible authorities must still listen to both sides. The localistic police forces of small towns and homogeneous suburbs work satisfactorily largely because they need not handle profound social conflicts; little is expected of them except to perform in middle-class areas a service function or in working-class areas a watchman function.

These cautionary remarks, it should be understood, are directed against plans to *disperse the authority* that governs the police; they are not directed at ways to *decentralize the functions* of the police. To decentralize an administrative apparatus is to give its component units greater freedom, within well-defined general policies, to handle local situations in a manner appropriate to local conditions. Decentralization, properly understood, *strengthens* local units; the dispersal of authority, by contrast, weakens them.[8] Precinct commanders in a decentralized department would have greater freedom of action and more control over their patrolmen; precinct commanders in a dispersed department would surrender that control to whatever constellation of political forces the neighborhood might produce.

Given the difficulties that face a police administrator trying to define a patrolman's duty and induce him to perform it, the case in favor of allowing more such decisions to be made by neighborhood police commanders can at best be a partial and perhaps inconclusive one. Indeed, many police administrators believe the risks of corruption are so great as to outweigh any advantage to be gained in the supervision of the patrol function. Such risks can be

8. See the excellent discussion of decentralization in Irving Kristol, "Decentralization for What?" *The Public Interest*, no. 11 (Spring, 1968), pp. 17–25.

lessened by insuring that the chief has absolute authority over his commanders, unchecked by either local politics, departmental cliques, or restrictive civil service regulations. Even so, the risks cannot be eliminated altogether, but perhaps they can be offset by the advantages of such decentralization.

The central problem of the patrolman, and thus of the police, is to maintain order and to reduce, to the limited extent possible, the opportunities for crime. Neither objective is served by judging men on the basis of their arrest records. Both objectives *may* be served by organizing and supervising the patrolmen so as to increase their capacity to make reliable judgments about the character, motives, intentions, and likely future actions of those whom they must police. The officer's ability to make such judgments is improved by increasing his familiarity with and involvement in the neighborhood he patrols, even to the extent of having him live there. The better he knows his beat, the more he can rely on judgments of character and the less he must rely on objective characteristics (race, apparent social class, age) and empirical generalizations about the relationships between those characteristics and the causes of crime and disorder.

The police supervisor, in turn, would have to judge his patrolmen on the basis of their ability to keep the peace on their beat, and this, like the judgment the patrolman must make about the citizen, is necessarily subjective and dependent on close observation and personal familiarity. Those departments that evaluate officers by "objective" measures (arrests and traffic tickets) work against this ideal; so also do promotional requirements and civil service examinations that reward the officer best able to memorize the penal code or the departmental rule book. Moving away from these conventional standards, like moving away from rigid departmental centralization, creates opportunities for "favoritism" in personnel practices, but such tendencies can be at least partially checked by the willingness of the police administrator to hold his local commanders responsible for keeping the peace in their precincts. If order maintenance is the general standard, then such favoritism as is displayed will be used to a substantial degree to reward officers who can make their superiors "look good" in this regard just as the favoritism that now exists (in recommending men for assignment as traffic specialist or detective, for example) is often used to reward officers who make their superiors look good with respect to law enforcement.

Because often an arrest is not, in the eyes of the police and citizens alike, the best way to cope with real or potential disorder, a department that places proper emphasis on the order maintenance function would have to create a wider range of options than now exist for handling disorderly situations. Specialized units, at the precinct or departmental level, would have to be created to provide for nonarrest dispositions of family quarrels, neighborhood disputes, rowdy teenagers, and drunken derelicts. The patrolman, who now must either pacify the disputants himself, call for the wagon, or do nothing, should be able to refer the parties involved to specialized services (a family service unit, an alcoholic detoxification center, a juvenile bureau, a neighborhood legal office) or, in serious matters, call in the assistance of officers trained in riot prevention and suppression.

Law enforcement might, in such a department, continue to be performed under centralized command. This would be especially necessary for those crimes (gambling and narcotics) where the possibilities of corruption are the greatest; it would also be desirable for crimes more easily solved through specialization. Because law enforcement involves innocent victims rather than parties to a dispute and because an arrest is almost always the appropriate police response, detailed knowledge of neighborhoods would be less important than well-cultivated networks of informants among the criminal elements.

It makes little sense for a department that takes seriously its order maintenance function to reward officers who perform it well by making them law enforcement specialists. At present the principal rewards are promotion, which takes a patrolman off the street, or reassignment to a detective or specialized unit, which takes him out of order maintenance altogether; not surprisingly, patrolmen wanting more pay or status tend to do those things (that is, excel at law enforcement) that will earn them those rewards. The administrator, accordingly, must enable patrolmen to rise in pay and rank *without* abandoning their function.

A decentralized, neighborhood-oriented, order maintenance patrol force requires central command to insure a reasonably common definition of appropriate order, a reduction in the opportunities for corruption and favoritism, and the protection of the civil liberties of suspects and witnesses. Equity should be an important constraint on order maintenance as well as on law enforcement, and equity requires bureaucratic regularity. That bureaucratic regularity, which insists that people be treated as if they were legally equal, and order maintenance, which assumes that people must be handled in full awareness of their moral differences, are competing values is obvious; that having an organization alert to such competing values will produce strains is entirely clear; but all human values are to some degree in competition and most organizations exist to manage that strain by striking reasonable balances.

Some thoughtful observers of police practice have suggested that the strain can be reduced if the patrolmen are given clearer substantive guides to the use of their discretion. To the extent this is possible, it is of course desirable.[9] At the very least, certain obvious steps can be taken once the fiction that the police have no discretion

9. The Task Force on the Police of the President's Commission urged departments to "develop and annunciate police guidelines for exercises of law enforcement discretion." (*The Police,* pp. 21–27). The Commission relied heavily on the views of Professors Frank Remington and Herman Goldstein of the University of Wisconsin Law School. They and others had earlier published defenses of police discretion and arguments for the development of policy guidelines. See Charles D. Breitel, "Controls in Criminal Law Enforcement," *University of Chicago Law Review,* 27 (Spring, 1960), p. 427; Frank J. Remington, "The Role of the Police in a Democratic Society," *Journal of Criminal Law, Criminology, and Police Science,* 56 (1965), pp. 361–365; Herman Goldstein, "Police Discretion: The Ideal Versus the Real," *Public Administration Review,* 23 (September 1963), pp. 140–148; and Wayne R. LaFave, *Arrest* (Boston: Little, Brown & Co., 1965), pp. 492–495. In one article Herman Goldstein enumerates the areas in which policy guidelines might be developed. Though many of his suggestions in law enforcement areas seem excellent, he has (not surprisingly) no recommendations for order maintenance cases — here, domestic disturbances — except to call for more research. "Police Policy Formulation: A Proposal for Improving Police Performance," *Michigan Law Review,* 65 (April 1967), pp. 1123–1146.

is dropped.[10] Some attention can be given, and is in fact being given, to how the police should stop persons on the street, what language they may and may not employ, what warning must be given, and the like. Once it is admitted that the police spend more time settling family fights than they do chasing bank robbers, then more time in police training programs can be devoted to the family fight problem (it should offer opportunities for some rather vivid role-playing exercises) and less to the bank robber problem.

But there are limits on how useful such policy guidance can be. For one thing, it is very hard to do more than list "factors to be considered" by the police (such as demeanor, gait, manner, time of day, and the like); what is needed is guidance in *how* they are to be considered.[11] For another, if the police are too explicit about what they intend to take into account and how, some courts stand ready to throw out any ensuing arrest on the grounds that it was "discriminatory." Though the courts generally do not accept as a defense the claim that "Others have done the same thing and not been arrested," when a police commissioner in Philadelphia announced publicly that he did not have the resources to arrest every violator of a Sunday closing law, one arrest his officers did make was overturned because, the law enforcement policy having been made explicit, the arrest was a denial of the equal protection of the laws.[12]

Under certain circumstances, the race or color of the citizen may

10. Some authors have argued against the need for police discretion and have urged that a policy of "full enforcement" be followed with legislatures then repealing laws it did not wish to see enforced. Any other procedures, the argument goes, would remove police actions from the possibility of judicial review. (See Joseph Goldstein, "Police Discretion Not to Invoke the Criminal Process: Low-Visibility Decisions in the Administration of Justice," *Yale Law Journal*, 69 (March 1960), pp. 543–594.) Whatever the merits of this view with respect to law enforcement matters, it is hardly applicable to order maintenance situations. To argue that we should have "full enforcement" of the disorderly conduct or breach of the peace statutes is to assume that somebody knows what full enforcement requires — that is to say, somebody can give an unambiguous definition of "orderly conduct" or "public peace." The debate between Goldstein and his critics (see note 9 above) is an interesting one and especially relevant to laws governing essentially private conduct (such as gambling, the use of addictive and hallucinatory drugs, prostitution, and homosexuality) but it is not relevant to — indeed, it has tended to obscure — the function of the patrolman.

11. President's Commission, *The Police,* pp. 38–41.

12. *Bargain City v. Dilworth,* 29 U.S. Law Week 2002 (1960).

be a very important "factor to be considered" — as, for example, constituting reasonable grounds for stopping and questioning a Negro carrying a suitcase late at night in a white neighborhood. Or, to cite an equally plausible case that might *prevent* the arrest of a Negro, a policy could suggest that because it is characteristic of lower-income Negroes and Puerto Ricans to socialize on the streets, arrests for disorderly conduct in such areas should only occur if disturbances are more serious than those that would produce an arrest in a middle-class white neighborhood. The courts have shown themselves extremely sensitive to any policy, explicit or implicit, that seems to make race a relevant factor in invoking legal processes, and it is hard to imagine that any police rules that did so would be sustained.[13]

If the police administrator is to have the freedom and resources to make the changes here suggested, he will have to be supported by public officials who understand that the police should not be evaluated solely or even primarily on the basis of the trend in the rate of serious crime. The police can do relatively little about preventing most common crimes, and those they can help prevent — street crimes — are precisely the ones that require the greatest knowledge of local conditions and persons and the greatest support, in terms of a willingness to report offenses and give information, from the populace. (A community concerned about lowering its crime rates would be well advised to devote its attention and resources to those parts of the criminal justice system, especially the courts and correctional agencies, which, unlike the police, spend most of their time processing — often in the most perfunctory and ineffective manner — persons who repeatedly perpetrate these crimes.) It is by no means clear, however, that the local political system will give the police administrator the support he needs to handle his order maintenance function properly. After all, the current emphasis on

13. The police investigated cars parked together in a Negro neighborhood and as a consequence discovered gambling; arrests ensued. The defendants appealed their convictions on the grounds (among others) that the police would ignore cars parked together in a white neighborhood and thus overlook white gambling. A new trial was ordered. See *People v. Harris,* 182 Cal. App. 2d Supp. 837 (1960) and also *People v. Winters,* 171 Cal. App. 2d Supp. 876 (1959).

law enforcement arose in great part out of political decisions and pressures. It was the Wickersham Commission that, in its 1931 report, concluded that the police should be judged by their ability to prevent major crimes such as bank robberies and burglaries, that they had failed in this task, and that accordingly they should be "taken out of politics" in order to perform this task better. The police have responded to that unreasonable charge in the most reasonable manner — either by suppressing reports on serious crimes in order to make themselves look better or by blaming the courts or correctional agencies for their failure to deal properly with the criminals after their arrest. The rates of certain crimes *are* rising,[14] though the desire of some departments in the past to protect themselves from criticism by suppressing that fact has made the recent increase appear to be greater than it actually is. Now that "crime in the streets" has become a major issue, it is probably too much to expect that public officials, sensitive to this popular concern, will be much inclined to encourage police administrators to do better those things the police *can* do (maintaining order) and to look elsewhere (primarily to the correctional agencies) for help in doing those things that the police cannot do (reducing the incidence of these crimes committed by repeaters).

But even if the politicians were to give the police the proper sort of encouragement, it would be a mistake to expect too much from even the most imaginative redirection of police efforts. That certain changes will enable the police to perform their task better does not mean that they will perform it to everybody's, or anybody's, satisfaction. Order maintenance means managing conflict, and conflict implies disagreement over what should be done, how, and to whom. Conflict is found in all social strata and thus in all strata there will be resentment, often justified, against particular police interventions (or their absence), but in lower-class areas conflict and disorder will be especially common and thus such resentment will be especially

14. Trends in most crime rates are difficult to interpret because of reporting errors, but the trend in the murder rate in big cities is known with some accuracy and it has gone up dramatically in these places over the last thirty years. The evidence on this matter is reviewed in some detail in James Q. Wilson, "Violence," in Daniel Bell, ed., *Toward the Year 2000* (Boston: Houghton Mifflin, 1968).

keen. It is hardly surprising that polls show young lower-income Negro males as being deeply distrustful of and bitter about the police; it would be a mistake, however, to assume that race is the decisive factor. No doubt race makes the potentiality for police-citizen hostility greater, but if all Negroes were turned white tomorrow this hostility, only slightly abated, would continue. Throughout history the urban poor have disliked and distrusted the police, and the feeling has been reciprocated; the situation will not change until the poor become middle class, or at least working class, or until society decides to abandon the effort to maintain a common legal code and a level of public order acceptable to middle-class persons.

Some advocates of communal law enforcement seem inclined to defend the model precisely on the grounds that it avoids the "middle-class bias" of the legal code and the moral order. If by "middle-class bias" is meant a concern for the security of person and property and a desire to avoid intrusions into one's privacy and disturbances of one's peace, it is not clear why such a "bias" is a bad thing or, indeed, why it should be called a "bias" at all. (If by middle-class bias is meant a dislike for eccentric dress and manners, that is something else, and perhaps the word "bias" is aptly chosen.) But there is another, and perhaps more important issue. We have had some experience in this country with the notion that different neighborhoods should be allowed to have radically different levels of public order, and the results have not been altogether encouraging. The southern double standard of justice may have contributed to the difficulties we now experience in our large cities. John Dollard in a classic account describes the high level of aggression among poor Negroes in a small southern town in the 1930's.[15] He finds several explanations for it — aggression that cannot be directed against whites is displaced and directed against other Negroes, the weak family structure means that a solution to the problem of sexual jealousy will involve violence to accomplish what familial and community norms cannot, and the degradation of the status of the Negro produces exaggerated efforts to affirm that status in other ways, one

15. John Dollard, *Caste and Class in a Southern Town* (Garden City: Doubleday Anchor Books, 1957; original edition published in 1937), chap. XIII.

of which is a conspicuous display of masculinity and an idealization of personal violence. But among the institutional features of southern life that sustain this is the double standard of justice: "Negro crime" is judged less serious than "white crime," and the difference is often defended on grounds of high-minded indulgence of "Negro ways." But the effects may be the very opposite of that intended. As Dollard writes:

> The formal machinery of the law takes care of the Negroes' grievances much less adequately than that of the whites, and to a much higher degree the Negro is compelled to make and enforce his own law with other Negroes . . . The result is that the individual Negro is, to a considerable degree, outside the protection of the white law, and must shift for himself. This leads to the frontier psychology . . . [This] condoning of Negro violence . . . may be indulgent in the case of any given Negro, but its effect on the Negro group as a whole is dangerous and destructive . . . So long as the law does not take over the protection of the Negro person he will have to do it himself by violent means.[16]

The problem becomes all the more critical with the relative lack of territorial differentiation among Negroes of different classes. Middle-class Negroes, sometimes because of enforced segregation, live close to lower-class Negroes. Though this is slowly changing as the size of all-Negro areas expands, it means that even if one might justify a level of law enforcement appropriate to lower-class culture and different from that provided to the community as a whole, middle-class persons unable to separate themselves physically from the lower class would be victimized in two ways: they would get less police protection than they want and, because black skin tends in the eyes of whites to conceal class differences, they are likely to be treated by the police (mistakenly) in ways not appropriate to their status.

One reason for the increasing complaints of "police harassment" may be that, in the large cities, Negroes are being brought under a single standard of justice; one reason for the complaints of discrimination may be that this process is proceeding unevenly and im-

16. *Ibid.*, pp. 274, 279, 280, 281.

perfectly. As the populations of our large cities become, through continued migration, more heavily Negro, more heavily lower income, and more youthful, we can expect these complaints to increase in number and frequency, especially if, as seems likely, organizations competing for leadership in the central cities continue to seek out such issues in order to attract followers.

In sum, the police can cope with their problems but they cannot solve them. If they were expected to do less, they might not be so frustrated by their inability to do much of anything. The bitterness between police and lower-class young males in our large cities — a bitterness that is pervasive and almost palpable — arises out of a situation neither can control: restless young men are driven by urges they do not understand, but which most of them outgrow, somewhat mysteriously,[17] and the police are asked to solve problems they cannot solve. The effort to manage the unmanageable leads both sides to define the conflict as one between competing rights, moralities, and tests of manhood.

These circumstances are not new, but the attention we pay to them, and especially the capacity of the mass media to make this conflict vivid, dramatic, and immediate, are new. What once occurred routinely, unobtrusively, and (to the police) under the aegis of an agreed-upon moral code now occurs more obviously, and hence more explosively, and (again, to the police) under the aegis of a shattered moral code and in a society in which the established institutions — the churches, the courts, the universities, the newspapers, and important public agencies — seem to take the side of the disorderly and the criminal and to blame the police for the "incidents" that occur. The "problems of the police" are long-standing and inherent in the nature of their function, but our definition of those problems has changed and, by changing, has misled or unsettled us.

17. David Matza, *Delinquency and Drift* (New York: John Wiley and Sons, 1964), pp. 21–27, notes that juveniles "drift" into delinquency but that in the vast majority of cases they drift out again; theories that "explain" the former often fail to explain the latter, and thus they "overpredict" delinquency.

Index

Atheneum Paperbacks

POLITICAL SCIENCE

2 POWER AND DIPLOMACY *by Dean Acheson*
15 CALL TO GREATNESS *by Adlai E. Stevenson*
20 DOCUMENTS ON FUNDAMENTAL HUMAN RIGHTS *edited by Zechariah*
A&B *Chafee, Jr., 2 vols.*
23 THE CONSTITUTION AND WHAT IT MEANS TODAY *by Edward S. Corwin*
27 COURTS ON TRIAL *by Jerome Frank*
34 THE DIPLOMACY OF ECONOMIC DEVELOPMENT *by Eugene R. Black*
40 THE UNITED STATES AND MEXICO *by Howard F. Cline*
41 THE DIPLOMATS, 1919-1939 *edited by Gordon A. Craig and Felix Gilbert,*
A&B *2 vols.*
44 CHINA'S RESPONSE TO THE WEST *by Ssu-Yü Teng and John K. Fairbank*
46 THE FUTURE OF FEDERALISM *by Nelson A. Rockefeller*
53 THE BILL OF RIGHTS *by Learned Hand*
54 STRATEGIC SURRENDER *by Paul Kecskemeti*
63 THE SINO-SOVIET CONFLICT, 1956-1961 *by Donald S. Zagoria*
72 MR. JUSTICE HOLMES AND THE SUPREME COURT *by Felix Frankfurter*
74 STALIN'S FOREIGN POLICY REAPPRAISED *by Marshall D. Shulman*
105 DILEMMAS OF URBAN AMERICA *by Robert C. Weaver*
107 RUSSIA LEAVES THE WAR *by George F. Kennan*
108 THE DECISION TO INTERVENE *by George F. Kennan*
110 DRED SCOTT'S CASE *by Vincent C. Hopkins, S.J.*
130 THE REVOLUTION OF THE SAINTS *by Michael Walzer*
138 OF LAW AND LIFE AND OTHER THINGS THAT MATTER *by Felix Frankfurter, edited by Philip B. Kurland*
147 AFTER IMPERALISM *by Akira Iriye*
148 POLITICAL CHANGE IN A WEST AFRICAN STATE *by Martin Kilson*
149 THE COMMUNIST CONTROVERSY IN WASHINGTON *by Earl Latham*
150 THE DECLINE OF AGRARIAN DEMOCRACY *by Grant McConnell*
156 VARIETIES OF POLICE BEHAVIOR *by James Q. Wilson*
157 AFRICA: FROM INDEPENDENCE TO TOMORROW *by David Hapgood*
160 UP AGAINST THE IVY WALL *by Jerry Avorn and other members of the staff of the* Columbia Daily Spectator
170 THE POLITICS OF AUTHENTICITY *by Marshall Berman*
175 SECOND CHANCE *by Robert A. Divine*
178 THE END OF THE AMERICAN ERA *by Andrew Hacker*
179 CONGRESS AND THE PUBLIC TRUST *by James C. Kirby, Jr.*
188 POLITICAL OBLIGATION *by Richard Flathman*
189 MACHIAVELLI AND THE NATURE OF POLITICAL THEORY *edited by Martin Fleisher*
195 MAN AND SOCIALISM IN CUBA *edited by Bertram Silverman*
196 THE RADICAL PROBE *by Michael W. Miles*
197 THE CRUEL CHOICE *by Denis Goulet*
198 POLITICS, LANGUAGE AND TIME *by J. G. A. Pocock*